My Boat Is So Small:
Creating a Safe Harbor of Hope and Health Care for *All* Children

**National Observance of
Children's Sabbaths® Manual**
Volume 16

By Shannon Daley-Harris

Children's Defense Fund

Acknowledgments

This book was made possible in part by funds granted by the Freddie Mac Foundation. The statements made and views expressed, however, are the sole responsibility of the authors.

This manual was written and compiled by Shannon Daley-Harris.

Thanks to the following Children's Defense Fund (CDF) staff for their contributions to the publication:
Elizabeth Alesbury, Editor; Anourack Chinyavong, Designer; Matt Rosen, Religious Action Coordinator; Casey Aden-Wansbury, Director of Communications; Neel Lattimore, Special Advisor to the President for Strategic Communication; Susan Gates, General Counsel; Mary Lassen, Acting Field Director; Taj Brown, Manager of Leadership Development for Freedom Schools

CDF thanks the following contributors who wrote portions of the Children's Sabbaths manual:
- Father Walter J. Burghardt, S.J., theologian, preacher, and author, Baltimore, Maryland (Catholic Homily Notes)
- Marc Katz, Legislative Assistant, Religious Action Center for Reform Judaism, Washington, D.C. (Jewish Sermon Notes)
- The Rev. Dr. Eileen W. Lindner, Deputy General Secretary for Research and Planning, National Council of the Churches of Christ in the U.S.A., New York, New York (Sermon Notes)
- National Spiritual Assembly of Bahá'ís of the United States, Evanston, Illinois (Bahá'í Resources)

In addition, CDF is deeply grateful to the following people for reviewing sections of the manual and providing other forms of assistance:
- The Rev. Patti Daley, Princeton, New Jersey
- Martha Bettis Gee, Director, Child Advocacy Office, Presbyterian Church (USA), Louisville, Kentucky
- Miriam Fink, Commission on Social Action, Union for Reform Judaism, New York, New York
- Mary Alice Gran, Specialist, Ministries with Children, General Board of Discipleship, The United Methodist Church
- Liz McCloskey, writer and doctoral candidate, Catholic University of America, Washington, D.C
- Afeefa Syeed, Director, Al-Fatih Academy, Herndon, Virginia

All scriptural references unless otherwise noted are from the New Revised Standard Version of the Bible, copyright 1989, by the Division of Christian Education of the National Council of the Churches of Christ in the United States of America.

Photographs by Photodisc and Alison Wright Photography
Illustrations by Sunny Chang, Sunny Kim and August Pollak

Table of Contents

All pages are perforated for easy removal.

Section 1

Dear Faithful Friend of Children,

Welcome to the National Observance of Children's Sabbaths, *"My Boat Is So Small: Creating a Safe Harbor of Hope and Health Care for All Children."* The title of this year's Children's Sabbaths celebration is taken from the Breton fisherman's prayer that has long served as the Children's Defense Fund's logo: "Dear Lord, Be good to me. The sea is so wide and my boat is so small," depicted by a young child's drawing.

Today, so many children are adrift in a wide sea of need, their small, frail craft unable to provide them the protection they need and deserve to withstand the tidal waves of poverty and violence, neglect and abuse that capsize their leaky boats.

In our nation today, why are there nine million children adrift on the sea without health and mental health coverage, vulnerable to the acute and chronic storms of illness and injury without the most basic life-giving protection all children need? Almost 90 percent of them live in working households. Every single one is God's child who needs and deserves health and mental health coverage. Millions more children are underinsured. Families are swamped by medical debt when they can no longer delay health care for their children but are unable to afford it. Millions of children are tossed about by preventable illness and untreated conditions that keep them from learning and thriving in school and in life. Our nation's uninsured children face preventable disease, illness, and even death in the richest nation on earth. Where is your persistent voice for health care for all children?

Tens of thousands of Katrina's children lost their homes, schools, neighborhoods, family members, friends, pets, hopes, and security and are still waiting for their nation and for adults of faith to rescue them from their purgatory of despair. In our nation today, why are children and their families whose lives were devastated by the flood waters of Hurricane Katrina still struggling to keep their heads above water and regain their footing amidst the ship wreckage of homes, schools, employment, health and mental health care systems, in a community and nation awash in bureaucratic incompetence and citizen indifference, left like so much debris on a beach? Where is your and my voice and action?

In our nation today, why are there nearly 13 million children adrift in a stormy sea of poverty? Hunger, homelessness, preventable illness, and even death in the richest nation on earth capsize and cast their tiny boats onto the deep sea. Our nation's vulnerable children living in poverty need the safe harbor of sufficient family income, safety nets, and safety. Where is our voice and action as people of faith?

In our rich nation today, why are so many children—especially Black, Latino, and poor children—being pulled into the treacherous undertow of the cradle-to-prison pipeline, struggling to stay afloat in choppy waters, denied the rudder of health care, good schools, high expectations, caring adult mentors, and positive alternatives to the streets, blown by powerful ill winds onto a course more likely to end up in prison than in a profession? Our children need us to reroute them from the cradle-to-prison pipeline with *lifelines* of hope and caring and safety that congregations cast through CDF Freedom Schools℠ programs in the summer and afternoons to bring them to successful adulthood.

We who want to mount a faithful witness today must remember another baby adrift in a small boat made of bitumen and pitch. When the Pharaoh's policy threatened all of the baby boys of a people, first the nurse-midwives and then Moses' birth family protected him as long as they could, and when they could do no more, Moses' mother and sister set him in a small boat and placed it in the

25 E Street, NW
Washington, DC 20001
Tel: (202) 628-8787
Fax: (202) 662-3570
Email: cdfinfo@childrensdefense.org
Internet: www.childrensdefense.org

reeds where another might discover and save him. Pharaoh's daughter found and rescued the baby in the boat. Just a few people working together can make a difference.

Remember, however, that Pharaoh's daughter didn't change the policy that had endangered the child to begin with, although she suspected he had been abandoned because of it. She just reached out to rescue one endangered child. Too many people of faith settle for well-intentioned but limited acts of service that leave in place the unjust systems that perpetuate the need. In the words of the late Rev. William Sloane Coffin, "We are not called to piecemeal charity, we are called to wholesale justice," what the prophets and all great faith traditions have understood as God's intention for our life in covenant community. It took the child, grown to adulthood, to accept the challenge of advocacy—going again and again to Pharaoh and demanding that he let the people go, change unjust policy. Moses returned to Pharaoh and kept demanding justice. He didn't give up. Finally, the one who had once been a baby set adrift in the wide waters became the one who followed God's mandate and led the people—children, mothers, fathers, grandparents—through the parted waters to safety, setting their feet on dry ground for the journey to a land of plenty, peace, and justice.

You and I must do so much more today than simply to pluck individual children in our congregations, communities, and nation, one by one, from the dangerous waters stirred up by unjust policies. We must challenge unjust policies and leaders that leave millions of our children adrift on a dangerous sea, and give all children sturdy gear to reach shore safely.

The Children's Defense Fund is committed to achieving comprehensive health and mental health coverage for all children in America this year and to implement it into the lives of every child to finish the job begun by Medicaid and the State Children's Health Insurance Program. It is crucial to guarantee coverage for *all* children, provide *all* of them an equal benefit package. God did not create two classes of children. We must make it simple for children to get and keep health care. We need to stop the costly maze of bureaucracy of two separate programs that results in over six million children falling through the cracks. And we must stand up to political leaders who claim our nation cannot afford to cover all children right now. This is not a budget issue; it is a moral and practical imperative. In Section 2, "Learn More," you will read more about our campaign to assure all children this health coverage and how you and your congregation can help us achieve it. It won't be easy. Like Moses, we will need to keep going to the leaders of our land and demand justice.

Every person of faith must stand up for children as a litmus test for our elected leaders—look at their votes in Congress. We must ask them how they will eliminate child poverty in 10 years? Ask how they will achieve a better balance between our military budget, which exceeds the military budgets of all other industrialized nations, and the need to stop the dying of mothers and babies from preventable causes including childbirth. Ask whether they will oppose any new tax cuts for the wealthy so children will not have to go hungry, homeless, and without health care and other basic needs. Ask if they will commit to guaranteeing a high quality early childhood system and closing the education gap between poor children and affluent children. What special commitments will they make to ensure children high quality, affordable child care? We must not take generalities for answers. Examine CDF's voting record to see if your elected officials' actions align with their words.

Moses' example of persistent advocacy and demands for justice from Pharaoh reminds me of another of my favorite advocates in the Bible. Like Moses, the powerless widow wore down the unjust judge. In Luke, Jesus tells this parable to remind us of the need to pray always and not lose heart. The widow—poor, powerless, easily ignored—comes to an unjust judge, who has no fear of God or respect for people, and demands justice. When he refuses, she comes again and again until finally the judge grants her justice, not because of a change of heart or new respect for God or people, but because she has worn him down.

We must be like Moses and the widow today and never take no, but, or maybe or half a loaf of justice for our children. Political leaders ask us to cut our child in half, by providing coverage for some but not all of them. Children don't come in pieces. We must demand health care coverage for *all* children. We need to have a powerful, continuing movement until every child not only has a Healthy Start but also a Head Start, a Fair Start, a Safe Start, and good education and the ability to become a successful adult.

Your congregation's participation in the interfaith National Observance of Children's Sabbaths is an important part of creating a persistent, faithful voice for justice. Through worship, proclaim God's call for justice and compassion, God's demand that we care first for the young, poor, and powerless. Through study and educational sessions, learn more about the faith basis for your advocacy for children's health and how you can help. Begin right now to plan activities that will immediately engage congregation members in meeting the needs of children and advocating for comprehensive health coverage for *all* children as the State Children's Health Insurance Program funding will likely come up for renewal this summer. Most importantly, use the Children's Sabbath weekend as a catalyst for new, urgent, long-term, year-round action on behalf of children at this defining time in our national life. Fighting for health care this year and children's needs don't end when the weekend is over, and neither should our faithful efforts with and for them.

Let me end with a few short prayers to help keep us strong in our commitment to advocate for and save our children.

Lord, we have pushed so many of our children into the tumultuous sea of life in leaky boats without survival gear.

Forgive us and help them to forgive us. Help us now to give all our children the anchor of faith, the rudder of hope, the sails of health care and education, and the paddles of family and community to keep them afloat when life's sea gets rough. Amen.

Lord, help me to persist although I want to give up.
Lord, help me to keep trying although I can't see what good it does.
Lord, help me to keep praying although I'm not sure You hear me.
Lord, help me to keep living in ways that seek to please You.
Lord, help me know when to lead and when to follow.
Lord, help me know when to speak and when to remain silent.
Lord, help me know when to act and when to wait. Amen.

O God,
Grant us creative patience
To persist until we see what the end may be.
Keep us from giving up just because the way is hard and uncertain.
Help us never to cease trying to get children their fair share of America's concern
because they are Your children. Amen.

I am grateful for all that you do to ensure children a healthy, safe, and hopeful journey, and pray that the Children's Sabbath will be for you and your congregation new inspiration for faithful and persistent work for justice.

With faith, hope, and determination,

Marian Wright Edelman

P.S. I cannot think of boats as a metaphor for children and their needs without recalling a marvelous story told by Dr. Eileen Lindner in her wonderful book, *Thus Far on the Way: Toward a Theology of Child Advocacy*. It is excerpted and reprinted on the next page. As they say, "That will preach!"

"Privileged Vessels"

Excerpted and adapted from *Thus Far on the Way: Toward a Theology of Child Advocacy*
by the Rev. Dr. Eileen W. Lindner

This whole question of relationship between the powerful and the powerless was revealed to me in an unexpected way. Now, as a mother, what passes for a leisure time activity is doing the Saturday chores. I'm a Calvinist, so I never leave the house without two or three days reading material, just in case there's a line wherever I'm going. Heaven forbid, I should just sit and do nothing.

It was my turn to take the car to the Jiffy Lube. Do you know Jiffy Lube, where you go and they clunk around under the car? I'm not entirely sure what they do but if you don't do it, your car stops or something. I'm not being too technical for you, am I? I don't know, maybe they change liquids. I don't know what they do, but you have to do it sometimes.

Anyway, I took the car and I went in to wait while they did whatever it is they do. To my great horror, I found that I had arrived without any reading material. Now, the Jiffy Lube is somewhat of a male precinct, I've got to say. There was something that I will euphemistically call a coffee table; that is to say, a flat surface, and on it were only two books.

One was a magazine called "Field and Stream." It's a most peculiar magazine. They sell things in there like worms. Worms— I said worms. By the gross. Now, I'm not really sure how many a gross is, but it's a very lot. I'm having a reasonably happy life. I have never even bought one worm. What do the people do who buy those grosses of worms? It costs you $20 to have a gross of worms and $50 not to have one. They also sell boots that come up to your armpits. I mean, honey, if it's that deep in there, I'd say don't go in. That would be my personal advice.

Well, I pretty soon thought I had about all the enlightenment I could stand from that little publication, so I picked up the other one. It was the manual that you study when you're getting your boat driver's license, like a driver's license for boats. You have to take a test and all that stuff.

Now, I'm a Calvinist, as I already confessed. Calvinists start at the back of the book, and we do that in case we run out of time. We always know how it came out. We don't know what it was about, but we know how it came out. So I start at the back, and it's talking about jigs and booms and ta rah rah boomdiyeas, for all I know. I didn't understand much of it. And then I got to a chapter on the rules for what happens when boats encounter each other on open sea—in open water, actually, it said. I thought, well, that's kind of interesting. You know, for cars we have traffic lights and traffic lanes and even that doesn't work out all that well. I mean, you may come from a place where you can turn right on a red light, but I work in Manhattan where you can't turn right on a green light. I thought, I wonder how they do that out there on the water where there are no lights or signs or anything. So I started to read and it said something like this:

There are two kinds of craft. One of them has access to great power. It can accelerate and push its way through the strongest of waves. It can change direction on command. It can even stop on demand. It has great power of its own. The other class of craft is dependent on the forces of nature, wind, tide, and human effort in paddling or rowing, or maintenance of the sails. And these two classes of craft are known as "privileged" and "burdened." This book said—this is getting pretty interesting, huh? I mean, for a boat story—that these two kinds of craft have two different terms or classes. One class is "privileged" and the other class is "burdened." But get this, now. The powerful boats, do you think they are considered privileged vessels or burdened? They, my friends, are the burdened vessels. The powerful boats that can make their way forward no matter what, under their own power, they are burdened vessels, burdened with responsibility to give way to the boats without power. And the powerless vessels, the ones who are dependent on the vagaries of tide and wind and weather, they are classified as privileged vessels. To them is accorded the right of way, for if the powerful vessels are not burdened with responsibility for giving way, these powerless vessels may not make safe harbor.

Imagine that: The powerful boats are burdened, and the powerless are privileged. And when these two kinds of craft meet each other on the open sea—the privileged and the burdened—the powerful are "burdened" and must give way if the powerless, the "privileged," are ever to make safe harbor.

The powerful must give way if the powerless are ever to make safe harbor.

I thought to myself, who wrote this thing, Billy Graham? Cornell West? Mother Teresa? Abraham Heschel? So I turned to the front and it said "New Jersey Department of Transportation." Now, you know what a notable theological institution that is!

Friends, what's going on? What's going on in our land when the Department of Transportation knows that the powerful must give way if the powerless are to make safe harbor—that the powerful are considered "burdened" and the powerless are "privileged"—and the government of the United States and the Church of Jesus Christ and all of our religious institutions are having trouble with the concept?

National Council of the Churches of Christ in the USA

OFFICE OF THE GENERAL SECRETARY

Dear Colleagues in Ministry,

Today in America, our children are too often adrift on the turbulent seas of inadequate health care, inconsistent policies and indifferent political leadership at all levels of government. Such a context places in harm's way God's children by denying them the adequate health care they need to grow in body, mind, and spirit.

In such perilous times, our children need a Sabbath rest and a time and place of sanctuary. The National Council of Churches of Christ in the USA has, since its inception, been an enthusiastic participant and endorser of the observance of Children's Sabbaths. This year it is with a special sense of faithfulness to Jesus that we urge every congregation to join in observing the Children's Sabbath.

Jesus said, "Whoever welcomes one such child in my name welcomes me." Every congregation can extend just such an invitation by observing Children's Sabbath and by utilizing the fine materials gathered in the Children's Sabbath Manual. These resources provide a rich treasury that pastors, mission teams, Christian educators, Sunday School superintendents, and others will turn to time and again in their own ministry in congregations on behalf of children and their families.

In these days then, let the church serve her Lord in measured and faithful ways in an ever ready welcome to all God's children. We thank God, too, for our long partnership with the Children's Defense Fund in preparing for the Children's Sabbath.

It is our prayer that each congregation will be blessed by this Children's Sabbath observance, and in turn, will be a blessing to children in every community. Together then, might children and churches ever more safely navigate through stormy seas in the name of that holy child of so long ago.

In His name,

Robert Edgar
General Secretary
National Council of Churches of Christ in the USA
Pentecost 2007

475 Riverside Drive, 8th Floor ▪ New York, NY 10115-0050 ▪ www.ncccusa.org
Phone: 212-870-2141 ▪ Fax: 212-870-2817 ▪ E-mail: redgar@ncccusa.org

Archdiocese of Galveston-Houston

Office of the Archbishop Emeritus

April 23, 2007

Dear Friends:

I am delighted to serve as a member of the Children's Defense Fund's Advisory Committee for the interfaith National Observance of Children's Sabbaths, which, since 1992 has united tens of thousands of people of faith to pray and advocate for the needs of the children of America who cannot speak, vote or lobby for themselves. The need to speak out for the health and well-being of America's children is urgent. Every 36 seconds in America, a baby is born into poverty. Every 36 seconds, a child is confirmed as abused or neglected. Every 46 seconds, a baby is born without health insurance.

On the third weekend of each October, congregations of many faiths focus their liturgies, education programs and hands-on service and advocacy activities on addressing the urgent needs of our nation's children such as poverty, violence and lack of health care. In addition to generating faithful action on the weekend itself, the Children's Sabbath aims to inspire new and renewed action for children throughout the year, as congregations respond with prayer, service and advocacy. I hope will use this comprehensive resource manual to plan a Children's Sabbath for your parish this year.

Catholic social teaching reminds us that, while God loves all people, God has a special love for those who are poor and oppressed. It is a teaching founded on the life and words of Jesus Christ, who came "to bring glad tidings to the poor...liberty to captives...recovery of sight to the blind" (Lk 4:18-19), and who identified himself with "the least of these," the hungry and the stranger (cf. Mt 25:45).

As Jesus served those who are poor and vulnerable, so must we serve the "least of these" in our midst. There is no more precious and vulnerable resource than our children. In the words of Pope Benedict XVI on the Feast of the Baptism of the Lord 2007, "Every child who is born brings us God's smile and invites us to recognize that life is his gift, a gift to be welcomed with love and preserved with care, always and at every moment."

I hope that you will take this opportunity to pray and advocate for the health and well-being of America's children. May God bless you as you serve as a light and a beacon of hope to the children of America who are suffering within our midst, and may your action make our world more healthy and safe for children of the poor and vulnerable.

Sincerely yours,

+Joseph A. Fiorenza

Most Reverend Joseph A. Fiorenza
Archbishop Emeritus
Catholic Archdiocese of Galveston-Houston

JAF/baf

NATIONAL SPIRITUAL ASSEMBLY
OF THE
BAHÁ'ÍS OF THE UNITED STATES
536 SHERIDAN ROAD, WILMETTE, ILLINOIS 60091-2849 • (847) 733-3537• EMAIL: secretariat@usbnc.org

April 24, 2007

To the American Bahá'í Community

Dear Friends,

Among the many valuable and creative initiatives being developed throughout the community in response to the pressing need for the care and nurturing for our community's children, the National Observance of Children's Sabbaths provides an excellent opportunity for the Bahá'í community to unite with Faith communities across the country in activities of worship, education and service on behalf of children.

The emphasis of this year's Sabbath, which is once again on healthcare for children, provides an occasion to reflect on how we express the value our Teachings place on children and the principles of nurturing and developing these precious trusts in our communities. In the words of the Master:

I give you my advice, and it is this: Train these children with divine exhortations. From their childhood instill in their hearts the love of God so they may manifest in their lives the fear of God and have confidence in the bestowals of God. Teach them to free themselves from human imperfections and to acquire the divine perfections latent in the heart of man...Therefore, make ye an effort in order that these children may be rightly trained and educated and that each one of them may attain perfection in the world of humanity. Know ye the value of these children, for they are all my children.

'Abdu'l-Bahá, The Promulgation of Universal Peace, pp. 53-54

The National Spiritual Assembly has been pleased to collaborate with the Children's Defense Fund by providing resources for inclusion in its manual for the National Observance of Children's Sabbaths. These materials, combined with those submitted by other Faith organizations, provide a wealth of ideas and activities to facilitate your planning process. These materials may be found by visiting the Children's Defense Fund website, www.childrensdefense.org. You may also download the Bahá'í materials on the Education and Schools website, www.education.usbnc.org.

We hope you will consult with your community to see how you may best utilize this opportunity to share with the greater community the value which the Bahá'í Faith bestows on all children.

With loving greetings,

Robert C. Henderson
Secretary General

بســـــــــــــر الله الرحمن الرحـــــيم

الإتحاد الإسلامي في أمريكا الشمالية

The Islamic Society of North America

Dear Brothers and Sisters,

Assalamu Alaykum.

We have all been given a tremendous opportunity to serve our community today with an effort that is both embraced by many faiths as well as an integral part of our own Islamic tradition. I implore you as concerned and passionate members of the American Muslim community to support and take part in the 2007 Children's Defense Fund National Observance of Children's Sabbaths.

This year's theme is particularly important because it addresses the issue of health care and hope. Too many of our neighbors are in dire need of care and too many are going without the attention they deserve. We reflect on our Prophet's urging to effect change when we witness an injustice or see someone in harm's way. When it is our children, our own future, that is being deprived of the basic need of well being, then we are even more accountable to our Creator.

I am heartened to see another chance for people of faith to come together and be strong in urging one another to do good for all. Reading through these sections, you will see that we have so much in common, and we share so many ideals. That gives us even more reason to be proactive in the preservation of the rights of our children over us.

Use the materials here to organize and implement a campaign for the sake of our children. Our schools, masajid and organizations need to take advantage of this manual as a tool to educate about, advocate for, and alleviate the stresses that accompany hopelessness when health care is unavailable and a non-option for so many. It is our fard kifaya, our communal duty, and the call to serve our Merciful Lord.

Dear Lord, give us the sense of perseverance we need to work tirelessly for our children so they may remember us when we return to You. Their remembrance should be one full of prayers for us because we have done the utmost to our capabilities to give them comfort in our lifetime.

With prayers for peace,

Sayyid M. Syeed
National Director
Interfaith and Community Alliances
Islamic Society of North America

P.O. Box 38 (mail) • 6555 South County Road 750 East (Express mail & packages) • Plainfield, IN 46168 U.S.A.
Phone: (317) 839-8157 • Fax: (317) 839-1840 • E-Mail: isna@surf-ici.com • Website: www.isna.net
Constituent organizations include: The Muslim Students' Association of the U.S. and Canada • The Association of Muslim Social Scientists • The Association of Muslim Scientists and Engineers • Islamic Medical Association of North America

UNION FOR REFORM JUDAISM
האיחוד ליהדות רפורמית
SERVING REFORM CONGREGATIONS IN NORTH AMERICA

Rabbi Eric H. Yoffie
President

April 12, 2007
24 Nisan 5767

Dear Friends:

I am writing to urge you to take part in the 2007 National Observance of Children's Sabbaths during the weekend of October 19-21, 2007. Each year, the Children's Defense Fund compiles a resource booklet that includes educational materials, sermon starters, and prayers for a variety of faith traditions. This year's Children's Sabbath theme is: *My Boat Is So Small: Creating a Harbor of Hope and Health Care for All Children*, which focuses on the need to provide affordable, high quality health care to all our nation's children.

Through your participation in Children's Sabbath, you can join other congregations, both Jewish and non-Jewish, in a unified call for action around this crucial issue. Currently, 9 million children lack health insurance; millions more are underinsured. Participating in the Children's Sabbath is an important first step in bringing this issue to the forefront and inspiring others to do the same. The materials in this guide will help to educate your members and make them effective and empowered advocates for this cause.

The Reform Movement has participated in the Children's Sabbath for many years and the event has a deep and profound impact on all who take part. Our clergy find the resource materials extremely helpful in promoting the cause of children within a worship setting, and our members are moved and inspired by the experience.

Indeed, health care is a critical issue and one that Judaism mandates should be available to all. In overlooking our children's health, we are neglecting our future. Our tradition teaches us that "The world endures only for the sake of the breath of school children" (Shabbat 119b). Without adequate access to health care, young lives with the potential to shape our world and preserve it for the future are being lost to our inaction. For this reason and so many others, I urge you to take an active role in the 2007 National Observance of Children's Sabbaths and, through prayer, education, and advocacy within your own community, to give this important issue the attention it deserves. I look forward to hearing about your participation.

Sincerely,

Eric H. Yoffie

Eric H. Yoffie

633 THIRD AVENUE, 7TH FLOOR, NEW YORK, NY 10017
P: 212.650.4150   F: 212.650.4159   PRESURJ@URJ.ORG   WWW.URJ.ORG

Welcome to the National Observance of Children's Sabbaths

Whether this will be your first or your 16th Children's Sabbath, welcome!

By participating in the interfaith National Observance of Children's Sabbaths, you are part of a powerful, diverse interfaith voice for children that spans our nation and crosses all lines of income, race, ethnicity, and political party. What unites us is the belief that God calls us to protect children, especially the poorest and most vulnerable, and the conviction that our faith calls us to live out God's justice and compassion.

Most of us, in our individual lives and in our life as a congregation, already celebrate God's gift of children, already strive to make the world just and safe for our children. The Children's Sabbath is an opportunity to affirm what we already do and at the same time deepen our understanding both of God's call and the current crises facing children so that we may more fully, persistently, effectively, and faithfully live out that calling not only on the Children's Sabbath weekend but throughout the year.

There is an extraordinary power in participating in the Children's Sabbath, knowing that all across the country, in congregations of many different faiths, we are united in our concern for children and in our commitment to respond.

This inspiring weekend focuses attention on the urgent plight of children in our nation and calls us to put our faith into action to meet children's needs through direct service and work for justice. Through the service of worship, educational programs, and congregational activities, you can affirm what your place of worship already does with and for children while challenging them to take new actions and commit to new efforts to meet the needs of children in your community, state, and our nation. When 12.9 million children in America live in poverty, nine million lack health insurance, and thousands are homeless each day, your concern and action are needed now more than ever.

What is the Children's Sabbath?

Every day, places of worship welcome children and families. Every day, congregations learn more about their faith and its implications for their lives. Every day, religious congregations provide food or clothing or other emergency assistance to families in need. Every day, religious leaders and members work for justice in their communities, nation, and world.

Already, there are congregations that celebrate June Children's Day, often to congratulate and celebrate youngsters who have completed Sunday school. Already, many congregations have Youth Days when they turn the service over to the young people to plan and lead. Already, there are places of worship that have separate services designed just for children to attend.

So what's so special about the Children's Sabbath?

The Children's Sabbath is a weekend that aims to unite religious congregations of all faiths across the nation in shared concern for children and common commitment to improving their lives and working for justice on their behalf. In that respect, it is bigger and more powerful and more inspiring than the efforts of any one congregation on its own. On the Children's Sabbath, congregations have a strong sense of participating in a larger movement for children. Some congregations plan services, educational sessions, and activities for their own place of worship. Others join with one or more places of worship in shared services bringing together their congregations. In some communities all of the congregations work together to sponsor an interfaith service to which the entire community is invited. Often, local organizations serving children or working on their behalf join in the planning of these community interfaith Children's Sabbaths.

The Children's Sabbath is sponsored by the Children's Defense Fund, guided by an interfaith advisory committee, and endorsed by hundreds of denominations and religious organizations. The Children's Defense Fund (CDF) Leave No Child Behind® mission is to ensure every child a *Healthy Start*, a *Head Start*, a *Fair Start*, a *Safe Start*, and a *Moral Start* in life and successful passage to adulthood with the help of caring families and communities. CDF provides a strong, effective voice for all the children of America who cannot vote, lobby, or speak for themselves. We pay particular attention to the needs of poor and minority children and those with disabilities. CDF educates the nation about the needs of children and encourages preventive investment before they get sick or into trouble, drop out of school, or suffer family breakdown. CDF is a private, nonprofit organization supported by foundations and corporate grants and individual donations, and has never taken government funds.

From its inception over 30 years ago, CDF has recognized the importance of the faith community's partnership in building a movement to Leave No Child Behind. A nation that lets its children be the poorest citizens has at its heart a spiritual and ethical crisis. Thus, the religious community must help to transform our nation's priorities so that we defend those who are youngest, weakest, poorest, and most vulnerable. For many years CDF has worked to support denominations and religious organizations as they develop and maintain child advocacy campaigns. The National Observance of Children's Sabbaths® celebration was launched in 1992 to coalesce these efforts into a united moral witness for children that crosses all lines of geography, faith tradition, race, and ethnicity.

The Children's Sabbath observance is guided by an interfaith advisory committee with Muslim, Jewish, Christian, Bahá'í, and Sikh members. It is endorsed by more than 200 denominations, faith groups, and religious organizations. If you are interested in having your organization become an official endorser of the National Observance of Children's Sabbaths, please call CDF's Religious Action Division at (202) 662-3555.

The Children's Sabbath seeks to affirm and celebrate the important work that congregations are already doing with and for children. Those faithful, week-in and week-out efforts make an enormous difference in children's lives, and the Children's Sabbath seeks to highlight, applaud, and build even greater support for those important, on-going efforts. Hopefully, by the end of the Children's Sabbath weekend, existing congregational efforts to help children and families will have more visibility, new volunteers, increased resources, and fresh energy.

At the same time, the Children's Sabbath provides an opportunity for each place of worship to consider in what new ways they might work—as a body or as individuals— to help children. Religious leaders, committees, and members may discover additional children's needs that aren't being met and come up with new ways to meet them. This might include starting a new program sponsored by the congregation. Or it might mean exploring and promoting opportunities for individual members to commit their time, services, or resources. Or it might mean forging a new partnership with another con-

gregation or community organization to help children. It could mean establishing a new child advocacy committee to guide the congregation's work for justice for children.

The Children's Sabbath is a time to look deeply at what one's faith tradition says about our responsibility to nurture and protect children. This is done through the worship service—in prayer, readings, songs, and sermon. It is also done in educational sessions, whether classes for children and youths or adult forums or discussions.

The Children's Sabbath is a time for action that springs from that faithful study and reflection. It is not only a time to pray but also to put prayer into action. It is not only a time to study but also a time to serve children directly. It is not only a time to sing, but also a time to speak out to elected leaders and others about the need for justice. So on the Children's Sabbath weekend, after worship/prayers or at another time, members and leaders should join in hands-on activities to help children as well as engage in working for justice—perhaps writing letters or planning a visit to an elected official.

The Children's Sabbath is intended to inspire new long-term efforts to help children and families. However wonderful the weekend celebrations may be, what matters most is what individuals and congregations do in the following weeks and months and years to help children. Some congregations will start new efforts (on their own or in partnership with other congregations or community organizations), such as an after-school tutoring program or housing a Head Start program or an outreach and enrollment campaign to help uninsured children get health care. Other congregations will not start a new program, but will work to encourage individual members to find new ways to volunteer time or resources to efforts helping children.

The Children's Sabbath is a poignant mix of joy and sadness, of celebration and sober commitment. To be sure, a Children's Sabbath exudes the happiness of a wonderful celebration. Children delight in their roles of the day, parents hug children a little tighter, more conscious of the gift that they are, balloons may adorn buildings, children's artwork may brighten hallways, child-friendly snacks may replace the usual after-services fare. It is a day that children and families look forward to, and those without children at their side can also appreciate the extra energy and excitement of the event.

At the same time, the Children's Sabbath is sobering, as the service and activities deepen our understanding of the terrible plight facing millions of children in our country. It is painful to think about children who are hungry or homeless or without health insurance or abused or neglected or victims of gun violence or without good quality child care or denied a place in Head Start. The Children's Sabbath can be an eye-opening experience. But done properly, the Children's Sabbath will do more than open eyes to the problems facing children—it also will lift up new ways to help children and families and inspire and motivate people to respond and get involved.

The Children's Sabbath is an annual event, taking place on the third weekend of October each year. Because it is an annual event, congregations participating for the first time can just "stick a toe in the water" and participate in small, simple ways... although some want to jump in completely right from the start. Others build their participation year by year, adding more elements to their observance. Because it occurs annually, congregations have the opportunity to evaluate what worked well and what didn't and improve their plans for the following year. Most importantly, because the Children's Sabbath takes place each fall, children look forward to it from year to year, having a consistent experience of their congregation as a place and community that cares about children and is committed to nurturing and protecting them.

The Children's Sabbath is flexible. While there is a suggested theme each year, congregations are encouraged to focus on the most urgent problems confronting children and families in their communities. This resource manual is chock-full of materials from which you can pick and choose those that are best suited to your congregation. Most can be used as is, or adapted, or simply serve as inspiration for you to create your own materials. Materials prepared for one faith tradition may be enriching for the congregation of another tradition. And while the suggested date is the third weekend of October, if that date doesn't work for your congregation's calendar, pick a different date that does. What is most important is finding a time to focus on the needs of children and our responsibility to nurture and protect them.

So if you want to get involved in the Children's Sabbath, where do you start?

Getting this manual is the first important step in getting involved in the Children's Sabbath, so you are already on your way! The next steps are outlined in Section 3: Planning and Promoting Your Children's Sabbath. One of the first decisions you and those who join you in the planning will need to make is whether to plan a Children's Sabbath just for your congregation or to join with congregations of other faiths or denominations to plan an interfaith or ecumenical Children's Sabbath in your community. (See Section 9 for planning an interfaith service.) Either option is a valuable way to participate. You should determine what is right for your congregation this year.

This manual provides planning suggestions, promotion ideas, worship resources, educational programs for all ages, activity ideas, and suggestions for building on your Children's Sabbath to help children throughout the year.

How congregations celebrated the Children's Sabbath last year

Like our children, Children's Sabbath celebrations are unique, no two are alike. They can be big or small, young or more experienced. Children's Sabbath celebrations reflect the diversity and unique gifts, resources, and concerns of the congregations that plan them. Some are celebrating their first-ever Children's Sabbath, some are building on a tradition of many years, and some are even reviving their congregation's Children's Sabbath participation after several missed years. As you'll see in the examples below, the emphasis and the extent of the celebrations vary—some congregations plan a full weekend of events, while others focus on just one element, whether worship or education or service. Together, they comprise a marvelous witness and work that bring our nation closer to the justice and compassion God intends for our life together.

A five-week adult discussion group, "How Are the Children?" was the core element of **Alexandria United Methodist Church's** Children's Sabbath in **Alexandria, Minnesota.** They used CDF data, a county profile, and the United Methodist Social Principles for their discussion, which included conversation with a social services director for the county.

First Congregational Church of West Springfield, Massachusetts, held their first Children's Sabbath service in more than five years. As a result, they now have information available at the church to help families access children's health insurance programs and are assembling children's health kits for kids in the community.

Guardian Angel's Catholic Church in Oakdale, Minnesota, involved parents, teachers, and children in the liturgy, which included a blessing of children. They distributed a bulletin insert from the area's Congregations Concerned for Children and had an advocacy table with handouts and information to help congregation members work for justice on behalf of children.

If you were listening to the radio in **Hattiesburg, Mississippi,** you might have heard the talk program discussion of Children's Sabbath coordinated by **Bentley Chapel Church.** Or, maybe you attended the community meeting they sponsored and learned more about children's needs and what the community could do to respond to those needs. At their Children's Sabbath service, the children took a leadership role.

First United Methodist Church in Ames, Iowa, celebrated the Children's Sabbath with a liturgy that included prayers from the Children's Sabbath manual, followed by a party with information on children's health insurance and a letter writing table so congregation members could communicate with their elected leaders to convey their concern for uninsured children and seek solutions.

A forum with school officials was just part of **Eagle Lake Lutheran Church's** Children's Sabbath celebration in **Battle Lake, Minnesota.** Their Children's Sabbath also featured children from the Sunday school singing, a coin collection for world hunger organized by the children, posters and bulletin inserts to focus attention on children's needs and how we can respond, and distribution of the seven-day devotional guide for adults provided in the Children's Sabbath manual.

Providence Presbyterian Church in Providence, Rhode Island, focused their Children's Sabbath on the worship service using resources from the Children's Sabbath manual. They also used it as an opportunity to recognize and affirm the church's connection to the Head Start program that meets in the church building.

Saturday fun activities and free health check-ups kicked off the Children's Sabbath weekend at **De Lisle Mount Zion United Methodist Church in Pass Christian, Mississippi.** Children of the community, legislators, and school personnel were especially invited to attend the Children's Sabbath service on Sunday.

St. Clare's Episcopal Church in Blairsville, Georgia, got the word out about the Children's Sabbath through an article in the local newspaper and distributing Children's Sabbath flyers to the congregation. Students in the Sunday school engaged in lessons from the Children's Sabbath manual and participated in the morning worship service. The worship service included a special sermon on the theme of the Children's Sabbath and an offering of school supplies for low-income children in the local child care center.

In **Scottsbluff, Nebraska, First United Methodist Church's** Children's Sabbath featured a community showcase of resources to help children and families and an invitation to mentor or volunteer, as well as other opportunities to serve as God's hands that help, heal, and build hope. **St. Paul's United Church of Christ in Mechanicsburg, Pennsylvania,** also sponsored a fair with several service organizations represented to enable members to volunteer time, talent, money, and/or gifts.

A weekend of Children's Sabbath events began at **First United Methodist Church of Palmetto, Florida,** with a Saturday morning CPR and Child-Youth Protection Training. That evening there was a prayer service and a fast in place of dinner, with prayers for hungry children. Sunday morning began with a pancake breakfast followed by the church service featuring a special sermon and offering for children in need.

Words from Children's Sabbath organizers

"Just a note and a few bits of sunshine to share with you. Our congregation celebrated Children's Sabbath this last Sunday. I have included our worship bulletin, an all-church mailing, and a copy of an upcoming newsletter article. As has happened each year that we have participated (this is our 9th year), our congregation has responded in an amazing way. From the time that the first newsletter article appeared in September to this very morning, contributions of money, bears, and offers of time and talent have been appearing in my office. As I type this to you, I am surrounded by a congregation's tangible gifts of love for children…a very large bunch of bears and over 200 'care kits' destined for Alpena Regional Medical Center's Emergency Room. This is one time I love the fact that my office is a complete, utter mess!

"Thank you for the work that you do, work that enables us to also help the children!"

Blessings and peace be with you,
Betsy Dee Adamus
Associate for Music and Christian Education
First Congregational United Church of Christ
Alpena, Michigan

"Good morning! Just wanted to let you know **St. Paul's Episcopal Church in Columbus, Indiana**, celebrated the first true Children's Sabbath yesterday, October 29th. It was a wonderful celebration beginning with the Forum as an inter-generational lesson. First, the Sunday school children acted out the play of the paralyzed man and his friends' visit to Jesus. After that, we discussed the health care issues that face our children and then handed out table-top discussions for young and old to talk about together. The results were very interesting. Also, there were word scrambles for the kids to complete, 'What Every Child Should Have/Do to Stay Healthy,' and a Bible hunt worksheet that asked questions about the play. Then we had six members of our congregation who are involved in health care or child development tell what they do and see in their jobs as it pertains to children's health and well-being. This was very interesting.

"During the church service two of our teens who were recently certified as Chalicers served on the altar. We had another teen do the lesson readings and the Sunday school children sang a song during the offering. For the prayers of the people, it was directed toward children, and the congregation replied with the song, 'Kum ba yah, my Lord,' after each prayer.

"It was a wonderful day and everyone truly enjoyed this special service. Thank you for helping us make it possible to share with our congregation!"

Peace,

Kim Swope

"We had our Children's Sabbath on September 22nd. I think this is the first time this church has celebrated. (I'm the new Director of Children's Ministry and have done it at other churches I've worked at.) We included an insert in our bulletin with concrete ways of helping children…everything from buying [canned food] every time you go grocery shopping to donate to the food bank, to volunteering to be a homework helper at the elementary school, to joining a gathering scheduled for November 14th to read and discuss *Thus Far On the Way: Toward a Theology of Child Advocacy* by Eileen W. Lindner, to praying for children, to purchasing school supplies and backpacks for the children who will be moving to the battered women's shelter and starting a new school during the year. Also, Sept. 22nd was "Undies Sunday," when we asked everyone to bring child-sized underwear as part of their morning offering; after the offering plate was passed, children carried big baskets down the aisle and collected the undies—all 303 pairs of them! They are for our local community clothing closet.

"Our children's choir and adult choir did a special piece of music for the service. The sermon was preached by our seminary intern who had been a Head Start teacher for twenty years before going to seminary; it gave the service a special depth and understanding. We are already thinking of ideas for next year!!!"

Peace,

Cheryl McDermott
Director of Children's Ministry
Conyers Presbyterian Church, Conyers, Georgia

Organizations Endorsing the National Observance of Children's Sabbaths

African American Women's Clergy Association

African Methodist Episcopal Church, Women's Missionary Society

African Methodist Episcopal Zion Church, Christian Education Department

Akron Area Association of Churches

Alliance of Churches, Ohio

American Baptist Churches, USA

Anti-Defamation League

Antioch Baptist Church

Arizona Ecumenical Council

Arkansas Interfaith Council

Armenian Apostolic Church of America

Armenian Orthodox Church

Arrowhead Council of Churches

Associated Churches of Fort Wayne and Allen Counties

Associated Ministries of Thurston County

Association of Brethren Caregivers

Bahá'ís of Sioux City, Iowa

Baptist Peace Fellowship of North America

Benedictine Sisters, Queen of Angels Monastery

Bergen County Council of Churches

B'nai B'rith International

Border Association for Refugees from Central America, Inc.

Bread for the World

California Council of Churches

Cape Cod Council of Churches

Carbondale Inter-Church Council

Catholic Archdiocese of Baltimore, Justice and Peace Commission

Catholic Archdiocese of Chicago, Office for the Ministry of Peace and Justice

Catholic Charities USA

Catholic Diocese of Cleveland, Social Action Office

Catholic Diocese of Covington, Family Ministry Office

Catholic Diocese of Savannah, Office of Black Ministry

Catholic Diocese of Youngstown

Center for Ethics and Economic Policy

Center for Ministry Development

Center for the Prevention of Sexual and Domestic Violence

Central Maryland Ecumenical Council

Chautauqua County Rural Ministry

Children's Ministry Team of Western Pennsylvania Annual Conference

Christian Children's Fund

Christian Church (Disciples of Christ)

Christian Communication Council of Metropolitan Detroit Churches

Christian Conference of Connecticut

Christian Council of Delaware and the Eastern Shore of Maryland

Christian Council of Metropolitan Atlanta

Christian Methodist Episcopal Church

Church Council of Greater Seattle

Church of Christ in Yale

Church of the Brethren

Church of the Brethren, Atlantic Northeast District

Church Women United

Church Women United in Pennsylvania

Churches United of the Quad City Area

Colorado Council of Churches

Communities of Christ

Community Ministries of Rockville

Congregational United Church of Christ, Arlington Heights, Illinois

Congregations Concerned for Children, Child Advocacy Network

Congregations Concerned for Children of the St. Paul Area Council of Churches

Congress of National Black Churches

Cooperative Metropolitan Ministries

Council of Bishops of the United Methodist Church

Council of Christian Communions

Council of Churches and Synagogues of Lower Fairfield County

Council of Churches of Greater Bridgeport

Council of Churches of Greater Springfield (Mass.)

Council of Churches of Santa Clara County

Council of Churches, the City of New York

Covenant to Care, Inc.

Cross-Lines Cooperative Council

Des Moines Area Religious Council

Dominican Sisters of Edmonds, Wash.

Dominican Sisters of San Rafael, Calif.

Downtown Cooperative Ministry, New Haven, Conn.

East Harlem Interfaith, Inc.

Ecclesia: The Ecumenical Mission of the Capital Area

Ecumenical Child Care Network

Ecumenical Communication Commission,
Northwest Ohio

Ecumenical Ministries of Oregon

Episcopal Church Center, Children's Ministries

Episcopal Diocese of Alaska

Episcopal Diocese of Arkansas

Episcopal Diocese of Bethlehem, Pennsylvania

Episcopal Diocese of Los Angeles

Episcopal Diocese of Maryland

Episcopal Diocese of Massachusetts

Episcopal Diocese of Newark, New Jersey

Episcopal Diocese of Northwestern Pennsylvania

Episcopal Diocese of Oregon, Education Department

Episcopal Diocese of Pennsylvania, Episcopal
Church Women

Episcopal Diocese of Southern Virginia

Evangelical Lutheran Church in America, Division for
Church in Society

Evansville Area Council of Churches

Faith Institute for Black Catholics

Federation of Reconstructionist Congregations
and Havurot

Florida Council of Churches

For the Love of Children

Franklin Township Ministerial Association

Friends United Meeting, Quaker Life

Georgia Christian Council

Grand Rapids Area Center for Ecumenism

Greater Dallas Community of Churches

Greater Flint Council of Churches

Greater Minneapolis Council of Churches

Gropo Shalom, Cammy, Puerto Rico

Hawaii Council of Churches

Illinois Conference of Churches

Inner City Renewal Society

Interfaith Center for Faith Action and Response
of St. Louis

Interfaith Community Council, Inc. (New Albany, Indiana)

Interfaith Conference of Greater Milwaukee

Interfaith Conference of Metropolitan Washington

Interfaith Ministries for Greater Houston

Interfaith Resource Center

International Institute for Islamic Thought

International League of Muslim Women

InterReligious Council of Central New York

Islamic Society of Greater Houston

Jesuit Social Ministries, National Office

Jewish Reconstructionist Federation

Jewish Women International Leadership Conference

Jordan United Church of Christ, Allentown, Pennsylvania

Lexington Theological Seminary

Lincoln Interfaith Council

Long Island Council of Churches

Lower Bucks Center for Church and Community

Lutheran Social Services of Washington and Idaho

Marin Interfaith Council

Metropolitan Area Religious Coalition of Cincinnati

Metropolitan Ecumenical Ministry

Metro-Toledo Churches United

Michigan Ecumenical Forum

Minnesota Council of Churches

Mississippi Religious Leadership Conference

Missouri Catholic Conference

Montana Association of Churches

Moravian Church, Northern Province

National Black Catholic Congress

National Committee to Prevent Child Abuse,
Indiana Chapter

National Council of the Churches of Christ in the USA

National Farm Worker Ministry

NETWORK, A National Catholic Social Justice Lobby

Network of Religious Communities

New Hampshire Council of Churches

New Jersey Council of Churches

New Mexico Conference of Churches

New York State Council of Churches

North Carolina Conference of Churches

North Dakota Conference of Churches

North Dallas Shared Ministries

North Snohomish County Association of Churches

Oak Park – River Forest Community of Congregations

Ohio Council of Churches

Ohio – West Virginia YMCA

Parenting for Peace and Justice Network

Pax Christi USA

Peace with Justice Week, National Council of the Churches
of Christ in the USA

Pennsylvania Council of Churches

Pomona Inland Valley Council of Churches

Presbyterian Child Advocacy Network

Presbyterian Church (U.S.A.) Child Advocacy Office

Presbyterian Health, Education, and Welfare Association

Presbyterian Women in the Presbyterian Church U.S.A

Presbytery of Cincinnati

Presbytery of New York City

Rabbinical Assembly

Reconstructionist Rabbinical Association

Reformed Church in America

Rhode Island State Council of Churches

Rochester Area Church Council

Rutgers Presbyterian Church

Sacred Heart School

Saint Luke United Methodist Church, Goldsboro,
North Carolina

San Fernando Valley Interfaith Council

San Francisco Interfaith Council

San Francisco Religious Council

Santa Clara Council of Churches

Service Employees International Union

Seventh Day Adventist Church, North American Division

Sisters of Charity, BVM, Women's Office

Sisters of the Holy Cross, Notre Dame, Indiana

Sisters of Notre Dame de Namur, Chesapeake Province
Sojourners

Solid Ground Franciscan Ministry (Ivy, N.Y.)

Solid Ground Ministry

South Carolina Christian Action Council

South Coast Interfaith Council

St. Paul Area Council of Churches

Tampa United Methodist Centers, Inc.

Tarrant Area Community of Churches

Temple of Understanding

Texas Baptist Christian Life Commission

Texas Conference of Churches

The Piarist Fathers

The Swedenborgian Church in North America

Trenton Ecumenical Area Ministries

Trinity College, Campus Ministry

Tulsa Metropolitan Ministry

Ukrainian Orthodox Church of America

Union of American Hebrew Congregations

Unitarian Universalist Service Committee

United Church of Christ, Connecticut Conference

United Church of Christ, Office of Church in Society

United Church of Christ, Penn Central Conference

United Church of Christ, Penn West Conference

United Church of Christ, Southeast Association
Indiana/Kentucky Conference

United Church of Christ, Wisconsin Women's Committee

United Methodist Church, General Board of Church
and Society

United Methodist Church, General Board of Global
Ministries, Women's Division

United Methodist Church, Harrisburg Area

United Methodist Church, Northern Illinois Conference

United Methodist Church, Rhode Island and Southeastern
Massachusetts District

United Methodist Church, South Carolina Conference,
Board of Church and Society

United Methodist National Youth Ministry Organization,
Steering Committee

United Synagogue of Conservative Judaism

Virginia Council of Churches

Voices for Illinois Children

Washington Association of Churches

Washington Ethical Society

Wesley Foundation, Merced, California

West Side Ecumenical Ministry of Cleveland

Western Pennsylvania Church and Society Committee

Westside Interfaith Council

Women of Reform Judaism

Women's League for Conservative Judaism

Worcester County Ecumenical Council

World Vision Relief and Development

Wyoming Church Coalition

Zen Mountain Monastery, Mount Tremper, New York

Response Form for Endorsers of the National Observance of Children's Sabbaths (for local, state, regional, and national religious organizations)

Yes! We will endorse the National Observance of Children's Sabbaths.

Name of Endorsing Organization: _____

Name of Contact Person: _____

City, State, Zip: _____

Telephone: _____   Fax: _____

Email: _____

Contact information for Media/Communications Staff

Person: _____

Please check the boxes below to indicate the support you plan this year:

☐ We will distribute Children's Sabbath manuals to our members.

☐ We will distribute Children's Sabbath flyers with ordering information to our members. Please send.

☐ We will print a camera-ready box about the Children's Sabbath manual in our publication. Please send.

☐ We will link our Web site to yours. Please send the necessary information.

☐ We will include the Children's Sabbath date on our calendar this year and next year.
(The 2008 Children's Sabbath dates are October 17-19, 2008.)

☐ We are interested in having a Children's Sabbath workshop at a meeting, conference, or convention.
(Please contact the Religious Action Division at (202) 662-3555 to discuss dates, times, locations, and other logistics.)

**Please return this form to Children's Defense Fund, Religious Action Division.
It may be faxed to (202) 662-3570 or mailed to 25 E Street NW, Washington, DC 20001.
Questions? Call the Religious Action Division at (202) 662-3555.**

Section 2

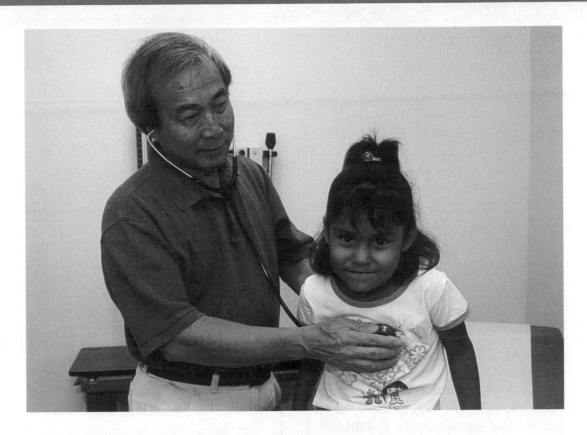

Nine million uninsured children in the United States. It is a problem that sounds too big to get our arms around. Listen to the stories of these children whose families have struggled to find health care coverage. Can you imagine putting your arms around one of them? If you can, then don't let go and don't give up. This effort to provide health care coverage for every child in our nation is about child after child after child after child like those you will meet in these stories. We can't embrace them all, but by embracing this calling to provide coverage, we will ensure that they are wrapped in the care that each needs and deserves. Open your eyes and your heart, your mouth and your arms.

This section provides an overview of the urgent need to solve the problem of nine million uninsured children in our nation. Read on for:

- A brief overview of Medicaid and the State Children's Health Insurance Plan (SCHIP)
- Snapshots of uninsured children: brief stories of real children who have struggled to get or keep health coverage
- The big picture: a look at the scope of the problem and a call to justice

Together, we can wrap our arms around this problem and solve it once and for all.

Medicaid is a joint federal- and state-funded health insurance program for low-income families, although it does not cover all children. Some of these children are now covered by the State Children's Health Insurance Program (SCHIP), which was created to help children in working families with incomes too high to qualify for Medicaid, but too low to afford private family coverage. Every state has some form of these two programs. Both provide for regular check-ups, immunizations, prescription drug coverage, and hospital care. Medicaid covers "all medically necessary care." Medicaid and SCHIP provide the opportunity for children from working families who do not have health insurance to receive the care they need.

However, millions of children are falling through the cracks between and in these two programs. Three million uninsured children don't qualify for SCHIP or Medicaid. Millions more children who do qualify aren't receiving coverage for a variety of reasons. Children don't receive health coverage through Medicaid or SCHIP automatically. Families need to know about these programs and seek them out. In many states, these programs have been given special names, so they may not be easily identifiable as "Medicaid" or "SCHIP." Parents must learn about the programs, apply for them, and maintain their eligibility over time. This can be difficult, confusing, and time-consuming, and some families will need help at every step of the process—learning about the program, applying for benefits, maintaining eligibility, and even seeking services. In many communities, concerned religious leaders, elected officials, businesses, and educators are spreading the word and helping with enrollment, but the most important thing we can do is to call for comprehensive health coverage for ALL children with simplified enrollment so that no child falls through the cracks.

Losing Hope

Ethel is a single mother caring for her two boys, ages 12 and 3. Her older son, Jeffrey, who is not adopted but for whom she is a legal guardian, suffers from major depression and Attention Deficit Hyperactivity Disorder (ADHD). Because he has been labeled disabled, he qualified for Medicaid. Her younger son suffers from severe asthma and is covered by SCHIP. Jeffrey's condition requires that he attend school in a controlled environment where there are doctors and counselors who can work with his aggression and constantly monitor his medication, but Medicaid recently cut him from this program.

Although Ethel works full-time, she earns only slightly more than $1,000 a month, and Jeffrey's situation has made it difficult for her to find constant supervision for him so she can continue to go to work. She said that she is working with her SSI caseworker to get his coverage back but admits she has lost all hope in the Medicaid system.

Can you imagine wrapping your arms around the slumped shoulders of Ethel, as she bears the burdens of work, raising children, and struggling with the system?

Snapshots of Uninsured Children

When the System Is Sick

Ten-year-old Robert is typical of a lot of children—no chronic conditions or serious illnesses so far. But like most kids, he needs preventive care to stay that way and for the routine injuries and illnesses of childhood that are bound to come along. When his SCHIP coverage needed to be renewed, Robert's grandfather, Richard Uhr, offered to take on what he thought would be a relatively routine task, since Robert's father is deaf. But it turned into a year-long nightmare of lost information and frequent and conflicting requests for more information. Mr. Uhr received eighteen letters with incorrect names and case numbers requesting information that he had already provided. He even went to the state capitol of Texas to testify about the difficulties he was having trying to renew his grandson's health coverage. Only after CDF intervened for him, did he finally receive an approval letter. He calls his year-long SCHIP ordeal, "the worst fight I've ever been in."

Can you imagine giving Robert a hug? Then wrap your arms around the problem of nine million children without health care coverage.

Reality Show

For most of us, our only regular "visit" to the emergency room is through a weekly television show like "Grey's Anatomy" or "ER." Yet for countless children and their families, visits to a real emergency room are their only access to health care for what could, with health coverage, be handled in a pediatrician's office. Kyle, 9, has chronic asthma, migraine headaches and Attention-Deficit Hyperactivity Disorder (ADHD), but his mother, who is a small business owner, cannot afford to pay for private health coverage. She learned about SCHIP three years ago and enrolled Kyle, who was eligible. But before SCHIP, Kyle had no pediatrician and had to go to the emergency room when his asthma or migraines got bad.

Can you imagine wrapping your arms around a child like Kyle enduring long waits for care amongst other sick children and stressed families? Solving the problem of uninsured children in our nation is the real emergency. Let's demand a cure.

What's Your Worry?

Being a teenager can bring an assortment of worries: Will you get your driver's license? A date? A good grade? A college acceptance letter? Imagine that your biggest worry is if you will get to see a doctor. Sixteen-year old Kayle was born with ataxia, a disease that causes damage to the nervous system resulting in lack of muscle control. Her family, which lives in Ohio, has been covered through her father's health insurance plan at work, but the physical, occupational and speech therapies that Kayle needs in order to function were regularly denied by his health plan because her therapy needs are not the result of an injury or accident. Kayle's younger brother, Gavin, also needs medication and therapy for a problem with acute double vision.

After a recent divorce, resulting in reduced income, Kayle's working mother, Twinkle, decided she had no choice but to apply for Medicaid to cover many of Kayle's medical expenses not included in her father's health plan. Twinkle explained that Medicaid will help pay for more of Kayle's expenses because of her disability, although not for some expenses that would seem to be basic. Medicaid said it would pay for a new wheelchair for Kayle, but not for the wheels.

Can you imagine putting an arm around Kayle's shoulders to comfort her?

Will the Doctor See You Now?

Elizabeth is just five. Can you remember what it feels like to be five and know you need to go for a shot? Even though shots are scary to a young child, they are essential to managing Elizabeth's severe allergies, so on this day she screwed up her courage and went with her parents, Marc and Patti, to the doctor they saw regularly, felt comfortable with, and trusted. Imagine their shock when they arrived for a routine appointment and were told the doctor wouldn't see them. He no longer provided medical services to those covered by Medicaid, like them, because of the low reimbursement rates paid to the doctor for those services compared to the rates he received from other insurance programs.

Marc and Patti try hard to take care of their four children on a very limited income. Marc is unable to work after being injured in a car accident, and health coverage is not available through Patti's employer. They have had particular difficulty in getting prescriptions for their children: Elizabeth, who requires medication for her allergies; Michael, who needs medicine for attention deficit hyperactivity disorder and Tourette Syndrome; and 17-year-old Steffy's health needs. All have had to go without the prescriptions that could significantly help or alleviate their conditions. To make matters worse, the family recently learned that they will no longer be eligible for Medicaid or SCHIP because Patti got a new job and will make just over the 200 percent federal poverty eligibility level. They now are forced to leave their home and move in with relatives.

Can you imagine wrapping your arms around a five-year-old like Elizabeth who can't get the shots she needs?

Could You Choose?

Do you remember the movie *Sophie's Choice* in which a mother was forced to choose which one of her children to save in the Holocaust? Can you imagine a situation where only some of our children get health coverage? How could we choose which children don't deserve care? Every day, families face the agonizing reality of having some children who are covered by health insurance and others who aren't.

Mekeal Cusic, a recently divorced mother, said her two children were dropped from SCHIP in January because her salary exceeds the annual income eligibility level by $2,000. She applied for private coverage through Blue Cross Blue Shield and was approved for her 3-year-old, Tracy, but not for her 10-year-old, Keyonna. She suspects it's because her daughter suffered from irritable bowel syndrome over three years ago. When she asked why Blue Cross Blue Shield refused coverage for her older daughter, they told her it was because of "strict underwriting." So now the family is trying to get by with no health insurance.

Can you imagine wrapping your arms around 10-year-old Keyonna when she gets the news that her little sister has health care coverage and can see a doctor when she needs to, but she doesn't?

Give Me Your Tired, Your Poor, Your Huddled Masses Yearning to Breathe Free...

Luminita and Sandor Tecsy live in Manhattan with their two daughters: Christina, 15, and Camilla, 12. Camilla has cystic fibrosis and requires ongoing health care, including daily medications, just to be able to breathe. Her mother, Luminita, works as an office manager and has health insurance through her employer but cannot afford to pay the premiums for the rest of her family. The father, Sandor, works as a taxi driver, and their combined income is $56,000 annually. Their daughters are enrolled in Child Health Plus B (New York's SCHIP), but because the family's income is just above the eligibility level for subsidized health insurance (currently 250 percent of the federal poverty level), they must pay a monthly buy-in fee of $150 per child. Sandor, who had colon cancer in the past, is uninsured because he is ineligible for any public health insurance program, and they cannot afford private health coverage for him.

In 1997 the family moved to Hungary after discovering, while there on vacation, that they could receive free medical care without any enrollment or approval process. Luminita said that although her daughter, Camilla, is a U.S. citizen, the doctors in Hungary immediately provided her with health care and the medicine she needed. They lived there for four years before returning to the United States. In stark contrast to their experience in Hungary, here their daughters periodically must go without health care because of bureaucratic processing problems that often occur when trying to renew their SCHIP coverage.

Before families and faith leaders visited members of Congress recently, Luminita sat next to Camilla in an interfaith service and wept. Can you imagine being the congregation member that moved next to Luminita and wrapped her arms around the mother as she sobbed? Will we wrap Christina and Camilla in health care coverage they can count on?

Lost in the Storm

Look around your home and imagine losing everything: your clothing, furniture, books, and photos. Imagine losing the house itself, your neighborhood, your job, your school, your friends, your neighbors. Imagine losing your sense of security, your emotional health, your hope. Now, imagine losing your health coverage on top of all of those other losses, when you are most in need of help. Valencia Allen and her three children, 12-year-old Kevin, 16-year-old Monica and 18-year-old Pedro, are still adjusting to life in Texas after relocating because of Hurricane Katrina. As if getting used to a new life in a new city wasn't enough to deal with, after emergency Medicaid ended for evacuee families, Valencia found it difficult to access health care for the children, and they lost their coverage. It took more than a year for the coverage issues to be resolved.

During the year that the children were uninsured, they were in desperate need of help. Valencia thought that the children were suffering from Post-Traumatic Stress Disorder (PTSD), but without insurance she was unable to get them evaluated for counseling or treatment. Her oldest child, Pedro, suffered episodes of depression and dropped out of school because the stress was too much. Sixteen-year-old Monica also went without treatment for her sickle cell anemia. The situation was traumatic for Valencia, who is disabled and provides for her family on a fixed income. Finally, their coverage was restored, and Valencia is able to get her children much needed health care.

Will we cry "compassion fatigue" and close ourselves off to the unsolved problems faced by families battered by Hurricane Katrina, or will we wrap them in the embrace of our concern?

When Justice and Compassion Come Too Late

Devante Johnson was a 13-year-old boy with advanced kidney cancer who went without any health coverage for four months while his mother attempted to renew his Medicaid coverage. Although his mother, Tamika Scott, submitted at least three renewal applications beginning in February 2006—one through the financial counselor at Texas Children's Hospital—and called the SCHIP/Medicaid hotline dozens of times, there was no record of Devante's case in the system when advocates contacted the call center on his behalf in August 2006. Because of a state staffing shortage, officials say his application went unprocessed. Meanwhile, Devante went without any health insurance and had to depend on clinical trials for care as his tumors continued to grow.

Only through personal intervention and extensive follow-up with the highest levels of the Texas Health and Human Services Commission was his coverage finally reinstated. He then was able to go to the University of Texas M.D. Anderson Cancer Center, where for a while radiation therapy helped take away his pain. After struggling courageously against his cancer, on March 1, 2007, Devante died at the age of 14 from complications of the disease. He is remembered as a thoughtful young man who was a devoted brother and son, and who never complained about his illness.

It's too late to wrap our arms around Devante. But try to imagine what it is like to be a mother like Tamika, who longs to wrap her arms around her son who died having struggled to secure the care he needed and deserved. It is too late to embrace that child, but not too late to embrace the responsibility for protecting other children who need us as he did.

Maybe you have your own story. Maybe there was a time when you or someone you love or someone you know faced the terrifying prospect of lacking health care coverage for a child. Maybe you needed us to wrap our arms around you and to wrap our minds around this challenge and make sure that every child has the health care he or she deserves.

Now is the time.

The Big Picture

So if we can hold in our mind's eye the individual children behind the huge numbers, we are better prepared to wrap our mind around the problem of uninsured children and to embrace the solution we can achieve.

Here's the big picture: Nine million children in the United States don't have health insurance. That means one out of every nine children is uninsured. Their families can't afford private insurance and they aren't receiving public health care coverage through either Medicaid or the State Children's Health Insurance Program—because they don't qualify, they aren't aware of the program, they don't know how to apply, or they are falling through the cracks. As the stories illustrate, even when you are doing everything right—you qualify and you apply—you still might not get coverage. Or, you are covered, but you can't find a doctor who will take your Medicaid coverage.

Why aren't all eligible children enrolled in either Medicaid or the State Children's Health Insurance Program?

More than 5.5 million children are eligible for but not enrolled in either SCHIP or Medicaid. There are several reasons for this: they don't know the programs exist, they don't think they qualify (seven out of ten families with children eligible for SCHIP or Medicaid do not think their children are eligible); they don't know how to apply or find the process confusing or difficult, especially if there are literacy or language challenges; and/or they don't understand the critical importance of health insurance, having walked the tightrope of being uninsured for so long out of economic necessity.

Without insurance, children are at risk of illness and disabilities that are preventable or treatable. They may not perform at their best in school because they cannot see or hear all that is being taught, or they may be distracted by physical or mental suffering. Nationally, one in five children and adolescents has a serious mental health impairment, yet only one-third receive services. Too frequently, children end up in the child welfare system or juvenile justice system because parents cannot afford or access mental health care. All families need health insurance in order to access health services in a timely and consistent way, rather than waiting until health conditions worsen.

Children with health insurance are healthier and get better overall care. Uninsured children are more likely to lack a regular source of health care, go without needed care, and end up worse off than children with health coverage in many measures of health. Instead of going to see a doctor when their child first shows symptoms of being sick, parents of uninsured children often wait, hoping the child will recover. Sometimes the child does in fact recover. Sometimes they do not. Sometimes they get sicker and their conditions get more serious and harder to treat. By the time families seek care in an emergency room, the child's condition is far worse and the medical bills are far higher than they would have been with preventive or early treatment. Uninsured children are almost nine times more likely than insured children to have no regular source of health care and over five times more likely not to have been to a doctor or other health care professional for two or more years.

As the costs of health insurance increase, so do the number of uninsured children. Most of these children are from working families who are playing by the rules, but still aren't able to afford insurance. Almost nine out of ten uninsured children live in families where at least one parent works, and more than half live in a two-parent household. However, the cost to employers and families to provide health insurance continues to rise, leaving more children uninsured. This is of particular concern to people who work in small businesses (where premiums tend to be more expensive) and to people working part-time or on a contract basis who usually aren't offered health insurance coverage at all.

Investing in Children's Health

Government can play a positive role in promoting policies that improve children's health. During the last half-century, we have witnessed tremendous progress brought about by public policies that have improved the health of the U.S. population. Access to public health programs, such as the Vaccines for Children program, and public insurance through Medicaid and the State Children's Health Insurance Program (SCHIP) has increased the primary and preventive health care that children receive, dramatically improving children's health. The many achievements of public policies include the eradication of devastating diseases such as smallpox, the virtual elimination of disabilities from diseases such as polio, the drastic decline in infant mortality, and the extension of life expectancy by more than a decade. Government can continue the progress in children's health care by further investing in these programs to improve health care and reduce health disparities, and by creating a seamless, comprehensive program that covers all children so that the millions of children falling through the cracks finally have a safety net that catches all of them before it's too late.

This investment is not only a moral commitment that must exist for our children; it is an imperative for the economic well-being of the nation. Studies have shown that preventive health care, such as newborn hearing screenings and immunizations, not only saves lives and improves health but also saves money. For every $1 spent vaccinating children against measles, mumps, and rubella, $16 is saved. Every parent knows that children do not stop getting sick simply because they lack health coverage. As children's medical needs remain untreated, the costs of treating the more serious conditions that develop are often passed on to communities through uncompensated hospital stays and clinic visits, contributing to higher premiums for the insured. For decades, Medicaid has provided critical health care, including primary and preventive care, for the poorest children in America. Providing preventive care for children is especially cost-effective in comparison to the cost of providing care to older populations. Children make up more than 50 percent of all Medicaid enrollees, but account for less than a quarter of total program spending. Per-capita health care costs for children are the lowest of all groups eligible for Medicaid.

Call for Justice

The faith community has long been a source of hope, healing, and wholeness for people. Our sacred texts, teachings, and traditions call us to care for people in mind, body, and spirit. Congregations and religious organizations are held in a special place of trust, providing members of the community a reliable source of information and resources.

Every week in the United States, millions of people attend religious services. Families turn to synagogues, churches, masjids, temples, gurdwaras, Baha'i communities, and other places of worship to have their spiritual needs met. But these religious institutions provide much more and play an ever-increasing role in the community, providing for people's basic needs including food, clothing, and shelter. These organizations also provide child care, educational programs, job training and readiness programs, and in a growing number of cases, health and mental health services.

For these reasons and others, places of worship and other religious institutions play a unique and important role in conducting outreach, enrollment, and justice-seeking activities in the community. Places of worship and faith-based organizations can play a vital role in informing eligible families and overcoming the barriers to accessing information about SCHIP and Medicaid, doubts about eligibility, difficulty navigating the enrollment process, and lack of awareness about the crucial importance of health insurance. And we can be a voice for justice calling for all children to have health care coverage.

In addition to helping with outreach and enrollment in Medicaid and SCHIP to connect the 5.5 million children who are eligible for but not enrolled in either program, the religious community can be a critical voice for justice, defending the health care services children depend on and reducing the inequalities of health care coverage related to income, race, age, disabilities, and immigration status. *All* children need simple access to comprehensive health and mental health care so no child is overlooked.

Because of the availability of public health programs, for five years before 2004, the percentage of children who were uninsured decreased, despite a rise in the number of uninsured adults. However, between 2004 and 2005, the percentage of uninsured children rose by three percent, increasing by almost 300,000 children. Progress covering children is further threatened by continued state budget shortfalls that have led to increasing cuts in public health insurance programs such as Medicaid and SCHIP. State variability and experimentation also place eligibility and coverage for children at risk.

The faith community can and should speak out against proposed cuts to these programs, which would result in more children without health coverage, limit the necessary services they provide, or increase the difficulty that families experience in applying for and maintaining enrollment in these programs. At the same time, the religious community has a prophetic role to play in calling for a more just approach that assures every child has health care regardless of where they live or how much their parents make. While Medicaid and SCHIP are providing critically needed services and improving the health of millions of children, millions more are falling through the cracks of these systems. America's children need health care that every child can count on, and they need it now.

Faith-based communities can also demand increased supports for community-based comprehensive mental health services for children. Families need access to prevention, early intervention and intensive mental health services for children and adolescents. It is a moral shame that families are forced to relinquish custody of their children to the child welfare or juvenile justice system because parents cannot afford or access the mental health services and treatment their children need. Parents turn to foster care or juvenile justice because of the limitation of both public and private health insurance in covering comprehensive mental health treatment; the inadequate supply of appropriate mental health services; the limited availability of mental health services through schools; difficulty in meeting mental health service eligibility requirements; and the lack of coordination among different child-serving agencies.

Additionally, the religious community can be a voice calling for justice to reduce the health coverage inequalities facing poor, immigrant, Black, Latino, and older children.

- The poorest quarter of children are more than five times as likely to be uninsured as the wealthiest quarter of children.
- There are more Latino children who are uninsured than there are any other single racial or ethnic group (3.3 million non-Hispanic White uninsured children and 3.4 million Hispanic uninsured children in the most recent data).
- A Black child is 2/3 more likely (or 70 percent more likely) and a Latino child is three times as likely to be uninsured as a White child.

The religious community must be a voice proclaiming that every child is precious, every child is equally beloved by God, every child deserves the same chance for a healthy start in life, and every child deserves health care regardless of income, race, age, or ethnicity. It is time to create a safe harbor of hope and health care for *all* children.

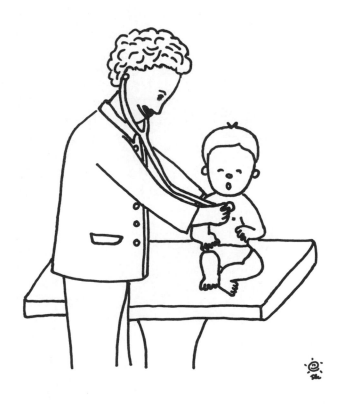

Section 3

This section provides guidelines for planning and promoting a Children's Sabbath celebration in your place of worship as well as reproducible resources: clip art and bulletin and newsletter inserts. See Section 9 for suggestions on organizing an interfaith Children's Sabbath involving congregations of many faiths.

Planning Suggestions for All Faiths

Steps for Planning a Children's Sabbath in Your Place of Worship

❑ **Begin with prayer.** The success of the Children's Sabbath—its ability to stir the hearts and minds and hands of people to nurture and protect children—ultimately relies on God's grace. Seek God's guidance for your Children's Sabbath, turn to God for the strength and commitment to plan it, pray for partners to help you in this venture, and thank God for the precious children God has entrusted to our care. (Those of the Christian faith may want to use the Daily Devotionals provided in Section 4.) Whatever your faith tradition, and whatever words you choose to pray, know that God is with you as you embark on planning a Children's Sabbath.

❑ **Secure support from appropriate religious leaders, staff, or committees.** In addition to obtaining approval for planning a Children's Sabbath, do some preliminary investigation into potential sources of financial support for your Children's Sabbath. Of course, you will have a better idea of your budget when you are further into the planning process. You may find that you can plan a Children's Sabbath with little additional expense.

❑ **Mark the date on your congregation's calendar. The 2007 Children's Sabbath is October 19-21.** Most Children's Sabbaths will take place on this third full weekend of October during a congregation's traditional worship and education time. If your congregation has a conflict with this date, select another. Keeping your celebration during the usual worship time promises greater participation and communicates that the Children's Sabbath is an integral part of your congregation's worship, work, and witness. If you select a time other than the traditional time for your place of worship, be prepared to do lots of extra promotion to ensure a strong turnout.

❑ **Recruit a committee to plan the Children's Sabbath and activities leading up to or following it.** Involving a broad range of people brings a wealth of gifts and experience, builds greater excitement and "ownership" of the Children's Sabbath throughout the congregation, and helps ensure that no single person gets overloaded. In addition to religious leaders and congregation staff, consider involving religious education teachers, social action committee members, children and youths, and any interested congregation members. Develop a meeting schedule that will allow sufficient planning time. Many committees find they need more frequent meetings in September and October as the Children's Sabbath draws near.

Who plans a Children's Sabbath?

- At *Lightstreet United Methodist Church* in *Lightstreet, Pennsylvania*, a layperson took the lead with one other planner, "many helpers" volunteered, and there was a point person who coordinated the Sunday school hour.

- The pastor and the director of the youth program led the planning at *St. Andrew's Church*, an Episcopal church in *Harrington Park, New Jersey*.

- The Children's Sabbath at *Aldersgate United Methodist Church* in *Jackson, Mississippi*, was the result of collaborative efforts of four local United Methodist churches.

- At *Highlands United Methodist Church* in *Highlands, North Carolina*, a co-pastor and the current and future children's coordinators collaborated on the planning.

- The pastor took the lead at *Fairview United Methodist Church* in *Washington, West Virginia*, with the help of the education chairperson and input from the nurture committee members.

- Wrote Clara Copeland of *First Baptist Church* in *Springfield, Ohio*, "I bought the books, then my pastor, husband and I ate dinner together and planned the service. I contacted all the other readers with their parts. My husband contacted the doctor (speaker)."

- At *Bethany Presbyterian Church* in *Spokane, Washington*, a retired pastor coordinated the planning.

(continued next page)

- The Sunday school took the planning lead at *St. Croix Falls United Methodist Church* in *St. Croix Falls, Wisconsin*.

- The past president of their United Methodist Women and two other United Methodist Women led the planning at *North United Methodist Church* in *North, South Carolina*.

- At *St. Alban's Episcopal Church* in *Indianapolis, Indiana*, an associate deacon and the director of Christian education teamed up to lead the planning.

❑ **Identify leadership within the committee.** Designate a chairperson or co-chairs to guide the planning and ensure that goals are set, responsibilities assigned and fulfilled, and that the process moves forward effectively. You also may want to name a secretary who will keep notes of committee meetings and communicate decisions and other information to those involved. (Be sure to involve or keep informed all who will be affected by Children's Sabbath activities, such as musicians, educational program teachers and volunteers, and secretaries.) A treasurer could keep tabs on the budget allotted for the Children's Sabbath and also oversee in-kind contributions donated by the community. As the Children's Sabbath planning proceeds, the chairperson(s) should assign new tasks and responsibilities as they arise.

❑ **Focus your vision for the Children's Sabbath.** What do you hope will happen during and as a result of your Children's Sabbath? Do you want the Children's Sabbath to highlight and affirm the gift and gifts of children? To underscore the responsibility of adults to nurture and protect children? Do you hope to increase awareness about the serious needs of many children today? To broaden the congregation's concern for children to encompass those in the community? Do you want to energize and increase participation in existing congregational programs serving children as a result of the Children's Sabbath? Do you hope to build excitement and commitment for starting a new congregational effort to help children? To stimulate new, individual commitments to giving time or resources to help children? Clarifying your vision for the Children's Sabbath and its impact will help guide your planning for a successful experience.

❑ **Determine the format of your Children's Sabbath.** You may decide to start small and build your celebration in future years, or you may want to plan an ambitious celebration now. Choose the approach that is right for your congregation and will provide a successful, affirming experience upon which you can build year after year. These are the major components to consider for your Children's Sabbath:

- **Service of worship/prayers:** This is the heart of most Children's Sabbath celebrations: lifting up, in prayer, sermon, and song, God's call to people of faith to nurture and protect children. (See Sections 4, 5, 6, 7, 8, and 9 for ideas and resources.)

- **Educational programs:** Educational programs for children, youths, and adults help everyone learn more about the problems facing children, the faith-based call to respond, and ways to make a positive difference. Lesson plans for a variety of faith traditions may be downloaded from the Children's Defense Fund Web site at www.childrensdefense.org/childrenssabbaths.

- **Advocacy and hands-on outreach activities:** When people have been inspired and called in the service of worship and have learned more through the educational programs, they are eager to start making a difference for children immediately. Providing concrete outreach and advocacy activities on the Children's Sabbath, perhaps following the service of worship, helps people respond and put their faith into action. (See Section 10 for ideas.)

- **Commitment to longer-term responses to children's needs:** The Children's Sabbath is about more than one weekend a year; it is about inspiring new, long-term responses to the needs of children. Provide opportunities for individuals to find out about, and make commitments to, ongoing action through information tables, presentations, and sign-up sheets. The ongoing action could include participating in existing programs in your congregation, volunteering with a community child-serving program or organization, or even joining a planning committee to develop a new program in your congregation. (See Section 11 for ideas and Section 12 for resources.)

❑ **Involve children and youths.** The Children's Sabbath is an important time to highlight the gifts, contributions, and leadership of children and youths. However, the Children's Sabbath should not be completely turned over to children, with adults serving only as the advisors and "audience." The Children's Sabbath is meant to be an intergenerational event that demonstrates and celebrates how everyone—children, youths, parents, singles, and seniors—must respond faithfully to God's call to nurture and protect children. (Other occasions celebrated by many congregations, such as Youth Sundays or Children's Day, are more appropriate times to put the service entirely in the hands of children and youths.) Be sure to involve children and youths in the planning process as well as in carrying out parts of the Children's Sabbath. The various sections of this manual offer specific suggestions on how children and youths can participate in promoting the Children's Sabbath, leading the service of worship, and engaging in outreach and advocacy activities. Be sure to solicit young people's ideas and suggestions to supplement those found here.

❑ **Involve resource people.** After you have determined the basic format and activities for your Children's Sabbath, involve resource people from the congregation and community. These may include health care professionals, public education teachers and administrators, staff of after-school programs, child care providers, Head Start teachers, staff of organizations serving families in poverty, juvenile justice professionals, police officers, staff of community organizations serving children, elected officials, and representatives of advocacy organizations working on children's behalf. Secular organizations working for children are often eager to find ways to link with religious congregations and draw on the rich resources congregations can offer. Forging these connections will not only assist you in planning your Children's Sabbath weekend, but also should create partnerships for long-term projects that build on the Children's Sabbath.

❑ **Recruit volunteers to help prepare for and conduct Children's Sabbath activities.** Some who may not have been able to join the ongoing planning committee would welcome responsibility for a specific task in preparation for the Children's Sabbath or during the weekend itself. In addition to recruiting volunteers through personal contact, publicize opportunities through the announcement time during the service, in the congregation's newsletter or bulletin, at meetings, and at gatherings. Tap seniors, children, youths, singles, parents—everyone! The Children's Sabbath is about the role each person can play to nurture and protect children.

❑ **Plan to build on the Children's Sabbath.** While you are planning the Children's Sabbath, keep your focus on the ultimate goal of stimulating new, long-term congregational and individual commitments to help children year-round. Don't wait until after the Children's Sabbath weekend to think about where you hope it will lead. Instead, make the long-term result of the Children's Sabbath a focus of the planning process. Some Children's Sabbath committees have found it useful to designate a sub-committee for follow-up to begin working on this from the start. (See Sections 11 and 12 for ideas and resources.) As you plan long-term follow-up, make sure that you involve the necessary religious leaders, staff, and committees, as well as other interested individuals. Your resource people can also provide input about community needs and opportunities for partnerships. Be sure you have a meeting date on the calendar after the Children's Sabbath to convene members of the Children's Sabbath Planning Committee and any others, as appropriate, to move ahead on the follow-up plans.

❑ **Take care of "wrap-up" details.** After the Children's Sabbath, be sure to attend to details to wrap things up. These may include evaluating the Children's Sabbath (what worked and what you would do differently next time); writing thank-you notes to those involved in the leadership and planning and any others who made contributions; marking next year's Children's Sabbath on the congregation's calendar; setting a date for the first planning committee meeting (even though the planning committee membership may change); and closing the books on the Children's Sabbath budget. Some congregations gather the planning committee members for a special appreciation luncheon and awards or other tokens of appreciation. If videotapes or photographs were taken during the Children's Sabbath, you may want to arrange a time to display them to extend the Children's Sabbath experience. Or, begin a scrapbook chronicling your congregation's Children's Sabbath, and plan to add to it next year.

❑ **Put next year's Children's Sabbath on the calendar.** The 2008 Children's Sabbath will be held October 17-19, 2008. Wrote the organizer of *Pilgrim Congregational Church-UCC's* first Children's Sabbath in *Bozeman, Montana*, "We will be putting together a Children's Sabbath Task Force as part of the Social Justice Team that will be brainstorming next year's celebration and how it ties into existing mission projects."

Promoting Your Children's Sabbath

Your Children's Sabbath will have the greatest impact if it is effectively promoted and publicized both within your place of worship and to the larger community. Here are some ways to do this:

Spreading the Word in Your Place of Worship

❑ Place the bulletin insert in this section announcing the Children's Sabbath in your congregation's bulletin or newsletter approximately one month before the date.

❑ Include other information in your congregation's newsletter. (Adapt the sample congregational newsletter article in this section.)

❑ Make posters announcing the Children's Sabbath and display them in the congregation's building. Involve the congregation's youths and children in making these posters.

❑ Request time to make an announcement during the worship service one or two weeks before the observance.

❑ If your place of worship has an email list of members, get permission to send an email to the members reminding them of the upcoming Children's Sabbath.

❑ Make a yard sign to place on the grounds in front of your place of worship, announcing the Children's Sabbath.

❑ Send the bulletin insert or a letter about the Children's Sabbath home with the children who participate in your place of worship's educational programs.

❑ If your congregation has a Web site, put an announcement on the Web site.

❑ After securing any needed permission to send a letter to the mailing list for your place of worship, write a letter describing the Children's Sabbath and encouraging members to join in the celebration on the designated weekend.

❑ Don't forget to continue to focus attention on the Children's Sabbath and the needs and opportunities for response *after* the weekend itself. Use these same media channels to report on the congregation's response, announce the total items and money collected, share stories of children and families who were helped, and encourage continued action.

Reaching Out to the Community and Media

❑ Introduce the Children's Sabbath to clergy and interfaith associations, civic groups, and other organizations that may be interested in supporting, attending, or publicizing your Children's Sabbath.

❑ Mail a letter to civic, social, and religious organizations in your community offering to speak about the Children's Sabbath at their meetings or gatherings. For example, you might contact the PTA, Lions Club, Rotary, interfaith associations, Boy Scouts and Girl Scouts, and others. Invite them to participate in your congregation's Children's Sabbath or to plan their own Children's Sabbath observance.

❑ Attend community events such as school open houses, local health fairs, and parades to distribute information about the Children's Sabbath, with permission of event organizers.

❑ Put up posters or flyers on community bulletin boards and in other permissible locations in the community.

❑ Adapt the sample news release in this section and submit it to the religion page of your local newspaper and to area religious newspapers or newsletters, including denominational publications as appropriate. Follow up with a telephone call to each.

❑ If you have any contacts who know a columnist for the local paper, solicit their help in pitching the Children's Sabbath to the columnist.

❑ Contact your local radio station to learn the requirements and formats for having your Children's Sabbath events publicized as a Public Service Announcement (PSA) or on its community calendar or community bulletin board. You may be asked to prepare a "live read" script—a brief (10 seconds) script giving the basic information. For example:

> "[Name of congregation] located at [cross streets or address] is planning a special celebration and events on [date] to involve young and old in responding to

Sample Article for Congregation's Own Newsletter

[Name of Congregation] to Celebrate Children's Sabbath To Create a Safe Harbor of Hope and Health Care for *All* Children

Can you imagine walking into a classroom of 27 children and picking out three children who don't deserve health care coverage that assures they can get preventive care to stay healthy and treatment for health and mental health illnesses, injuries, and other needs? In our nation today, nine million children—that is one out of every nine children—is uninsured.

[If desired, add a story of an uninsured child from your community or add one of the stories of uninsured children beginning on page 22.]

On *[date]*, *[name of your congregation]* will join with thousands of other congregations across the nation in the 16th annual interfaith National Observance of Children's Sabbaths® celebration sponsored by the non-profit, non-partisan Children's Defense Fund and supported by *[add the name of your denomination or religious tradition, if they have formally endorsed]*, Catholic Charities U.S.A., the Islamic Society of North America, the National Council of the Churches of Christ in the U.S.A., the National Spiritual Assembly of Bahá'ís in the U.S., the Sikh Council on Religion and Education, the Union for Reform Judaism, the United Synagogue of Conservative Judaism, and more than 200 other religious organizations and denominations.

The Children's Sabbath will focus on the needs of our nation's nine million children without health insurance. Together, congregations will commit to creating a safe harbor of hope and health care for *all* children.

At *[name of congregation]*, we will join in this united voice for children by *[describe the events, giving dates and times]*. This is *[name of congregation]*'s *[number—e.g., first or tenth]* time celebrating the Children's Sabbath. Leading the observance of Children's Sabbath here are *[names of several of those who will be involved]*. All are invited. This also will be a good time to invite other families or children to visit our congregation. For more information or to find out how you can help, contact *[name and phone number of contact person in the congregation]*.

the urgent needs of children. Can you believe that in our rich nation, nine million children don't have health insurance and may not be able to see a doctor when they need to? On the Children's Sabbath, congregations of many faiths will stand for healthy children. Together, we can create a safe harbor of hope and health care for all children. For more information, call [name of congregation]."

Type it, double-spaced, with accurate names, times, and addresses. Be sure to include your name as a contact for the station, with daytime and evening phone numbers. Send it to the station at least two weeks in advance.

❑ Invite the local media—television, radio, and print—to attend and publicize the Children's Sabbath. Tell them about aspects of the events that promise to be visually interesting and emotionally compelling. Point out that the Children's Sabbath is a way to focus attention on serious problems facing children and on positive ways to make a difference. Let them know about any well-known speakers who will be participating in your Children's Sabbath.

❑ Arrange for a local spokesperson or an interfaith panel of speakers to participate on a radio or television talk show program about an issue of concern for the children in your community.

❑ If your community has a cable or public access television station, contact the station's producers to arrange an interview. Ask if they will also air the Children's Sabbath video. Also check if they will list the Children's Sabbath on their billboard of local events.

❑ Write a letter to the editor about the crises facing uninsured children and call for justice so that every child has health coverage. Offer the Children's Sabbath as a way to learn more and become involved. Watch the newspaper for articles about health care, poverty, and children in general so that you can relate your letter to those articles and time it appropriately.

❑ Think outside the box to come up with creative and effective promotional ideas. Organizers of an interfaith Children's Sabbath in Kalamazoo, Michigan, printed paper placemats with information about their event and distributed them to restaurants that had agreed to use them in the weeks leading up to the Children's Sabbath.

News Release for Local Media

One of the goals of the National Observance of Children's Sabbaths is to reach a wider, secular audience with a message about children's needs and the religious community's concern and commitment to meeting those needs. We encourage you to use the sample news release on page 38 as a model for explaining the Children's Sabbath to your local newspaper's religion or community news editor and as a means of generating a news story. If you know of other congregations in your community that will also be celebrating the Children's Sabbath, contact them about preparing a joint news release.

Here are steps to follow:

1) **Call your newspaper** to obtain the name of the religion writer or city editor. If you know someone who works for the newspaper or has contacts there, ask for his or her help in getting the news release into the right hands.

2) **Mail the news release** to the right person at the paper in early October, two to three weeks before your Children's Sabbath.

3) **Follow up with a telephone call** a few days later. Remember, the news media are looking to cover a newsworthy story, not to promote a particular event. In your communication with them, emphasize that the Children's Sabbath is about children's issues of concern to many people and is a practical and inspiring example of how people are taking action. Emphasize that your celebration is part of a growing national movement among religious congregations to improve the well-being of America's children. Suggest that reporters contact the Children's Defense Fund's Communications Department at (202) 628-8787 for background information and a national perspective to supplement your own.

4) **Send a letter of thanks** to the reporter if the paper does cover your story, with copies to superiors. Building and maintaining a good relationship with the religion writer or other reporter may help gain coverage of follow-up efforts developing from your Children's Sabbath and of the Children's Sabbath in subsequent years.

5) **Send a copy** of any coverage you receive to the Religious Action Division of the Children's Defense Fund to assist in further promotion of the Children's Sabbath.

Sample News Release for Community Newspapers

FOR IMMEDIATE RELEASE

October [date], 2007

[YOUR CONGREGATION'S NAME] JOINS THE CHILDREN'S DEFENSE FUND IN THE INTERFAITH NATIONAL OBSERVANCE OF CHILDREN'S SABBATHS® CELEBRATION

[Name of your town, state]— [Your congregation's name] will [describe events planned, such as holding a special worship service or conducting service and advocacy activities] on [date and time] to draw attention to the needs of the children in our nation who are without health coverage.

[Your congregation's name] is one of thousands of churches, synagogues, mosques, Bahá'í communities, and other places of worship around the nation celebrating the Children's Sabbath this weekend as part of the Children's Defense Fund (CDF)'s 16th annual observance. The interfaith National Observance of Children's Sabbaths® celebration seeks to inspire congregations and religious organizations to work on behalf of children through prayer, service, and advocacy throughout the year.

The Children's Sabbath theme this year, "My Boat Is So Small: Creating a Safe Harbor of Hope and Health Care for All Children," focuses attention on the nine million children in the United States who do not have health insurance and may not be able to see a doctor when they need to. Most of them live in working families. The theme is drawn from a traditional fisherman's prayer, "Dear Lord, be good to me. The sea is so wide and my boat is so small," that serves as CDF's logo, depicted in a small child's drawing.

"Millions of children are adrift in a wide sea of need," notes Marian Wright Edelman, founder and president of the Children's Defense Fund. "They need us to create a safe harbor of health care for *all* children that will protect them from the storms of illness and injury. Without the protection of health care, children go without treatment, receive delayed treatment when conditions have worsened, and even die needlessly. Families are overwhelmed by medical debt. The richest nation on earth, with the most advanced medical technology, cannot stand by as one out of every nine children lacks health coverage. It is immoral, irresponsible, and short-sighted. The time is *now* to do the right, smart, and achievable thing and ensure *all* children health coverage."

[Add a statement from a local religious leader or young person.]

The interfaith National Observance of Children's Sabbaths is sponsored by the non-profit, non-partisan Children's Defense Fund and supported by Catholic Charities U.S.A., the Islamic Society of North America, the National Council of the Churches of Christ in the U.S.A., the National Spiritual Assembly of Bahá'ís in the U.S., the Sikh Council on Religion and Education, the Union for Reform Judaism, the United Synagogue of Conservative Judaism, and more than 200 other religious organizations and denominations.

For more information about [your congregation's name]'s celebration of the Children's Sabbath, contact [contact person's name, title, group affiliation, telephone number, and email address, if available].

###

Reproducible Resources for All Faiths

The following pages provide several resources that may be photocopied. No additional permission is needed.

Announcement Bulletin Insert (pages 40-41)

This bulletin insert announces to members of your congregation your plans to participate in the 2007 National Observance of Children's Sabbaths. Photocopy these two pages back-to-back on 8-1/2" x 11" paper and cut down the middle to make two bulletin inserts per photocopy. Distribute this bulletin insert one month before your Children's Sabbath to alert congregation members and build excitement and participation.

Children's Sabbath Service Bulletin Inserts (pages 42-46)

There are several bulletin inserts that may be used on the day you celebrate the Children's Sabbath or thereafter. If you are able, compile a list of specific ways that congregation members can serve by volunteering with or donating to community- or congregation-based programs serving children or advocating on their behalf, with local contact information. Photocopy it and distribute along with the bulletin insert.

Bulletin insert #1 begins "Dear Lord, be good to me… and ends with "What You Can Do…" and is a 4-page insert to be copied front and back and folded in the middle.

Bulletin insert #2 begins "Snapshots of Uninsured Children" and ends with "What Can We Do?" and is a 4-page insert to be copied front and back and folded in the middle.

Bulletin insert #3 begins with "Top 10 Facts About Children's Health" and is a 2-page insert to be copied front and back and cut down the middle.

Children's Sabbath Clip Art (pages 47-49)

Reproduce the images on these pages to enhance your newsletter, worship bulletin, flyers, posters, letters, and other materials related to the Children's Sabbath.

We Will Be Joining the
16th Annual Interfaith National Observance of Children's Sabbaths

My Boat Is So Small: Creating a Safe Harbor of Hope and Health Care for All Children

Don't miss this special occasion to join with congregations and other places of worship of all faiths all across our nation as we:

- learn more about the urgent needs of children in our nation, especially the needs of our nation's nine million children without health insurance and the needs of children who are pushed into the "cradle to prison pipeline" without the lifelines of high expectations, parent and community support, good schools, and more to guide them toward a hopeful and productive future;

- reflect on the call of our faith to respond to the needs of the young and the poor;

- create a harbor of hope and health care for children through hands-on service and work for justice; and

- commit to help children throughout the year through prayer, compassionate service, and justice-seeking advocacy.

Date: _____

Time: _____ Place: _____

For more information or to help, contact:

_____

_____

DEAR LORD
BE GOOD TO ME
THE SEA IS SO
WIDE AND SO
MY BOAT IS
SO SMALL

Children's Defense Fund

Today, America's children are adrift in a wide sea of need:

Nine million children bear the brunt of injury and illness without health insurance, their frail craft needing a harbor of health care.

Nearly 13 million children live in poverty, swamped by hunger, homelessness, poor health, and other difficulties without a harbor of hope and adequate family income.

Countless children are still displaced by Hurricane Katrina, as they struggle to pick up the pieces of their lives that were submerged in a flood of natural disaster and bureaucratic failure.

Nearly 100,000 young people are incarcerated, without the rudder of guidance, sails of good education and high expectations, or lifeline of opportunities.

On the Children's Sabbath and throughout the year to come, we will create a safe harbor of hope and health care for all children in our congregation, community, and nation.

DEAR LORD
BE GOOD TO ME
THE SEA IS SO
WIDE AND SO
MY BOAT IS
SO SMALL

Children's Defense Fund

Today, America's children are adrift in a wide sea of need:

Nine million children bear the brunt of injury and illness without health insurance, their frail craft needing a harbor of health care.

Nearly 13 million children live in poverty, swamped by hunger, homelessness, poor health, and other difficulties without a harbor of hope and adequate family income.

Countless children are still displaced by Hurricane Katrina, as they struggle to pick up the pieces of their lives that were submerged in a flood of natural disaster and bureaucratic failure.

Nearly 100,000 young people are incarcerated, without the rudder of guidance, sails of good education and high expectations, or lifeline of opportunities.

On the Children's Sabbath and throughout the year to come, we will create a safe harbor of hope and health care for all children in our congregation, community, and nation.

**We Will Be Joining the
16th Annual Interfaith National Observance of
Children's Sabbaths**

**My Boat Is So Small: Creating a Safe Harbor of
Hope and Health Care for All Children**

Don't miss this special occasion to join with congregations and other places of worship of all faiths all across our nation as we:

- learn more about the urgent needs of children in our nation, especially the needs of our nation's nine million children without health insurance and the needs of children who are pushed into the "cradle to prison pipeline" without the lifelines of high expectations, parent and community support, good schools, and more to guide them toward a hopeful and productive future;
- reflect on the call of our faith to respond to the needs of the young and the poor;
- create a harbor of hope and health care for children through hands-on service and work for justice; and
- commit to help children throughout the year through prayer, compassionate service, and justice-seeking advocacy.

Date: _____

Time: _____   Place: _____

For more information or to help, contact: _____

_____

Dear Lord,
Be good to me.
The sea is so wide
and my boat is
so small.

O n this Children's Sabbath day, we turn first to God with the prayers of children and the prayers of our hearts. We know that we can trust in God's goodness to us. We recognize the wide sea of need in which our children are adrift, and we know that they and we are too small to make it safely into a harbor of hope and health care by dint of our efforts alone. And so we start with prayer—our own—and the prayers of the children.

But we don't end with the prayers of our hearts. We must engage in study to understand more about the problem and how we can and must respond. We will take action to immediately meet the needs of children and be a voice for justice on their behalf. And we will use the inspiration and information of this weekend to guide us into new, long-term efforts to help children.

Children's Defense Fund

What you can do to create a safe harbor of hope and health care for all children:

Pray for children. When you read an article or hear a news story that mentions children in difficult circumstances, stop and pray for them. Listen for God's word to you about how you should respond.

Pray for yourself. It is easy to feel inadequate when facing a sea of need, and sometimes the natural response is to give up and not even try to respond. Trust in God's goodness and care for you even when you feel small in the face of big challenges and draw on God's strength to do all that you can to help children.

Chart the course to get all children into a safe harbor: Get connected to information and action steps. Sign up for the Children's Defense Fund's monthly newsletter to find out how you can help throughout the year at www.childrensdefense.org/newsletter. Find at least one other person—a member of your family, congregation, neighborhood, or work place—who will take action with you. Support each other and hold each other accountable. Plus, it will be more fun to do it together.

Put an oar in the water: Serve children directly. Commit to a volunteer opportunity that will meet children's immediate needs, such as helping with outreach and enrollment in children's health programs. In addition to providing needed help, it will deepen your understanding and strengthen your voice as you advocate for systemic justice so all children have what they need, like health care coverage.

Demand a lifeline for every child: Be a voice for justice. God didn't create different classes of children, and God doesn't expect us to treat some as worthy of health care and others as expendable. Be a persistent voice for justice until *all* of our children have guaranteed health care coverage that provides uniform benefits and automatic enrollment. For more information about how you can be a voice for justice, visit www.childrensdefense.org.

America's children are adrift in a wide sea of need:

Nine million children don't have any form of health insurance—public or private. That is one out of every nine children. Most uninsured children live in working families. Uninsured children are less likely to receive health care when they need it, more likely to delay care and receive it when their health has worsened, or their families assume crushing medical debt for care they can't afford. They are children who are falling through the cracks of Medicaid, the State Children's Health Insurance Program (SCHIP), and private insurance. They are children who need our nation to guarantee all children comprehensive child health coverage with uniform benefits and automatic enrollment now.

Meet just a few of the children who need not only our prayers but our voices to demand justice now.

Vivian

Vivian is a lively and beautiful two-year-old with cute pigtails, a contagious laugh, and a charming smile. When you look at her, you'd never know how hard it is sometimes for her to breathe. You see, Vivian has chronic respiratory problems, including asthma. A mild attack leaves her coughing and gasping for air. A serious attack leaves her feeling like she is suffocating. If she does not have the tools to manage her asthma, like an inhaler, or if she does not receive prompt treatment in the case of a serious attack, then her life could be in danger. The other thing you do not know about Vivian when you look at her is that she has just lost her health coverage. Her father works full-time delivering linens and earns about $550 a week. His job does not offer health insurance, and private health coverage is too costly to afford, averaging $900 a month for family coverage. Vivian used to receive coverage through the state Children's Health Insurance Program (SCHIP). She first enrolled in

SCHIP when she had to be hospitalized for serious pneumonia. The medications cost $100 a piece, which the family never could have afforded without health coverage. However, some commissions from her father's job put the family's income above the income eligibility limit for SCHIP by just $37 and, as a result, Vivian lost her health care coverage.

James

Fifteen-year-old "James" loves to play football. After evacuating from New Orleans during Hurricane Katrina, James and his mother "Jennifer" settled in Texas. Jennifer has a job but cannot afford private coverage through her job, which would cost $285 a month for the family. She earns $8.00 over the income limit for a family of two to be eligible to get SCHIP coverage for her son and cannot afford insurance for her own chronic health problems. She cannot even afford the $80 physical required for James to participate in extracurricular activities like football.

Snapshots of Uninsured Children

Nine million uninsured children in the United States. It is a problem that sounds too big to get our arms around. Listen to the stories of these children who have struggled to find health care coverage, falling through the cracks between Medicaid, the State Children's Health Insurance Program (SCHIP), and private insurance. Can you imagine putting your arms around one of them? If you can, then don't let go and don't give up. This effort to provide health care coverage for every child in our nation is about child after child after child, like those you will meet in these stories. We can't embrace them all, but by embracing this calling to provide coverage, we will ensure that they are wrapped in the care that each needs and deserves. Open your eyes and your heart, your mouth, and your arms.

When the System Is Sick

Ten-year-old Robert is like a lot of kids—no chronic conditions or serious illnesses so far. But like most kids, he needs preventive care to try to stay that way and for the routine injuries and illnesses of childhood that are bound to come along. When his SCHIP coverage needed to be renewed, Robert's grandfather, Richard Uhr, offered to take on what he thought would be a relatively routine task, since Robert's father is deaf. But it turned into a year-long nightmare of lost information and frequent and conflicting requests for more information. Mr. Uhr received 18 letters with incorrect names and case numbers requesting information that he had already provided. He even went to the state capitol of Texas to testify about the difficulties he was having trying to renew his grandson's health coverage. Only after CDF intervened for him, did he finally receive an approval letter. He calls his year-long SCHIP ordeal, "the worst fight I've ever been in."

Can you imagine giving Robert a hug? Then wrap your arms around the problem of nine million children without health care coverage.

Reality Show

For most of us, our only regular "visit" to the emergency room is through a weekly television show like "Grey's Anatomy" or "ER." For countless children and their families, a real emergency room is their only source of health care for what could, with health

arms around her son who died without the care he needed and deserved. It is too late to embrace that child, but not too late to embrace the responsibility for protecting other children who need us as he did.

Lost in the Storm

Look around your home and imagine losing everything: your clothing, furniture, books, and photos. Imagine losing the house itself, your neighborhood, your job, your school. Your friends, your neighbors. Imagine losing your sense of security, your emotional health, your hope. Now, imagine losing your health coverage on top of all of those other losses when you are most in need of help. Valencia Allen and her three children, 12-year-old Kevin, 16-year-old Monica, and 18-year-old Pedro, are still adjusting to life in Texas after relocating because of Hurricane Katrina. As if getting used to a new life in a new city wasn't enough to deal with, after emergency Medicaid ended for evacuee families, Valencia found it difficult to access health care for her children, and they lost their coverage. It took more than a year for the coverage issues to be resolved.

During the year that the children were uninsured, they were in desperate need of help. Valencia thought that the children were suffering from Post Traumatic Stress Disorder (PTSD), but without insurance she was unable to get them evaluated for counseling or treatment. Her oldest child, Pedro, suffered episodes of depression and dropped out of school because the stress was too much. Sixteen-year-old Monica also went without treatment for her sickle cell anemia. The situation was traumatic for Valencia, who is disabled and provides for her family on a fixed income. Finally, their coverage has been restored, and Valencia is able to get her children much needed health care.

Will we cry "compassion fatigue" and close ourselves off to the unsolved problems faced by families battered by Hurricane Katrina, or will we wrap them in the embrace of our concern?

What Can We Do?

Pray for children without health coverage and their families. Pray for the strength to do all you can do to bring justice and care to every uninsured child. Visit www.childrensdefense.org to find out how you can help. It is time to wrap our minds, hearts, and arms around this problem and solve it once and for all.

coverage, be handled in a pediatrician's office. Kyle, 9, has chronic asthma, migraine headaches, and Attention Deficit Hyperactivity Disorder (ADHD), but his mother, who is a small business owner, cannot afford to pay for private health coverage. She learned about the State Children's Health Insurance Program (SCHIP) three years ago and enrolled Kyle, who was eligible. But before SCHIP, Kyle had no pediatrician and had to go to the emergency room when his asthma or migraines got bad.

Can you imagine wrapping your arms around a child like Kyle as he/she endures a long wait among other sick children and stressed families waiting for care? Solving the problem of uninsured children in our nation is the real emergency. Let's demand a cure.

Could You Choose?

Do you remember the movie Sophie's Choice in which a mother was forced to choose which of her children to save in the Holocaust? Can you imagine a situation in which only some of our children get health coverage? How could we choose which children don't deserve care? Every day, families face the agonizing reality of having some children who are covered by health insurance and others who aren't.

Mekeal Cusic, a recently divorced mother, said her two children were dropped from SCHIP in January because her salary exceeds the income eligibility level by $2,000. She applied for private coverage through Blue Cross Blue Shield and was approved for her 3-year-old but not for her 9-year-old. She suspects it's because her daughter suffered from irritable bowel syndrome over three years ago. When she asked why Blue Cross Blue Shield refused coverage for her older daughter, they told her it was because of "strict underwriting." So now the family is trying to get by with no health insurance.

Can you imagine wrapping your arms around your 9-year-old Keyonna when she gets the news that her little brother has health care coverage and can see a doctor when he needs to, but she doesn't?

Losing Hope

Ethel is a single mother caring for her two boys, ages 12 and 3. Her older son, Jeffrey, who is not adopted but for whom she is a legal guardian, suffers from major depression and Attention Deficit Hyperactivity Disorder (ADHD). Because he has been labeled disabled, he qualified for Medicaid. Her younger son suffers from severe asthma and is covered by SCHIP. Jeffrey's condition requires

that he attend school in a controlled environment where there are doctors and counselors who can work with his aggression and constantly monitor his medication, but Medicaid recently cut him from this program.

Although Ethel works full-time, she earns only slightly more than $1,000 a month, and Jeffrey's situation has made it difficult for her to find constant supervision for him so she can continue to go to work. She said that she is working with her SSI caseworker to get his coverage back but admits she has lost all hope in the Medicaid system.

Can you imagine wrapping your arms around the slumped shoulders of Ethel as she bears the burdens of work, raising children, and struggling with the system?

When Justice and Compassion Come Too Late

Devante Johnson was a 13-year-old boy with advanced kidney cancer who went without any health coverage for four months while his mother attempted to renew his Medicaid coverage. Although his mother, Tamika Scott, submitted at least three renewal applications way before the deadline, beginning in February 2006—one through the financial counselor at Texas Children's Hospital—and called the CHIP/Medicaid hotline dozens of times, there was no record of Devante's case in the system when advocates contacted the call center on his behalf in August 2006. Because of a state staffing shortage, officials say his application went unprocessed. Meanwhile, Devante went without any health insurance and had to depend on clinical trials for care as his tumors continued to grow.

Only through personal intervention and extensive follow-up with the highest levels of the Texas Health and Human Services Commission was his coverage finally reinstated. He then was able to go to the University of Texas M.D. Anderson Cancer Center, where for a while radiation therapy helped take away his pain. After struggling courageously against his cancer, on March 1, 2007, Devante died at the age of 14 from complications of the disease. He is remembered as a thoughtful young man who was a devoted brother and son, and who never complained about his illness.

It's too late to wrap our arms around Devante. But try to imagine what it is like to be a mother like Tamika, who longs to wrap her

Top 10 Facts About Children's Health

1. Nine million children in the United States—one in nine—have no health insurance coverage.

2. Every 51 seconds, another baby is born without health insurance.

3. It costs less to provide health insurance coverage to children than to any other group of people. In fact, children's health coverage costs less than half as much as adult health coverage.

4. The majority of uninsured children live in two-parent households, and more than nine out of ten live in families where at least one parent works. Increasingly, families that are working hard need help paying for health insurance for their children.

5. Increases in private health insurance costs are dramatically outpacing increases in wages. Over the past three years, the cost of health insurance premiums has increased at more than three times the rate of workers' earnings. Even if an employer offers health insurance, the family may not be able to afford its share of the costs.

6. Ensuring that children have timely, affordable access to health care is a smart economic move. Every dollar spent vaccinating children against measles, mumps, and rubella, saves $16 in medical costs to treat those illnesses.

7. Children's health status affects children's academic performance. Reading scores and school attendance of uninsured children improve dramatically after they become insured and are able to access health care. Good health status in childhood is also associated with increased future earning potential.

8. The United States leads the world in health care spending per person, yet lags behind other nations in key health outcomes. U.S. spending on health care per person is more than twice the average spent in industrialized countries, yet we rank near the bottom among those nations in infant mortality rates.

9. Existing health care programs for low-income children vary widely, with different standards for eligibility, cost sharing, and benefits in each of the 50 states and the District of Columbia. This "lottery of birth" is a game that can have, literally, life or death consequences for millions of the most vulnerable members of our society.

10. Americans over 65 have access to health coverage under the Medicare program, regardless of income. Children deserve the same guarantee.

Children's Defense Fund

Children's Defense Fund

Children's Defense Fund

My Boat Is So Small:
Creating a Safe Harbor of Hope and Health Care for *All* Children

National Observance of Children's Sabbaths 2007

My Boat Is So Small:
Creating a Safe Harbor of Hope and Health Care for *All* Children

National Observance of Children's Sabbaths 2007

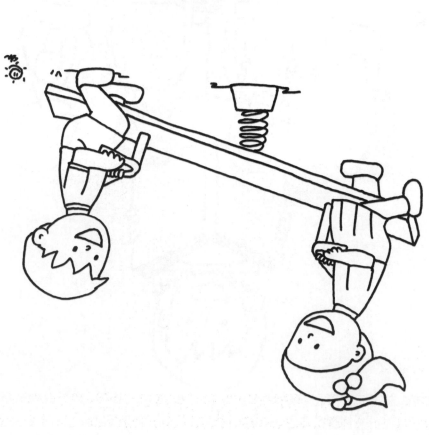

Section 4

Worship is at the heart of most Children's Sabbaths. It is in worship that we praise God who has blessed us with children and charged us with their care. It is in worship that we hear again the prophets and their warnings against injustice and their call to justice. It is in worship that we renew our commitment to follow Jesus who said to welcome the children because in doing so we welcome him and not just him but the one who sent him. As we go forth from worship, may we continue to praise God with our work to nurture and protect all children.

In this section you will find:

- **Worship suggestions** drawn from Children's Sabbath worship services celebrated by congregations all across the country. Use or adapt those that would be appropriate for your church.

- **Suggestions for creative ways to include the children and youths** of your congregation in the Children's Sabbath service. Remember: The Children's Sabbath should not be turned over to the children with adults only serving as "audience," since this is meant to be an intergenerational event that underscores the role people of all ages have to play in meeting children's needs. At the same time, it is an important time to fully engage children and youths. Be sure to involve them in the planning and leadership of the day.

- **Sample worship services** from a variety of traditions: Protestant, Catholic, and Episcopal. Use or adapt them as appropriate for your congregation's tradition. There are additional worship resources provided to use in your service.

- **A list of suggested hymns.**

- **Sermon resources** providing exegetical notes and other materials related to the Roman Catholic lectionary, the Episcopal lectionary, and the Revised Common lectionary, as well as sermon notes on a text for those who don't follow a lectionary. These resources are intended to spark your reflection and assist your study as you seek to discern the Word that you will proclaim on the Children's Sabbath.

- **A sample Children's Sermon** that provides an example of a conversation a worship leader might have with the children of the congregation during the service.

- **A Daily Devotional Guide (for adults)** that can be photocopied and distributed to adult congregation members the week before the Children's Sabbath to help them prepare their hearts and minds through reading scripture, reflecting, and praying throughout the week leading up to the Children's Sabbath. (Please note: This devotional is written for adults, not children.)

- **Children's Activity Bulletins** for younger and older children that can be distributed on the Children's Sabbath.

- **Lesson plans** for all ages can be downloaded from the Children's Defense Fund's Web site at www.childrensdefense. org/childrenssabbaths. The lesson plans on health care prepared for the 2006 Children's Sabbath are available now. Lesson plans for 2007 will be available after September 1, 2007. The religious education hour is a valuable time to engage congregation members of all ages in learning more about the needs of children, studying the sacred texts and teachings of their faith that call us to work for justice on behalf of children and those who are poor, and exploring faithful responses that they can make.

Worship Suggestions

- The week before the Children's Sabbath, **distribute copies of the Daily Devotional Guide** in this resource to help adult congregation members prepare their hearts and minds for the Children's Sabbath, as did *First United Methodist Church in De Soto, Missouri,* and many other congregations. Members of *Clearview Baptist Church in Anderson, South Carolina,* took it one step further and wrote and distributed their own devotional guide!

- **Decorate the sanctuary with images and materials that bring to life the theme, "My Boat Is So Small: Creating a Harbor of Hope and Health Care for All Children."** Possibilities include: a fishing net to collect prayers; a small rowboat (or boat constructed from cardboard) to collect donated items such as food or diapers; lengths of rope, "lifelines" from which dangle cards bearing words or images of what we can do to assure our children have what they need to survive; life jackets with words taped to them describing what children need to keep them safe (e.g., family, health care, food, faith, safe communities); white cloth cut into triangular sail shapes, emblazoned with words or images of what will propel our children forward in life; images of water and words of the kinds of need in which our children are adrift; strings of origami boats (see following pages for instructions), perhaps a symbolic number of boats such as 72, representing the number of children who are born without health insurance each hour.

- **Invite on-site child care or Head Start staff, administrators, parents, and children, and others** to attend your Children's Sabbath. *De Lisle Mount Zion United Methodist Church in Pass Christian, Mississippi,* invited children of the community, legislators, and school personnel to attend their Children's Sabbath service.

- **Use bulletin covers that emphasize the Children's Sabbath,** as did *First Congregational United Church of Christ in Alpena, Michigan,* whose bulletin cover depicted a child bandaging another and the words, "Children are God's apostles, day by day sent forth to preach of Love, and Hope, and Peace. James Russell Lowell" and "Suffer the little children to come unto me, and forbid them not: for of such is the kingdom of God. Luke 18:16."

- **Leading up to and on the Children's Sabbath, distribute the bulletin inserts** beginning on page 40, as did *St. Andrews Church in Harrington Park, New Jersey.* If you don't use the bulletin insert, prepare your own announcement about the Children's Sabbath to include in the bulletin so that worshipers, especially visitors, will understand the special focus and significance of the service. *Fairview United Methodist Church in Washington, West Virginia,* prepared a special insert listing 32 specific ways that congregation members could "stand for children" in the church and community, listing relevant contact information.

- **On the Children's Sabbath, distribute the children's activity bulletins** in this section, along with crayons, markers, or pencils.

- **Distribute special tokens to every child** attending the Children's Sabbath, such as ribbons or stickers. *Highland United Methodist Church in Highlands, North Carolina,* distributed little bags of pink and blue M&Ms they had specially printed with the words "Hope and Healing" and "4 God's Children." The children of *First United Methodist Church in Ames, Iowa,* each made a handprint with their name on Shrinky Dink (craft) material. They attached the completed handprints to cards that read: "Pray for me and all God's kids because we all need hope and healing" and handed them out to each family in the church.

- **Use or adapt some of the prayers and other worship resources provided in this section,** as did *St. Alban's Episcopal Church in Indianapolis, Indiana.* Or, use readings from prayer and worship books that include a social action theme, or create your own materials on the theme of putting our faith into action to seek justice for children and families who are poor.

- **Explore the resources of other faith traditions.** Don't miss the Children's Sabbath worship resources in sections for other faith traditions and in the interfaith section; some may be appropriate to include in your service. The bulletin for *Camp Hill-Wesley United Methodist Church* opened with a reading for reflection before worship that was from the Jewish section of the Children's Sabbath manual and included a prayer from the Jewish Children's Sabbath service as their opening prayer.

Origami Boat Instructions
From DLTK's Bible Crafts for Kids

These can also be found at http://www.dltk-bible.com/crafts/mboat.htm.

Yes, the boat will really float, but as the paper gets saturated with water, it will sink and be ruined. This can actually start an interesting discussion about what made the boat float to begin with and then what made it sink.

- Fold the paper (or the 1/2 sheet of newspaper) in half.

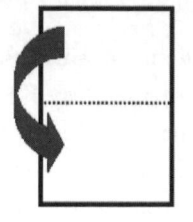

- Fold down each side to make triangles.

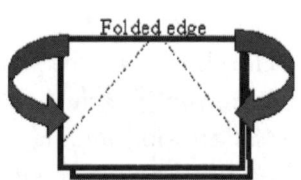

- At the bottom, fold the top strip upward on the blue line.

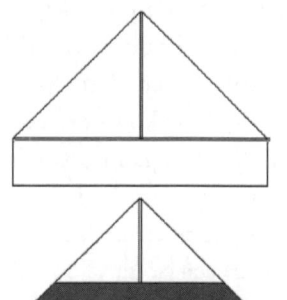

- Fold the two small triangles on the left and on the right backwards to make them disappear.

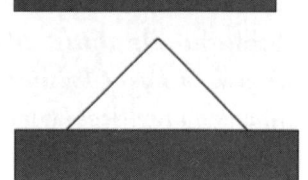

- Turn the paper over and fold the other strip upwards. You have formed the well-known paper hat. (If you're finding the origami too challenging for the group, you can always just stop here and wear your hats as sailor hats.)

- To continue to make a boat, turn the hat 90 degrees and open it so you're looking inside the part you would wear on your head. The thumbs must be inside.

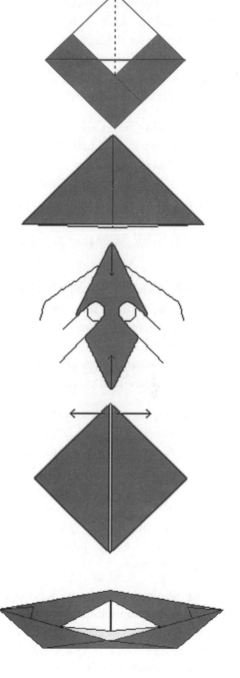

- Lay the upper and lower parts on each other so it looks like a diamond.

- Fold the lower front triangle upwards on the blue line.

- Turn the paper over and fold the other triangle up. It basically looks like the hat without the brim this time.

- Open the hat again and put the upper part on the lower one to make a diamond shape again.

- Pull the upper corners of the triangles in the direction of the arrows. As you pull these corners you'll see the boat forming before your eyes.

- Stretch the boat both to the right and left, and then separate it slightly so it can float.

- **Incorporate resources from your denomination that focus on children and child advocacy.** See the resources in Section 12.

- **Select hymns and anthems that focus on children** and our responsibilities to them, as did *Conyers Presbyterian Church in Conyers, Georgia.* Wrote their Director of Children's Ministries, "Our children's choir and adult choir did a special piece of music for the service, 'The People Came from Everywhere.' It started with the children singing a question and the adults answering, and then the congregation joined in at the end with 'As once you took your hands and blessed the children on their way, O bless us, Jesus, in our quest to find a faith today.'" This section includes music suggestions on page 76.

- **Focus the sermon or homily on children and our responsibility to act on their behalf.** The sermon resources in this manual are based on the lessons designated in the Revised Common Lectionary, Roman Catholic Lectionary, and the Episcopal Lectionary for the third weekend of October. Other sections of this resource provide information and stories about children that you may want to include in your sermon or homily.

- **Use or adapt the suggested Children's Sermon** in this manual during a special time with children in the service. Or, in a role reversal, have one of the children give an "Adults' Sermon"—a short message from a child to the adults. At *Pleasant Union United Methodist Church in Julian, North Carolina*, a nurse gave the children's sermon.

- **Offer prayers for children.** Specifically name problems afflicting children in your community, as well as crises affecting children across our nation and throughout our world. Invite congregation members to pray for the children in your church, too. *North United Methodist Church in North, South Carolina,* wrote the name and birthday of a child at the bottom of each bulletin. The adult who received the bulletin was asked to pray for and mentor that child throughout the year.

- **Dedicate ministries/programs serving children or commission staff and board members of child-serving programs affiliated with the congregation** and celebrate their work as part of the congregation's ministry. *First United Methodist Church of Salina, Kansas*, reported, "At offering time we recognized all of the children's ministries we currently provide for our congregations, ministries that involve children from the community and ministries carried out *by* our children." The Children's Sabbath was an occasion for *Providence Presbyterian Church in Providence, Rhode Island,* to recognize and celebrate their connection to Head Start, which meets in the church's building.

- **Incorporate a special blessing of children,** as did *Guardian Angels Catholic Church in Oakdale, Minnesota.*

- **Honor people who work with and for children.** At an appropriate point in the service, invite these professionals and/or volunteers (contacted in advance) to come forward for a brief time of recognition for their work putting their faith into action to seek justice for children, with prayers for God's guidance in their work and prayers for the children they serve. Present them with a flower, ribbon, or other token so that later others might identify them and offer personal appreciation. *First Christian Church (Disciples of Christ) in Frankfurt, Kentucky,* recognized members of the congregation who care for children with an Elder's "Litany for the Children of the World" and candle-lighting. (See Additional Worship Resources on page 69.) *Grace United Methodist Church in Williamston, South Carolina,* invited doctors, nurses, and educators in the community to be their special guests.

- **Collect special offerings for children and families.** In addition to monetary offerings, consider collecting items to help children and families, such as toothbrushes and children's toothpaste, nutritious food, or diapers. Announce the special offering in advance. *First United Methodist Church in Salina, Kansas*, had an "Undie Sunday" project and collected new underwear and socks for Ashby House, a transitional housing program for women and their children and for an elementary school. *St. Clare's Episcopal Church in Blairsville, Georgia*, collected a special offering of school supplies for children in need at the local child care center.

- **Invite guest speakers to preach or give another address on the needs of children and our call to respond.** Encourage the speaker to highlight opportunities for members to become involved themselves and to speak out for children. A doctor from a neighboring health clinic was the speaker at *First Baptist Church's* Children's Sabbath in *Springfield, Ohio.* For their first Children's Sabbath, *First United Methodist Church of Erie, Pennsylvania*, had a "sermon dialogue" titled "Promises to Keep: Our Service to All," during which the pastor, the United Methodist Women's president, and co-chairs of Christian education addressed commitment to children, Sunday schools, health care insurance, and families worshipping together. Guest speakers from the state public health office addressed *Eastern Shore Chapel Episcopal Church's* Children's Sabbath in *Virginia Beach, Virginia*.

- **Use various media to focus more powerfully on children and their needs.** Some congregations create PowerPoint presentations or slide shows with images of children in need. *Clearview Baptist Church in Anderson, South Carolina*, showed the DVD "Prayer for Children" from CDF while diapers were brought forward to donate to Anderson Interfaith Ministries. *Faith United Church of Christ in Cincinnati, Ohio*, took a unique approach to helping adults connect with the experience of being a child. "In order for adult members to reconnect with their own childhood, we asked each person to bring along one of their favorite books when they were growing up. The books were displayed in the sanctuary. Following the worship service, we held a pot luck luncheon, again asking each person to bring a favorite food from their childhood." After the service, books could be donated to a health clinic waiting room, Head Start program, homeless shelter, or other program serving children in need.

- **Include a dramatic presentation of *Swimmy*, or another, to especially engage children and young people, as well as adults.** This year, consider having the young people act out *Swimmy*, a children's book by Leo Lionni (New York: Dragonfly Books), which presents a wonderful metaphor for our working together as advocates and fits well within the theme of being small in the midst of a wide sea. See page 156 for more about *Swimmy*.

- **Invite members to light candles for the 40 days leading up to the Children's Sabbath,** as suggested by the Christian Church (Disciples of Christ) and the United Church of Christ, and then light a symbolic 40th candle on the Children's Sabbath. (For more information, visit http://www.homelandministries.org/FamilyandChildren/candle.htm.) *Crown Heights Christian Church in Oklahoma City, Oklahoma*, reported, "As part of that [Forty Days of Prayer] process and to remind our participants to pray each week, a flyer highlighting an issue related to child health concerns is included with the bulletin. The first was an introduction to the subject, the next six included

discussions regarding the plight of children in Darfur, the psychological needs of children recovering from Hurricane Katrina, environmental risks impacting child health, 14 ways to show love for your children, child health status in Oklahoma, and a final piece on ways to help address the issues. Elementary-age children light the candles on the communion table each Sunday year-round; during this special time of prayer an additional candle is added to 'light a candle for children.'"

Involve Children and Youths

The Children's Sabbath, unlike a traditional Youth Sunday or Children's Day, is intended to involve adults in the planning and leadership of the day. As members of the congregation, adults must recognize the challenges facing children in our nation and their collective responsibility to respond. However, the Children's Sabbath is an important time to include children and youths in the planning and leadership of the worship service and all other events.

For example, children and youths can:

- **Prepare for the Children's Sabbath during a "Kids' Night Out," overnight, or other event.** *St. Andrew's Lutheran Church in Grand Rapids, Minnesota,* held an intergenerational forum the week before the Children's Sabbath. The prayers that participants wrote during the forum were then read during the Children's Sabbath the following week. *Herndon United Methodist Church in Herndon, Virginia*, conducted a Homelessness Experience Camp from Friday to Saturday, followed by a special guest speaker on children, homelessness, and poverty at the Sunday morning service. *Highlands United Methodist Church in Highlands, North Carolina*, devoted a month of Wednesday night lessons to focus on the mission projects supported by the United Methodist Children's Fund. The children collected an offering in decorated tin cans to support it.

- **Review the Children's Sabbath service the week before** (perhaps in church school classes) and practice responses and hymns so they may join more fully in the Children's Sabbath service.

- **Design and paint the paraments (such as the cloth draping the pulpit).** The fifth grade class of *First United Methodist Church in Salina, Kansas*, made an altar cloth depicting children's faces.

- **Draw pictures for the bulletin cover**, as did *Lightstreet United Methodist Church in Lightstreet, Pennsylvania.*

- **Decorate the sanctuary with drawings or banners that the children have made.** *El Pueblito United Methodist Church in Taos, New Mexico*, displayed the children's art work in addition to having the children greet, read Bible passages, and take up the collection. The sanctuary at *First United Methodist Church in Skidmore, Pennsylvania*, had on display on the altar a "Love Quilt" made by the children from squares of cardboard and decorated with a background of puzzle pieces. On each piece, the children illustrated and wrote words to show ways they can "Love God" and "Love Others." On cut-outs of children they also drew themselves and hung foam puzzle pieces from them with the same words, "Love God" and "Love Others."

- **Bake the communion bread (if appropriate for your tradition).**

- **Assist and greet worshipers as they arrive or leave, light candles, or collect the offering.** At *St. Paul's Episcopal Church in Columbus, Indiana*, two teens recently certified as Chalicers served on the altar. Reports an organizer of the Children's Sabbath at *Downtown United Presbyterian Church in Rochester, New York.* "The 'Light a Candle for Children' theme captured their imagination, and one of the things they did was cover the communion table with candles, gathered statistics concerning children, and lit a candle as they read each statistic."

- **Lead a procession to begin the Children's Sabbath**, as did the children of *First Presbyterian Church in Marietta, Georgia*, who also sang, made handprints for prayers, and participated in a mother-daughter tea.

- **Sing a special anthem, play an instrumental piece, or perform a song in sign language.** The fourth through sixth grade youth group at *Jordan Memorial United Methodist Church in Ramseur, North Carolina,* led the service, which included an anthem with sign language (and taking up a "teddy bear offering" for the County Sheriff Teddy Bear Program). At *Christ Reformed United Church of Christ in Martinsburg, West Virginia*, children sang a song and two children played a duet; others ushered, collected the offering, and served as acolytes.

- **Read prayers and scriptural passages and lead responsive readings.**

- **Write a prayer to be used in the service.**

- **Deliver the sermon or other presentation.**

- **Prepare a dramatic skit** for the service, as did the children at *Liberty Hill United Methodist Church in Greer, South Carolina,* and *Highlands United Methodist Church in Highlands, North Carolina.* At *Princeton Presbyterian Church in Princeton, West Virginia*, the children acted out a story from the Children's Sabbath manual and collected items for a local women's and children's shelter. See the suggestion on page 57 for acting out the children's book *Swimmy* by Leo Lionni (New York: Dragonfly Books).

- **During the offertory procession, place items on the altar that serve to remind the congregation of the love and care our children require.** *Spring Glen United Methodist Church in Jacksonville, Florida,* placed a globe encircled with children on their altar along with the crosses, candles, and other symbols.

- **Invite friends to attend.** The children and youth of *West-Park Presbyterian Church in New York City* invited friends from the neighborhood food pantry that works with the church.

Congregations whose children usually depart for church school classes during the worship service (often after the Children's Sermon or time with children) will need to reflect thoughtfully about the plan for the Children's Sabbath.

Some will choose to follow their customary schedule and have the children engage in the Children's Sabbath lesson plans while the adults remain in worship. This may free the preacher to speak more seriously to the adults about the plight of children and their responsibility to respond without concerns about trying to engage or upsetting the children. The children can learn about the concerns in an age-appropriate setting in their classes.

Other congregations will see the Children's Sabbath as a good opportunity for the children to remain in worship throughout the service. If the children are not accustomed to this, however, it will require forethought. The whole service, including the sermon, can be carefully planned to be engaging and accessible to all ages. The more children are involved in the planning and implementation, the more interested they will be. Or, the Children's Activity Bulletins and other quiet activities can be distributed to engage the children during the sermon and other "listening" times.

Protestant Service of Worship

For the 29th Sunday in Ordinary Time, Year C

Call to Worship

Come, let us worship our God who creates each child in God's own image;

Come, let us worship our God who blesses the children with enfolding grace;

Come, let us worship our God who sustains us in the work for justice.

Come, let us worship the Triune God.

Hymn *(For this and other hymns, see suggested hymns on page 76.)*

Call to Confession

Like a mother who searches for a lost coin, like a father who welcomes a straying child home, God seeks us and loves us even when we have lost our way. Trusting in God's forgiveness, let us confess our sins before God and one another.

Prayer of Confession

Gracious God, we come to you with our brokenness. We confess that though you call us to compassion, we have hardened our hearts. Though you call us to extend our embrace, we have withheld our touch. Though you have called us to speak out, we have remained silent. Though you have called us to community, we mostly have cared just for our own. We see our brokenness as a nation, resulting in children without health care, families left in poverty, youths limited by low expectations and little support, and in the growing canyon between rich and poor. (*time for silent prayer*)

Heal us, O Great Physician. Create in us new hearts that love, hands that reach out, voices that proclaim your justice, and a mended community that cares for all and not just for some. Amen.

Assurance of Pardon

There is healing in the name of the Lord, whose mercy is everlasting. Friends, believe the Good News of the Gospel: In Jesus Christ we are forgiven.

The Peace

Hymn

Prayer for Illumination

Mighty God, in Jesus you gave sight to the blind, unstopped the ears of the deaf, gave voice to the mute, and restored those who could not walk. By your Spirit, open our eyes and unstop our ears that we may behold your Word to us this day and, in joyful response, seek to do your will as we speak and stand for children. In Jesus Christ we pray. Amen.

First Reading: Jeremiah 31:27-34*
(*for churches following the Revised Common Lectionary; other churches may wish to select other passages, such as Genesis 21:16, Jeremiah 31:15-17, Exodus 2: 1-10, or Exodus 3:7-12)

Second Reading: 2 Timothy 3:14-4:5*
(*Churches that do not follow the Revised Common Lectionary may prefer to select a passage such as James 2:1-10 or James 2:14-26.*)

Time with Children/Children's Sermon
(*See sample Children's Sermon, "When Whining is Wonderful," in this section or the sample Time with Children, "Swimmy," in the Interfaith Section.*)

Anthem/Hymn

Gospel Reading: Luke 18:1-8*
(*for churches following the Revised Common Lectionary, there are many texts that point to children in need of healing and the lengths that family and friends will go to bring them to a source of care. A few examples are Mt. 17:14, Mark 2:1-12, Mark 5:23, and Jn. 4:46.*)

Sermon
(*See Sermon Resources in this section. The reflections in the Daily Devotional Guide may also spark sermons on other scripture passages.*)

Hymn: God of Justice, God of Mercy

Affirmation of Faith

(Select one from your tradition that most closely relates to the day's theme. See Additional Worship Resources for two options.)

Other Liturgical Responses to the Word

(According to your tradition, one or more of the following may be incorporated into the service: baptism, reaffirmation of baptismal vows, or other pastoral rite of the church.)

Offering

Offertory Hymn

Prayers of the People

Let us turn to the Holy One, Healer of our hearts and minds, spirits and lives, saying, "Bind up our wounds, O Lord."

For the wounded places in the Body of Christ, your Church, where division and discord harm our witness and work on behalf of the last, the least, the little, and the lost, we pray,

Bind up our wounds, O Lord.

For the wounded places in our world, where starvation and slavery, disease and debt cripple children and families, communities and countries, that we bring healing and wholeness, justice and peace, restoring the strength of peoples everywhere that they may live lives of dignity and purpose, we pray,

Bind up our wounds, O Lord.

For the wounded places in our nation, fractured along lines of race and ethnicity, income and education, politics and place, that we align with your purpose and, as one, nurture and protect your children, empower the oppressed, prepare paths of promise and purpose for young people, and strengthen families, we pray,

Bind up our wounds, O Lord.

For the wounded places in our community, where children are hurt, where families suffer, where young people can't find their way, especially for the nine million children without health or mental health coverage and the families that struggle to get them care, that we ensure that every child has the care that they need and families can afford, we pray,

Bind up our wounds, O Lord.

For the wounded places in all who sorrow—the battered hopes, the aching hearts, the tortured minds, the suffering spirits, that they are restored with the balm that only you can provide, and that we are filled with your spirit to ease another's pain, we pray,

Bind up our wounds, O Lord.

For the wounded place in ourselves that fails to seek your justice—for the dashed spirit, the hopeless heart, the limited vision, the weak voice, that you strengthen us and sustain our spirits, raise our hopes, expand our vision, amplify our voice so that we faithfully seek justice especially for the last, the lost, and the least, we pray,

Bind up our wounds, O Lord.

O God, we ask these things and the silent prayers of our hearts in confidence that you can make all things whole. In the name of Christ we pray, **Amen.**

The Eucharist

(Congregations that will be celebrating the Lord's Supper should include the appropriate liturgical material. See the Episcopal Liturgy.)

Closing Hymn

Charge and Blessing

Beloved, encourage the fainthearted, help the weak, be patient with all of them. See that none of you repays evil for evil, but always seek to do good to one another and to all. Rejoice always, pray without ceasing, give thanks in all circumstances, for this is the will of God in Christ Jesus for you. Do not quench the Spirit. Do not despise the words of prophets, but test everything; hold fast to what is good; abstain from every evil. *(1 Thessalonians 5:14-22)*

May the grace of our Lord Jesus Christ, who welcomes every child; the love of God who created each of us for lives of health and wholeness; and the communion of the Holy Spirit who moves in and among us to create communities of justice, be with you now and forever more. Amen.

Catholic Liturgy for Children's Sabbath

This sample liturgy provides suggestions for incorporating the focus of the National Observance of Children's Sabbaths into the standard liturgy for the 29th Sunday in Ordinary Time, Year C. All hymn numbers refer to *Worship*, GIA Publications. See page 76 for additional music suggestions.

Introductory Rites

Entrance Song: Gather Us In (#665), Immortal, Invisible, God Only Wise (#512), Tell Out My Soul, the Greatness of the Lord (#534)

Greeting

In the name of the Father, and of the Son, and of the Holy Spirit.
Amen.

The grace of our Lord Jesus Christ and the love of God and the fellowship of the Holy Spirit be with you all.
And also with you.

We greet you on this day that is celebrated as the Children's Sabbath by congregations of many faiths across our nation. In the words of Pope Benedict XVI on the Feast of the Baptism of the Lord 2007, "Every child who is born brings us God's smile and invites us to recognize that life is his gift, a gift to be welcomed with love and preserved with care, always and at every moment." On this day, we renew our commitment to welcoming with love and preserving with care all of the children God has entrusted to us, creating a harbor of hope and health care for all children. We will worship our God of justice and compassion with our hearts and voices always and at every moment as we serve and seek justice for children in need.

Penitential Rite

Option 1:
Priest: Coming together as God's family, with confidence let us ask the Father's forgiveness, for he is full of gentleness and compassion.

Lord Jesus, you gathered the little children to yourself.
Lord, have mercy.
People: Lord, have mercy.

Priest: Lord Jesus, you warned us not to put a stumbling block before one of these little ones who believe in you. Christ, have mercy.
People: Christ, have mercy.

Priest: Lord Jesus, you called us to welcome children in your name.
Lord, have mercy.
People: Lord, have mercy.

Option 2:
Lord Jesus, you healed the sick.
Lord, have mercy.
People: Lord, have mercy.

Lord Jesus, you forgave sinners.
Christ, have mercy.
People: Christ, have mercy.

Lord Jesus, you give us yourself to heal us and bring us strength.
Lord, have mercy.
People: Lord, have mercy.

May almighty God have mercy on us,
Forgive us our sins,
And bring us to everlasting life.
Amen.

Gloria

Opening Prayer

Almighty and ever-living God,
our source of power and inspiration,
give us strength and joy
in serving you as followers of Christ,
who lives and reigns with you and the Holy Spirit,
one God, for ever and ever. Amen.

Liturgy of the Word

First Reading: Exodus 17:8-13

Responsorial Psalm: Psalm 120

Second Reading: 2 Timothy 3:14-4:2

Gospel Acclamation

Priest: Alleluia.
People: Alleluia.

Priest: Whoever welcomes this child in my name welcomes me, and whoever welcomes me welcomes the one who sent me; for the least among all of you is the greatest. (Luke 9:48)
People: Alleluia.

Gospel: Luke 18:1-8

Homily

(*See Sermon Resources in this section.*)

Profession of Faith: The Nicene Creed (or Apostles, per *Directory for Masses with Children*)

General Intercessions (Prayer of the Faithful

(*See also the U.S. Conference of Catholic Bishops' Intercessions for Life on "The Marginalized" on page 63, which may be incorporated or substituted.*)

My brothers and sisters, in the name of Christ who brought his healing touch to all, especially the least, the last, and the lost, let us pray to the Lord saying, Bind up our wounds, O Lord.

For the holy Church of God: that we heal the wounded places in the Body of Christ where division and discord harm our witness and work on behalf of the young and poor and vulnerable, we pray to the Lord,

Bind up our wounds, O Lord.

For the wounded places in our world, where starvation and slavery, disease and debt cripple children and families, communities and countries, that we bring healing and wholeness, justice and peace, restoring the strength of peoples everywhere that they may live lives of dignity and purpose, we pray,

Bind up our wounds, O Lord.

For all our brothers and sisters in need, especially the millions of children without health care whose suffering is unceasing, whose illness is untreated, whose anxiety is unrelieved, that they know your love and compassion and our care, we pray to the Lord,

Bind up our wounds, O Lord.

For the wounded places in our community, where children are hurt, where families suffer, where young people can't find their way, and for the wounded place in ourselves that fails to seek your justice; for the dashed spirit, the hopeless heart, the limited vision, the weak voice, let us pray to the Lord,

Bind up our wounds, O Lord.

Priest: God of love,
who shelters us like a mother hen
and welcomes us like a father,
hear the prayers of your Church
and grant us today
what we ask of you in faith.
We ask this through Christ our Brother. Amen.

Liturgy of the Eucharist

Preparation of the Altar and the Gifts

Offertory Song: Lord of Our Growing Years (#556)

Prayer over the Gifts

Lord God,
May the gifts we offer
Bring us your love and forgiveness
And give us freedom to serve you with our lives.
We ask this in the name of Jesus the Lord.

Eucharistic Prayer

Communion Rite

The Lord's Prayer

Doxology

Sign of Peace

Breaking of the Bread – Agnus Dei

Communion

Communion Song: You Satisfy the Hungry Heart (#736), Draw Us in the Spirit's Tether (#731)

Song of Praise: There's a Spirit in the Air (#531), For the Beauty of the Earth (#557)

Prayer after Communion
Let us pray.
Lord,
May this Eucharist help us to remain faithful.
May it teach us the way to eternal life.
Grant this through Christ our Lord. Amen.

Concluding Rite

Greeting

The Lord be with you.
And also with you.

Blessing

May almighty God bless you,
The Father, and the Son, and the Holy Spirit.
Amen.

Dismissal

Go in peace to love and serve the Lord.
Thanks be to God.

---

*The Marginalized

For those deprived of their human needs
and their human rights,
that they may be given the dignity
which God confers on all his people;
We pray to the Lord.

For all who are forgotten or thrown away,
and especially for the poor, the sick and the aged,
that God might change our hearts
and move us to love them as the image of Christ
We pray to the Lord.

For all who are lonely or afraid,
for teenagers on the street,
old people in nursing homes,
prisoners with no one to visit them,
and all whom the world has forgotten;
that Christ might lead us to them;
We pray to the Lord.

For all who are forgotten or cast off,
that we might value each human life,
as a priceless gift from God;
We pray to the Lord.

* From the U.S. Conference of Catholic Bishops
  Intercessions for Life

Episcopal Liturgy for the Children's Sabbath

Proper 24, Year C

This sample liturgy provides suggestions for incorporating the focus of the National Observance of Children's Sabbaths into the standard Episcopal liturgy for Proper 24, Year C, which falls on October 21, 2007. Throughout the liturgy, we have provided two options, one from *The Book of Common Prayer* and the other from *Enriching Our Worship: Supplemental Liturgical Materials* prepared by The Standing Commission on Liturgy and Music of The Episcopal Church. (Where noted, hymn suggestions are from *Wonder, Love, and Praise: A Supplement to The Hymnal 1982* [WLP]; otherwise, hymns are from *The Hymnal 1982*.) See page 76 for additional music suggestions.

The Word of God

Hymn: Immortal, Invisible, God Only Wise (#423); God the Sculptor of the Mountains (#746, WLP)

Opening Sentences

Option 1:
(From *The Book of Common Prayer*, hereafter referred to as BCP)

Celebrant: Blessed be God: Father, Son, and Holy Spirit.
People: **And blessed be His kingdom, now and forever. Amen.**

Option 2:
(From *Enriching Our Worship: Supplemental Liturgical Materials prepared* by The Standing Commission on Liturgy and Music, hereafter referred to as EOW)

Celebrant: Blessed be the one, holy, and living God.
People: **Glory to God forever and ever.**
Celebrant may say:
          Almighty God, to you all hearts are open, all desires known, and from you no secrets are hid: Cleanse the thoughts of our hearts by the inspiration of your Holy Spirit, that we may perfectly love you, and worthily magnify your holy Name; through Christ our Lord. Amen.

Song of Praise: God Is Love (#379); Creating God, Your Fingers Trace (#394)

The Collect of the Day

Option 1:   (BCP)
Celebrant: The Lord be with you.
People: **And also with you.**
Celebrant: Let us pray.

Proper 24   (BCP)
Almighty and everlasting God, in Christ who came as a child you have revealed your glory among the nations. Preserve the works of your mercy, that your Church throughout the world may persevere with steadfast faith in the confession of your Name; through Jesus Christ our Lord, who lives and reigns with you and the Holy Spirit, one God, forever and ever.
People: **Amen.**

Option 2:   (EOW)
Celebrant: God be with you.
People: **And also with you.**
Celebrant: Let us pray.

On the Children's Sabbath

Tender God, with Christ's healing touch and inclusive embrace you showed us your will that we be restored to health, wholeness, and community. Make us now agents of your love and justice that we bring hope and healing to your beloved children, through Jesus Christ our Lord who lives and reigns with you and the Holy Spirit, one God for ever and ever.

People: Amen.

The Lessons
A Reading from Genesis 32:3-8, 22-30

> **Option 1:** (BCP)
>
> *After each reading, the Reader says:*
> The Word of the Lord.
> **People:** **Thanks be to God.**
>
> **Option 2:** (EOW)
> *After each reading, the Reader says:*
> Hear what the Spirit is saying to the churches.
> **People:** **Thanks be to God.**

Gradual Hymn

A Reading from 2 Timothy 3:14-4:5

Gospel Announcement

> **Option 1:** (BCP)
> The Holy Gospel of our Lord Jesus Christ, according to
> St. Matthew.
> **People:** **Glory to you, Lord Christ.**
>
> **Option 2:** (EOW)
> The Holy Gospel of our Savior Jesus Christ, according to
> St. Matthew.

Gospel: Luke 18:1-8a
After the Gospel, the Reader says:
The Gospel of the Lord.
People: **Praise to you, Lord Christ.**

The Sermon
(*See Sermon Resources in this section.*)

The Nicene Creed

The Prayers of the People and Confession of Sin
(*Alternative Prayers of the People may be found in the Catholic Liturgy and Protestant Service.*)

> **Option 1:** (BCP)
> We pray to you also for the forgiveness of our sins.
>
> **Leader and People:**
> Most merciful God,
> we confess that we have sinned against you

in thought, word, and deed,
by what we have done,
and by what we have left undone.
We have not loved you with our whole heart;
we have not loved our neighbor as ourselves.
We are truly sorry and we humbly repent.

For the sake of your Son, Jesus Christ,
have mercy on us and forgive us;
that we may delight in your will,
and walk in your ways,
to the glory of your Name. Amen.

Option 2:
With all our heart and with all our mind, let us pray to the Lord, saying, "Lord, make us whole."

For the body of Christ, that we reach out with Christ's healing touch that cared for all and excluded none, restoring those who suffer to health, hope, and community,

Lord, make us whole.

For our nation and our leaders, grant us the wisdom, compassion, and commitment to justice that ensures that all receive the care they need, especially the youngest and most vulnerable, we pray to the Lord,

Lord, make us whole.

In a world in which disease knows no boundaries, suffering is a common language, and pain is a shared experience, that we heed your cry to us in the voices of our brothers and sisters around the world, we pray to the Lord,

Lord, make us whole.

For ourselves and our community in which it is easier to be entertained than to take action, to be casual rather than committed, to be unconcerned rather than uncompromising when it comes to demanding justice, we pray to the Lord,

Lord, make us whole.

On this Children's Sabbath day, we pray especially for the children and families without health care, as they suffer, pain unabated, sickness untreated, anxiety unrelieved, that they know your love and our care, we pray to the Lord,

Lord, make us whole.

For all who have died, especially those who died from lack of care, we pray to the Lord,

Lord, make us whole.

Leader and People:
God of all mercy,
We confess that we have failed to live our lives as ones made in your image,
We have not loved each other as sisters and brothers,
We have not welcomed all children and so welcomed you,
We have left stumbling blocks in the way of too many children.

Forgive us our sins,
As a woman searching for a cherished coin,
As a father welcoming a beloved child home,
And uphold us by your Spirit
That we may do justice, love kindness, and walk humbly with you,
Through our Savior, Jesus Christ. Amen.

Absolution

Option 1:   (BCP)
The Bishop when present, or the Priest:
Almighty God have mercy on you, forgive you all your sins through our Lord, Jesus Christ, strengthen you in all goodness, and by the power of the Holy Spirit keep you in eternal life. Amen.

Option 2:   (EOW)
Almighty God have mercy on you, forgive you all your sins through the grace of Jesus Christ, strengthen you in all goodness, and by the power of the Holy Spirit keep you in eternal life. Amen.

The Peace
The Celebrant says to the people:
Let us share the peace of Christ with one another, and give thanks for the children among us who show us new ways to walk in peace together.

Option 1:	(BCP)
Celebrant:	The peace of the Lord be always with you.
People:	**And also with you.**
Option 2:	(EOW)
Celebrant:	The peace of Christ be always with you.
People:	**And also with you.**

The Holy Communion

Offertory: For the Beauty of the Earth (#416), For the Fruit of All Creation (#424), Tell Out My Soul, the Greatness of the Lord (#438), Lord, You Give the Great Commission (#528, The Hymnal 1982; #780, WLP), We Are All One in Mission (#778, WLP)

(*You may wish to include the Act of Commitment as a way for parishioners to make an offering of themselves—their time, commitment, voices.*)

The Great Thanksgiving

Option 1: Eucharistic Prayer B (BCP)

Proper Preface for Children's Sabbath
Because you have blessed us with children and have given your own child, Jesus Christ, to reveal the fullness of your love and mercy.

Option 2: Eucharistic Prayer for the Children's Sabbath

Celebrant:	The Lord be with you.
People:	**And also with you.**
Celebrant:	Lift up your hearts.
People:	**We lift them to the Lord.**
Celebrant:	Let us give thanks to the Lord our God.
People:	**It is right to give our thanks and praise.**

Celebrant: We give you thanks and praise, amazing God,
who made heaven and earth and sea, and
all that is in them,
who keeps faith forever,
who executes justice for the oppressed,
who gives food to the hungry;
You watch over the strangers,
uphold the children and most
vulnerable parents,
and have triumphed over sin and evil.
(from Psalm 146)

On this Children's Sabbath day, we give you thanks, O God, especially for children, for the blessing they are and the blessing we may be to them, as we seek to do justice, love kindness, and walk humbly with you.

And so we join the saints and angels in
proclaiming your glory, as we sing (say),

Celebrant and People:
Holy, holy, holy Lord, God of power
and might, heaven and earth are full of
your glory.
Hosanna in the highest.
Blessed is the one who comes in the name
of the Lord.
Hosanna in the highest.

The **Celebrant** continues:
We praise you, O God,
for sending your beloved child Jesus
born as a baby
nurtured by his family,
and protected by strangers,
who grew as a child
who was taught in his temple,
surrounded by his community,
and guided by his parents,
who became an adult
who loved and blessed the children,

who cared for those who were sick,
poor, and left out,
who taught that God loves us like a parent,
and who called us his friends.
This one who was born a baby needing us
died our Savior whom we all need,
triumphant even over death,
freeing us to live as your beloved children.

(At the following words concerning the bread, the Celebrant is to hold it, or lay a hand upon it; and at the words concerning the cup, to hold or place a hand upon the cup and any other vessel containing the wine to be consecrated.)

On the night before he died for us, Jesus was at the table with his friends. He took bread, gave thanks, broke it, and gave it to them, and said: "Take, eat: This is my Body, which is given for you. As you do this, remember me."

As supper was ending, Jesus took the cup of wine.

Again, he gave thanks, gave it to them, and said: "Drink this, all of you: This is my Blood of the new Covenant, which is poured out for you and for all for the forgiveness of sins. Whenever you drink it, remember me."

Around your table, as your children,
O God, we remember Jesus Christ,
Who came in love, lived in love, and died in love,
Who was and is and is to come.

We offer to you our gifts of bread and wine,
And we offer to you our lives.

Pour out your Spirit upon these gifts that they may be for us the body and blood of Christ, that they strengthen us to welcome the children, to show your love, to work for your justice. Through Christ and with Christ and in Christ, in the unity of the Holy Spirit, to you be honor, glory, and praise, for ever and ever. Amen.

The Lord's Prayer

The Breaking of the Bread

> **Option 1:** (BCP)
> Alleluia. Christ our Passover is sacrificed for us;
> Therefore let us keep the feast. Alleluia.
>
> **Option 2:** (EOW)
> We break this bread to share in the Body of Christ.
> We who are many are one body, for we all share in the one bread.

Communion Hymn: As We Gather at Your Table (#763), Go Forth for God (#347)

Post Communion Prayer

> **Option 1:** (BCP)
> Let us pray.
> Eternal God, heavenly Father,
> You have graciously accepted us as living members of your Son our Savior, Jesus Christ, and you have fed us with spiritual food in the Sacrament of his Body and Blood.
> Send us now into the world in peace, and grant us strength and courage to love and serve you with gladness and singleness of heart, through Christ our Lord.
> Amen.

> **Option 2:** (adapted from EOW)
> Loving God,
> we give you thanks
> for restoring us in your image
> and nourishing us with spiritual food
> in the Sacrament of Christ's Body and Blood.
> Now send us forth
> a people, forgiven, healed, renewed;
> that we may proclaim your love to the world
> through serving the children
> and continue in the risen life of Christ our Savior.
> Amen.

The Blessing (EOW)

May the blessing of the God of Abraham and Sarah, and of Jesus Christ born of our sister Mary, and of the Holy Spirit, who broods over the world as a mother over her children, be upon you and remain with you always. Amen.

The Dismissal

Celebrant: Remembering especially all our children, let us go in peace to love and serve the Lord.

People: **Thanks be to God.**

Additional Worship Resources

Following are worship resources from a variety of sources. Use or adapt any of the following resources that would be appropriate for your tradition. In addition, you may want to consider the prayers and other worship resources in the interfaith section (Section 9) and sections for other faith traditions to see if any would be appropriate for your service.

Call to Worship: A Litany of Awareness
from the Children's Sabbath at *First Christian Church (Disciples of Christ) in Frankfort, Kentucky*

Leader: Every 10 seconds a high school student drops out. (*tolling of bells for 10 seconds*)

People: Jesus loves me, this I know.

Leader: Every 35 seconds a child is abused or neglected. (*tolling of bells for 35 seconds*)

People: For the Bible tells me so.

Leader: Every 40 seconds a baby is born into poverty. (*tolling of bells for 40 seconds*)

People: Little ones to him belong.

Leader: Every 51 seconds a baby is born without health insurance. (*tolling of bells for 51 seconds*)

People: They are weak but he is strong.

All: Yes, Jesus loves me. The Bible tells me so.

A Litany for Children of the World

Leader 1: The children in our congregation need a voice… a voice filled with praise and commitment…
A voice inspired by a God of covenant promises and steadfast love.
We light a candle for the children of our congregation.

Leader 2: The children in our neighborhood need a voice… a voice filled with vision and accountability…
A voice inspired by a God who calls us to love neighbor and stranger.
We light a candle for the children of our neighborhoods.

Leader 3: The children of this nation need a voice… a voice filled with compassion and strength…
A voice inspired by a God of love and justice for all people—especially children.
We light a candle for the children of our nation.

Leader 4: The children of the world need a voice… a voice brought out of our congregations, our neighborhoods, and our nation [and theirs].
Through prayer and action let us together commit to making a difference for children everywhere, so that they, and we, may grow into the fullness of God's creation.
We light a candle for the children of our world.

Let All the Little Children Come
Let the little children come unto me and forbid them not, for such is the kingdom of Heaven, Jesus said.

He did not say let only rich or middle-class White children come.

He did not say let only the strapping boys but not the girls come.

He did not say let only the able-bodied children come.

All the children He bade come.

He did not say let all my children or your children or our friends' children or those in our families and neighborhoods and who look and act like us come.

He did not say let only the well-behaved nice children come or those who conform to society's norms.

He did not say let a few, a third, half, or three-fourths come—but all.

Jesus said let the little children come and forbid them not, for such is the kingdom of heaven.

(By Marian Wright Edelman)

Call to Worship (based on Jeremiah 31:15-17)

Child 1: Every day in our nation, more than 2,500 babies are born into poverty.
Child 2: Every day in our nation, more than 1,800 children are reported abused or neglected.
Child 3: Every day in our nation, more than 600 babies are born to mothers who received late or no prenatal care.
Child 4: Every day in our nation, more than 700 babies are born too small to be healthy.

Child 5: Every day in our nation, more than 100 babies die before their first birthday.

Leader: "A voice is heard in Ramah, lamentation and bitter weeping. Rachel is weeping for her children; she refuses to be comforted for her children, because they are no more."

People: We come together with hearts that weep for our nation's children.

Leader: "Thus says the Lord: Keep your voice from weeping and your eyes from tears; For there is a reward for your work, says the Lord."

People: We come together to be moved from weeping to hear the promise of the work we can do.

Leader: "[The children] shall come back from the land of the enemy; there is hope for your future says the Lord: Your children shall come back to their own country."

People: We come together to glimpse your vision of home-coming that would bring our nation's children from an experience of need to one of safety, plenty, and love.

Unison: Be with us in our worship and our work, O God. Prepare us by the power of your spirit that we may commit our hearts and hands and minds to realizing your vision of homecoming for the children of our nation. Amen.

(By Shannon Daley-Harris)

Call to Worship (Based on Psalm 147)

Leader: Praise God!

People: **How good it is to sing praises to our God.**

Leader: God builds up the city; God brings together those who have been left out.

People: **God heals the brokenhearted and makes their wounds better.**

Leader: Great is our God, and abundant in power; God's understanding is beyond measure.

People: **God lifts up those who are beaten down and puts down those who hurt others.**

Leader: Praise God,
For God strengthens our communities;
God blesses our children within us.
God grants peace.

People: **Praise God.**

(By Shannon Daley-Harris)

Prayer of Confession

Dear God, you sent Jesus your son that all might have life abundant. We confess that we have not done what we can to help all children live into that promise. We have not assured care for the millions of children in need of a doctor. We have let poverty, not promise, define the lives of millions of children.

Forgive us, we pray. Help us to bring your promise of life abundant to children through our care, our guidance, and our work for justice. In Jesus' name we pray. Amen.

Assurance of Pardon

There is a balm in Gilead, to make the wounded whole. There is a balm in Gilead to heal the sin-sick soul. Friends, believe the Good News of the gospel: In Jesus Christ we are forgiven!

(By Shannon Daley-Harris)

A Prayer for Healing

Mighty and merciful God, you sent Jesus Christ to heal broken lives. We praise you that today you send healing in doctors and nurses, and bless us with technology in medicine. May we work with justice and compassion to assure that the blessing of this care is available to all and not just to some. We claim your promises of wholeness as we pray for those who are ill in body or mind, who long for your healing touch. Make the weak strong, the sick healthy, the broken whole, and confirm those who serve them as agents of your love. Then all shall be renewed in vigor to point to the risen Christ, who conquered death that we might live eternally. Amen.

(Adapted from the Presbyterian Church (USA)
Book of Common Worship)

For Doctors and Nurses

Sanctify, O Lord, those whom you have called to the study and practice of the arts of healing, and to the prevention of disease and pain. Strengthen them by your life-giving Spirit, that by their ministries the health of the community may be promoted and your creation glorified. Guide us, your people, to assure that these ministries of health are available to all and not just to some, through Jesus Christ our Lord. Amen.

(Adapted from the Episcopal *Book of Common Prayer*)

Collect: Saint Luke

Almighty God, who didst inspire thy servant Luke the physician to set forth in the Gospel the love and healing power of thy Son: Graciously continue in thy Church the love and power to heal, to the praise and glory of thy Name; through the same thy Son Jesus Christ our Lord, who liveth and reigneth with thee, in the unity of the Holy Spirit, one God, now and for ever. Amen.

(From the Episcopal *Book of Common Prayer*)

Prayer

Holy One, Healer of all wounds, be with us as we search for faith to be your people. Help us see the wounds around us, especially those inflicted on children. Guide us to bring a healing touch of love and care, not given at a distance or hidden from view, but person to person. We pray all this in the name of Jesus Christ, whose gaze avoided no one and whose touch healed the sick. Amen.

(By the Rev. Dr. Eileen W. Lindner)

Affirmation of Faith

God has not taken God's people out of the world, but has sent them into the world to worship God there and serve all humankind. We worship God in the world by standing before our Lord on behalf of all people. Our cries for help and our songs of praise are never for ourselves alone. Worship is no retreat from the world; it is part of our mission. We serve humankind by discerning what God is doing in the world and joining in that work. We risk disagreement and error when we try to say what God is doing here and now. But we find guidance in God's deeds in the past and promises for the future, as they are witnessed to in Scripture. We affirm that the Lord is at work, especially in events and movements that free people by the gospel and advance justice, compassion, and peace.

(From *A Declaration of Faith*)

Affirmation of Faith

We believe in God, the Creator Spirit, who moved upon the face of the deep at the beginning of creation, who created all that is, and who spoke through the prophets of old.

We believe in Jesus Christ, into whom God's Spirit was poured in fullness and in power, that the whole creation might be restored and unified; and who promised that the Spirit would come and fill the faithful with power to witness to the mighty love of God.

We wait on that Spirit today, with longing hearts, seeking to be empowered to witness to God's love in Christ, with fresh words and courageous actions of love and hope.

Glory be to God—Creator, Christ, and Holy Spirit—now and always. Amen.

Call to Confession

Let us honestly confess before God the things that we have done or have failed to do, which have caused us to be less effective servants.

Prayer of Confession

Dear God, whom we so quickly and easily call Lord: Forgive us for failure to understand and accept the great demands placed upon us by your lordship. We enlist in your causes, but find ourselves losing interest. We promise to be courageous, but find ourselves afraid. We want to be sensitive, but find ourselves hard and callous. We are confronted with great opportunities, but fail to take advantage of them. Forgive us, God; take our limitations and turn them into possibilities for service. Hear our prayer and grant us new life, through Christ our Lord. Amen.

(From First United Methodist Church of San Diego's Order of Worship)

Prayer of Confession

God, we confess that we have not loved you with all our hearts, with all our souls, with all our might. We have not loved our neighbors as ourselves.

When nine million of our children are left by the wayside, without health care coverage, we confess that we have looked away and passed by on the other side.

We confess that when more than 12 million children in our nation are beaten down by poverty, we look away and pass by on the other side.

We confess that when millions of poor, Black, and Latino children have the odds stacked against them and are routed to jail more often than Yale, we look away and pass by on the other side.

We confess that when half a million children languish in the foster care system, many of them waiting for adoption, we look away and pass by on the other side.

Fill us with your compassionate spirit, that our hearts will be moved with concern for children in need, that we will reach out with caring hands, and that we will give of ourselves and our resources, and our time and our treasure.

Help us to love you with all our heart, all our strength, and with all our mind, and our neighbors—especially children and families in need—as ourselves.

(By Shannon Daley-Harris)

Prayer of Confession

Loving God, we know there are big problems facing children and families—too little food and too much hunger. Not enough love and too much violence. Too little family time and too much despair. Too little money and too many bills. Too many illnesses and not enough health or health care.

We confess that there are times we want to turn away from the problems or pretend they don't exist. We say they are someone else's concern or someone else's fault. We fear that we can't make a difference. We fear that making a difference will change our lives in ways we won't like. We want to give up—to give up on others, give up on ourselves.

Forgive us for our faint-heartedness—for failing to love others as you would have us, for failing to believe in ourselves as you do. Remind us that you never give up on others and you never give up on us. Amen.

(By Shannon Daley-Harris)

Prayer for a New Society

All-nourishing God, your children cry for help
Against the violence of our world:
Where children starve for bread and feed on weapons;
Starve for vision and feed on drugs;
Starve for love and feed on videos;
Starve for peace and die murdered in our streets.

Creator God, timeless preserver of resources,
Forgive us for the gifts that we have wasted.
Renew us for what seems beyond redemption;
Call order and beauty to emerge again from chaos.
Convert our destructive power into creative service;
Help us to heal the woundedness of our world.

Liberating God, release us from the demons of violence.
Free us today from the disguised demon of deterrence
That puts guns by our pillows and missiles in our skies.

Free us from all demons that blind and blunt our spirits;
Cleanse us from all justifications for violence and war;
Open our narrowed hearts to the suffering and the poor.

Abiding God, loving renewer of the human spirit,
Unfold our violent fists into peaceful hands:
Stretch our sense of family to include our neighbors;
Stretch our sense of neighbor to include our enemies
Until our response to you finally respects and embraces

All creation as precious sacraments of your presence.
Hear the prayer of all your starving children. Amen.

(Pax Christi USA)

Prayers of Intercession

Leader: Eternal God, we know that you are ever-present, waiting for us to turn to you. By asking you to "kum ba yah," to "come by here," we really seek a more profound awareness of your presence as we pray. Infuse us with your spirit, Lord, and in your mercy—

People (sing): **Kum ba yah, my Lord, kum ba yah. Kum ba yah, my Lord, kum ba yah. Kum ba yah, my Lord, kum ba yah. Oh Lord, kum ba yah.**

Leader: Someone's crying, Lord. A baby born too soon, too small, too sick. A child aching with hunger. A teenager who lost a friend to gunfire. A parent who can't afford to take her sick child to the doctor. Someone's crying, Lord. In your mercy, Lord—

People (sing): **Kum ba yah, my Lord, kum ba yah. Kum ba yah, my Lord, kum ba yah. Kum ba yah, my Lord, kum ba yah. Oh Lord, kum ba yah.**

Leader: Someone's singing, Lord. A child whose parent praised her good job on homework. A teenager who feels valued by his parents and teachers. A parent lulling his child to sleep. Someone's singing, Lord, with thankfulness for your love. In your mercy, Lord—

People (sing): **Kum ba yah, my Lord, kum ba yah. Kum ba yah, my Lord, kum ba yah. Kum ba yah, my Lord, kum ba yah. Oh Lord, kum ba yah.**

Leader: Someone's praying, Lord. A child whose parents are fighting. A teenager who fears she may be pregnant. A parent who can't see how to make ends meet. Someone's praying, Lord, that your justice and mercy will spread through our land. In your mercy, Lord—

People (sing): Kum ba yah, my Lord, kum ba yah. Kum ba yah, my Lord, kum ba yah. Kum ba yah, my Lord, kum ba yah. Oh Lord, kum ba yah.

Leader: Someone in need of your guiding presence asks you to come by here, Lord. Elected officials, as they make decisions that will affect millions of children and families. Parents, as they seek to nurture strong values in their children. Those serving children and families, as they try to discern the right action to take. In your mercy, Lord—

People (sing): Kum ba yah, my Lord, kum ba yah. Kum ba yah, my Lord, kum ba yah. Kum ba yah, my Lord, kum ba yah. Oh Lord, kum ba yah.

(By Shannon Daley-Harris)

Prayers of the People

Leader: Tender God, we come before you with prayers on our hearts. We seek the balm that only you can provide.

People (sing): There is a balm in Gilead, to make the wounded whole. There is a balm in Gilead, to heal the sin-sick soul.

Leader: We pray for all children, that they may know wholeness in their lives and flourish as God intends. We pray especially for children who are sick or injured, that while they wait for healing, they may know the love and presence of God.

People (sing): There is a balm in Gilead, to make the wounded whole. There is a balm in Gilead, to heal the sin-sick soul.

Leader: We pray for communities that are divided by racism, violence, selfishness, or ideology that they may find ways to work together to improve the lives of children, families, and all who live in them.

People (sing): There is a balm in Gilead, to make the wounded whole. There is a balm in Gilead, to heal the sin-sick soul.

Leader: We pray for leaders—leaders of our nation, states, and communities, of businesses and congregations, of schools and child care centers, of scout troops and soccer teams, of hospitals and homeless shelters—that they may lead in a way that embraces diversity while promoting unity for the well-being of children and families and communities.

People (sing): There is a balm in Gilead, to make the wounded whole. There is a balm in Gilead, to heal the sin-sick soul.

Leader: We pray for ourselves. For the dashed dream, the bruised spirit, the wounded heart, the battered hope. Come touch our hearts with the tenderness and healing that only you can provide, that we may be healed and renewed for the work we are called to do.

People (sing): There is a balm in Gilead, to make the wounded whole. There is a balm in Gilead, to heal the sin-sick soul.

(By Shannon Daley-Harris)

Prayers of the People

(The prayer here is written as a "bidding prayer." Leader 1, perhaps a lay leader or youth, invites the congregation to pray about a particular concern. Congregation members may pray in silence or add their own brief, spoken prayer about the concern. Then, Leader 2, perhaps the pastor, concludes the time of silence and spoken prayer with a brief prayer about the concern. For another form of intercessory prayer, please see the Catholic and Episcopal liturgies and the sample interfaith service.)

Leader 1: Let us pray for peace in our homes, schools, communities, nation, and world.

A time of silence follows during which congregation members may add their own brief prayers for peace—silently or aloud.

Leader 2: We pray that your peace will bind together families in discord and schools and neighborhoods that have become battlefields, and that our community and nation will work to provide positive, peaceful, and productive futures for all children.

Leader 1: Let us pray for those in need of healing.

A time of silence follows during which congregation members may add their own brief prayers for healing—silently or aloud.

Leader 2: We pray for your healing, especially for children who suffer in mind, body, and spirit—for those tormented by thoughts from which they cannot find peace, for those wracked by pain and without health insurance to see a doctor, for those plunged into the darkness of despair and unable to see your light.

Leader 1: Let us pray for our church.

A time of silence follows during which congregation members may add their own brief prayers for the church—silently or aloud.

Leader 2: We pray that we will welcome the children as Jesus bid us to do, that we will remove the stumbling blocks before them, and that our church will become a place of sanctuary—peace, protection, and well-being—for children.

Leader 1: Let us pray for leaders in our community, state, and nation.

A time of silence follows during which congregation members may add their own brief prayers for these leaders—silently or aloud.

Leader 2: We pray that your vision will guide their leadership, that their commitment will be sustained, and that they will do what is right to protect children and families.

Leader 1: Let us pray for ourselves as we seek to be faithful guardians of God's children.

A time of silence follows during which congregation members may add their own brief prayers for the gathered community—silently or aloud.

Leader 2: We pray for ourselves, that our work with and for children be guided by faith, motivated by love, and sustained by hope. Amen.

Prayers of the People

By faith and religious fervor we have come. Let us now pray as one:

For calling us into community—in our places of worship and our places of work, in families and in friendships, in common concern and common cause, **we give you thanks.**

For the blessing of children and the blessing of being your children, **we give you thanks.**

For opening our eyes to the needs of children and opening our hearts to respond, for opening our hands to give and our mouths to speak out for justice, **we give you thanks.**

For children and families who face illness and injury without the resources to get help and healing, **we ask your comfort.**

For the children who live in despair or fear and are not safe in their homes, schools, neighborhoods, or country, **we ask your comfort.**

For those who grieve the loss of a loved one, especially the children lost needlessly to violence, incarceration, illness, or injury we could have prevented, **we ask your comfort.**

For the leaders of our communities, state, and nation, that they lead with vision and courage, pursuing the health and safety of our children, **we ask for guidance.**

For leaders of our faith communities, that they manifest your will and help us together to live out our faith in the care of children, **we ask for guidance.**

For ourselves, that we are led by your vision, sustained by our faith, and sustained by hope as we work for children, **we ask for guidance.**

These things we ask in confidence, knowing that our children are held in your love before we even reach out, and our prayers are heard before we even think to ask. **Amen.**

(By Shannon Daley-Harris)

Prayer

Lord, make our hearts bigger
Our love deeper
Our faith stronger
Our hope unwavering
Our strength greater
Our efforts unceasing
Our voices unflinching
Our vision Yours
as we seek justice and care
for all your beloved children. Amen.

(By Marian Wright Edelman)

A Franciscan Benediction

May God bless you with DISCOMFORT…
At easy answers, half-truths, and superficial relationships
    So that you may live deep within your heart.

May God bless you with ANGER…
At injustice, oppression, and exploitation of people,
    So that you may work for justice, freedom, and peace.

May God bless you with TEARS…
To shed for those who suffer pain, rejection, starvation,
and war
    So that you may reach out your hand to comfort them
        And to turn their pain into JOY.

And may God bless you with enough FOOLISHNESS…
To believe that you can make a difference in the world,
    So that you can DO what others claim cannot be done.
Amen.

Commissioning Pastoral Caregivers and Health Professionals

The following service is offered as an example of a commissioning service to recognize and empower individuals in ministry. Following the reading of scripture and the sermon, those persons to be anointed and commissioned come forward.

Message from the Minister: Jesus healed those who were sick and hurting. By restoring them to health, Jesus showed God's love and desire that we be made whole. God's shalom, God's intention for health and wholeness, extends to every area of life. God longs for healthy minds, bodies, and spirits, for healthy relationships, healthy societies, and a healthy world. Each person is called to be a bearer of God's love and care in our hurting world.

As health care providers, you have accepted a special and important role as an instrument of healing. When mothers get good prenatal care, when babies are born into welcoming hands, when children's cuts are stitched, eyes and ears are checked, when ear aches are treated and asthma relieved, when the last moments of a body's life in this world are eased, when you tend these and any of God's people, you are an agent of God's love and caring.

Ministers in Christ's service, witnessing our faith, embrace with hope the healing power of God who attends your art and science of medicine and health with blessing and honor. May Jesus Christ, whose love and compassion you know, touch your head and heart and hands, granting you his healing grace.
(Adapted from *The Presbyterian Whole Health Catalog*, produced by the Presbyterian Health Network)

Prayer: We pray for health professionals, including [*insert names*] and all those whose names we do not know.

We pray for those they tend, and all who are in need of healing and care, especially (*may insert specific names or categories of patients, such as "premature babies"*).

We pray for those who do not receive the health care they need and for our nation, that we will work together to assure health care for all.

We pray that we may find our own roles as healers and comforters, for the hurting places in people's minds, bodies, and spirits, and for the broken places in our society that need justice and restored relationship. In the name of Christ we pray, Amen.

Music Suggestions

The following hymn suggestions that lift up children, families, and God's call to justice and love can be found in many hymnals including the New Century Hymnal, the United Methodist Hymnal, the Presbyterian Hymnal, Chalice, the Lutheran Book of Worship, the African American Heritage Hymnal, and Worship: Hymnal and Service Book for Roman Catholics.

Hymns of Praise

All Things Bright and Beautiful
Bring Many Names
For the Beauty of the Earth
Gather Us In
God Whose Love Is Reigning o'er Us
God Is Here
How Can We Name a Love
Immortal, Invisible, God Only Wise
Lift Every Voice and Sing
Let the Whole Creation Cry
Lord of Our Growing Years
My Heart Is Overflowing
O God in Heaven
Tell Out, My Soul, the Greatness of the Lord
There's a Wideness in God's Mercy

Hymns After Passing the Peace

A hymn such as "I've Got Peace Like a River" or "Jesus Loves Me" would be a good choice here, since the children may already know it or could learn it in preparation for the Children's Sabbath.

Hymns of Thanksgiving and Communion

For the Fruits of This Creation
God Whose Giving Knows No Ending
Draw Us in the Spirit's Tether

Hymns of Petition

God, Omnipotent, Eternal
Kum Ba Yah
Lord of All Hopefulness
O God, We Bear the Imprint of Your Face
Our Father by Whose Name
This World, My God, Is Held Within Your Hand

Hymns of Commitment and Closing Hymns

All Who Love and Serve Your City
Called as Partners in Christ's Service
Christian Women, Christian Men
Guide My Feet
Help Us Accept Each Other
Here I Am, Lord
I'm Gonna Live So God Can Use Me
Jesu, Jesu, Fill Us with Your Love
Let Justice Flow Like Streams
Like a Mother Who Has Borne Us
Live into Hope
Lord of All Nations, Grant Me Grace
Lord, Whose Love in Humble Service
Lord, You Give the Great Commission
Now Praise the Hidden God of Love
O For a World
Our Cities Cry to You, O God
Song of Hope (Canto de Esperanza)
The Church of Christ in Every Age
There's a Spirit in the Air
Today We All Are Called to Be Disciples
We Are Your People
What Does the Lord Require
When a Poor One
When We Are Living

Sermon Resources

The sermon or homily is one of the most powerful opportunities to proclaim God's love and concern for all of God's children and God's call to us to put our faith into action by loving and protecting children.

The lectionary texts designated for this Children's Sabbath Sunday offer deep connections and powerful messages related to the Children's Sabbath themes for those churches that follow these designated cycles of readings. The Revised Common Lectionary, the Roman Catholic Lectionary, and the Episcopal Lectionary share a common Gospel lesson and Epistle. Even pastors who do not follow a lectionary will find food for thought and study in these sermon resources, which include sermon notes by **Shannon Daley-Harris, M.Div.,** on the lectionary texts for the Revised Common Lectionary, Episcopal Lectionary, and Lutheran Lectionary, and a sample homily by **Father Walter J. Burghardt, S.J.,** on the Roman Catholic Lectionary texts.

For preachers who do not follow a lectionary, sermon notes on Exodus 2:1-10 are provided by the **Rev. Eileen W. Lindner, Ph.D.,** Deputy General Secretary for Research and Planning, The National Council of the Churches of Christ in the U.S.A.

Episcopal Lectionary for Proper 24:
Genesis 32:3-8, 22-30
Ps. 121
2 Timothy 3:14-4:5
Luke 18:1-8a

Revised Common Lectionary for 29th Sunday in Ordinary Time
Jer. 31:27-34
Ps. 119:97-104
2 Tim. 3:14-4:5
Luke 18:1-8

Roman Catholic Lectionary for the 29th Week
Exodus 17:8-13
Ps. 120
2 Tim. 3:14-4:2
Luke 18:1-8

A sample Children's Sermon, "When Whining Is Wonderful," follows these sermon resources (on page 88) for use with the children of the congregation in a special conversation or "time with children."

Revised Common Lectionary Sermon Notes

29th Sunday in Ordinary Time
By Shannon Daley-Harris, M.Div.

Jeremiah 31:27-34
2 Timothy 3:14-4:5
Luke 18:1-8

Jeremiah 31:27-34

Context of the Passage

The book of Jeremiah contains both warning and consolation. While there was still time to warn the people and urge them to change their ways, Jeremiah did so in strong, painful language. When it was "too late," and Israel was already suffering from the dislocation they saw as a result of their injustice and faithlessness, Jeremiah offered words of comfort. Jeremiah, like other prophetic literature in the Old Testament, reflects this transition from a period of judgment to the coming of renewal and restoration, and the need to offer an authoritative word of hope to sustain the people.

A Closer Look

The Sins of Others: In verse 30, our passage reads, "But all shall die for their own sins; the teeth of everyone who eats sour grapes shall be set on edge." Notes one scholar, "The point of this saying was clearly not to express a doctrine or give a legal defense for the principle of shared family responsibility but rather to give voice to despair." While it does not immediately strike the listener today this way, for Jeremiah to move to a declaration that "they shall die for their own sins," was actually a word of hope: no longer would children suffer for the sins of their parents.

Covenant: In Jeremiah, the term "covenant" comes from the language of international relations, comparable to "treaty." Covenant represented a mutual commitment in which two parties had an agreement and responsibility, a relationship between God and Israel. However, Israel broke the covenant so egregiously and repeatedly that Israel essentially rendered the covenant null and void, so that it was no longer in force. In this passage, as elsewhere in Deuteronomistic use, law and covenant are used synonymously. Israel is promised not a new law, but a new way to understand and fulfill the original covenant revealed to Moses. Just as God promised and

instructed, "These words which I command you this day shall be upon your hearts," (Deut. 6:6) words Jews repeat even to this day, so too Jeremiah promises that God will write this law on the hearts of God's people. This fresh start is another chance to live in obedience from the inside out.

Note that instead of the term "nation," our passage uses the more general "house of Israel." Jeremiah acknowledged that Israel was no longer a "nation" as it had been but was now a diaspora, a scattered community. This people was now more loosely defined not only geographically but also more genetically; to be of the house of Israel was less about who one's ancestors were and more about how one was prepared to live one's life that day with a deep understanding in one's heart and a renewed commitment to live in relationship with God.

Themes for Preaching

Covenant, from the least to the greatest
No more shall they teach one another, or say to each other, "Know the Lord," for they shall all know me, from the least to the greatest, says the Lord; for I will forgive their iniquity, and remember their sin no more. (31:34)

Imagine our communities, nation, and world if we all knew God, if God's law were written on our hearts and revealed in our lives. Would children still be the poorest Americans? Would one of every nine of our children lack health and mental health care coverage and live sicker as a result? Would we allow families to be buried under a mountain of medical debt instead of assuring that every child has health care coverage that is easy to access? Would half a million women die from child-birth related causes around the world? Would 11 million children die each year globally from largely preventable malnutrition and disease? Would millions of poor and minority youth be pushed along the "cradle to prison pipeline" instead of being set on the path to successful, hopeful futures?

If God's law were written on our hearts and revealed in our lives, would we, in our rich nation, instead ensure that children have the food, family income, health care, and other basic things they need to live out their lives with the health and wholeness God intends? Would ours be a world in which no child dies from preventable malnutrition and disease, in which no woman bears a child for calamity, in which every young person is guided on the path to a hopeful future full of promise? What would it look like if we really lived as God's people?

Sins of our parents...

Jeremiah heralds this "new day" with the oddly good news that now one will only die for their own "sins," not for the sins of others. How is this "good news"? We've seen all too often what it means for children to die for the sins of others. We see that every few seconds around the world, an innocent child dies of malnutrition and disease that could have been prevented. We see that every minute somewhere around the world a woman dies unnecessarily in childbirth. We've seen children like Devante and Diamonte die because they didn't have health coverage and the access to a doctor that most of us take for granted. We've seen children die from causes we could have prevented. We know all about children dying because of the sins of others—from injustice, inequality, indifference. It's time for that new day to dawn, when no child dies from what we failed to do or because of what we have done.

2 Tim. 3:14-4:5

Context of the Passage

Unlike 1 Timothy, in which Paul is presented as a free apostle, 2 Timothy is written as though Paul is in prison and near death, abandoned by almost all of his friends; it has the tone of a "final testament," conveying a dying parent's exhortation, blessing, and warning to a "child." We don't know the author who assumed Paul's name in writing this letter which, with 1 Timothy and Titus, is commonly referred to as the Pastoral Epistles. We also don't know the precise date of composition, but it is believed to be in the early second century C.E.

The "Timothy" to whom the letter was supposedly addressed is one of Paul's closest co-workers, active in work with the churches of Thessalonica, Corinth, and Ephesus. Timothy is held up as a model and ideal, contrasted sharply with false teachers. Lois and Eunice, mentioned in 2 Tim 1:5 are Timothy's grandmother and mother, Christians before him who nurtured him in faith.

A Closer Look

Points out Fred Craddock in *A New Testament Commentary*, the "sacred writings" and "All Scripture" refer to the Old Testament, as Christian writings were not yet considered Scripture. Though at the time this epistle was written, some writings, such as Paul's letters, were beginning to be highly revered, in the fictive setting represented here the Scriptures that "Timothy" would have known in his youth could only be the Jewish Scriptures.

Preaching Themes

Be Persistent

I solemnly urge you: proclaim the message; be persistent whether the time is favorable or unfavorable; convince, rebuke, and encourage, with the utmost patience in teaching. (4:1b-2)

On this Children's Sabbath weekend, the urging to proclaim the message and persist whether the time is favorable or unfavorable is a powerful message. The Rev. Jim Wallis, founder of Sojourners and author of *God's Politics*, jokes that you can recognize elected leaders in Washington because they are the ones walking around with their fingers in the air to see which way the wind is blowing. In our day, elected leaders do consult polls and focus groups and lead with an eye to campaign contributions and getting votes. This makes our steady witness as people of faith all the more important. We don't decide what is right by what is popular, we aren't called to speak up when it is convenient and bite our lip when it is not. Instead, we are called to proclaim God's intention for justice, God's demand that we protect those who are poor and powerless and young and vulnerable first, whether it is popular or not, whether the political climate is favorable or unfavorable.

Itchy Ears

For the time is coming when people will not put up with sound doctrine, but having itching ears, they will accumulate for themselves teachers to suit their own desires, and will turn away from listening to the truth and wander away to myths. (4:3-4)

Do you remember as a child, asking your mother for something, and if her answer was "no," going to your father and asking him the question, hoping to get the answer you wanted? Our passage from Timothy warns us of the danger of "itchy ears," looking for those who will tell us what we want to hear, not the truth. In an election season, it is particularly hard to find those who are willing to tell the truth and not to pander to "itchy ears." Who wants to hear a candidate say that we need to invest more resources to provide for the needs of others? Who wants to hear that our lack of investment in children's health care has cost children their lives? Who wants to hear that we as parents, teachers, communities, and a nation have turned our backs on too many poor and minority youths, or, worse, that we have pushed them into the cradle to prison pipeline instead of on to paths of promise? Who wants to hear that tax breaks for millionaires and billionaires have driven our nation deeper into debt and caused us to cut programs serving the poor? Wouldn't we rather hear the smooth words of a slogan, the easy words of a false promise, the comforting words of simple assurance? Wouldn't we rather hear candidates sling mud at each other than tell the truth about the quicksand on which our nation now stands, sinking in a culture of power, greed, violence, and superficial distraction? Wouldn't we rather hear that we can't afford to provide for the needs of our nation's children than that we have simply chosen not to make it our priority?

In this election season, we must decide if we will indulge our itchy ears and pursue leaders who will suit our own desires, or if we will attune our ears to hear the truth—difficult as it may be to hear. If we will seek silence to listen to our hearts and the call of our God to do justice for the least, the last, and the left out. If we will listen with careful discernment that sees through the rhetoric, sound bite, and slogan to discover who is willing to tell the hard truth about what our nation needs to do to live out God's intention for justice and compassion.

Luke 18:1-8

Context of the Passage

Luke, writing toward the end of the first century C.E., was addressing a community that was several generations removed from Jesus. His readers were enduring abuse and persecution and hard times because of their faith.

Our passage is situated in the midst of Jesus' teachings on his final journey to Jerusalem. The preceding passage, like our passage, is unique to Luke's gospel. Both address the longing of the disciples for the advent of the kingdom and their final vindication, both speak to the question of "when" and "how long." The preceding passage addresses the longing of the disciples for the coming of the Son of man and their deliverance from the suffering they endure. Our parable assures the disciples that God will not long delay, but leaves them with the challenging question: Will they have persisted faithfully until that time? The parable that follows our passage cautions the listeners against self-righteousness and complacency, and is then followed by the beloved story of Jesus blessing the children.

A Closer Look

The main characters in our parable represent two extremes. First, there is the judge. A judge, then as now, was a symbol of power, one with responsibility to exercise fairness in settling disputes, to restore justice. A good and impartial judge was the best hope of weaker and powerless members of the community who were dependent on him to help secure justice for them. Our judge, who neither feared nor had respect for people, was unjust. (Note that in the parable, we are "hearing" his inner thoughts, what he is saying to himself, so we know they are his true sentiments.)

At the other end of the power spectrum stands the widow. Fred Craddock in *The People's New Testament Commentary* elaborates, "Widows in Israelite tradition were extremely vulnerable—they could not inherit their husband's property, there was no organized social welfare program, and for the most part no opportunity for independent employment for them. They were often dependent on the judge for protection and fairness, since they were easily victimized. In this story the judge is the widow's only hope for justice, and he is a bad judge." (p. 249)

In our passage, the phrase translated "wear me out" literally means "hit me in the eye." It may be meant literally or metaphorically—that she might "beat him up" in the view of the public.

So what does the bad judge do? Astoundingly, he grants the widow justice. This big, bad judge, who isn't afraid of God or people, grants the poor and vulnerable widow justice.

Note that the judge *does the right thing for the wrong reason.* In our advocacy on behalf of children, we can look for the best intentions of our elected leaders, can appeal to their deepest desires to do the right thing. However, there may also be times that we simply need to exert enough pressure, persistently enough, that even those who aren't inclined to do the right thing for our children will, simply because we successfully pressure them to.

Note also that the widow, who was presented as a poor and vulnerable figure, was not powerless. Often, advocates speak of "empowering" those who are poor or vulnerable. But no one *gave* the widow her power—she discovered and exercised it herself. Part of our work for justice isn't about "empowering" others but is about getting out of their way as they tap and exercise their own inherent power, lift their own voices to express their own best understanding of their need and the justice they demand.

Will not God grant justice? This is one of the "how much more" parables that makes its point by moving from the lesser to the greater. That is, the unjust judge certainly isn't the stand-in, equivalent figure for God in this parable. The point is that if an *unjust* judge grants justice, *how much more* quickly will a just and loving God, who is so much greater than the miserable unjust judge, grant justice. Be careful that listeners, especially children and young people, understand this point.

What are we to make of the word "quickly"? Luke was addressing believers who, several generations after Jesus' time, were enduring long years of persecution and hard times. The preceding passage (Luke 17:20-37) acknowledges their earnest, eager longing for the end time of vindication. Now this parable promising that God will "quickly" grant justice to God's chosen ones. Craddock points out that in this instance *"quickly" is not about calendar or clock time, but means instead that God won't hesitate (unlike the judge) to bring vindication and justice.* We don't need to wait for God to come around to our side because God is already there. It is the difference between *chronos*, calendar time, and *kairos*, God's time. This is an important, and challenging, distinction to raise for listeners—especially those who are enduring suffering themselves, for whom help seems slow to come, for those who have spent long years advocating for justice, for whom a better world for our children seems slow to arrive. We can't promise the date or the time by which God's healing will be experienced in our lives, the date or time by which justice will be realized in our world. What we can promise is that we don't have to persuade God to yearn for our wholeness, don't have to change God's mind to make God intend us to live in a world of justice. God already does.

Craddock notes that Luke's phrase, "When the Son of Man comes" links our parable to the preceding passage that sought to discourage speculation that the end will come soon. The question was phrased in a way that the expected response is "no." Rather than suggesting that there will not be any faithful ones at that time, Luke was reminding his readers that this journey of faith will be a marathon and not a sprint, and the greatest danger is complacency and self-righteousness, a point underscored by the parable that follows in 18:9-14.

Preaching Themes: Power, Persistence, and Prayer

Widow and the Judge: Persistence of the powerless up against the powerful

The parable effectively evokes the experience of powerlessness before power, of dismay when one who is supposed to protect you and your interests fails to do so. And of the determination of those with less power to demand justice from the powerful. Millions of parents today know that feeling of powerlessness and frustration when their uninsured children are in urgent need of help and health care, and the systems and providers and bureaucracy seem to be no respecters of persons. Imagine appealing again and again to secure care for your sick child. Imagine being turned away again and again. Sarah Guerrero doesn't need to imagine what that would be like. She has lived it.

> Since 2004, Sarah Guerrero's three children, seven-year-old Damian, ten-year-old Arturo and eleven-year-old Crystal, had been enrolled in SCHIP, the state Children's Health Insurance Program for low- and moderate-income families. SCHIP coverage allowed Sarah to take the children to the doctor for regular checkups, prescriptions, exams and routine follow-ups for Crystal's allergies and Damian's frequent ear problems.

> One Friday afternoon in November 2006, that all changed. When Sarah took her kids to the doctor for high temperatures, she was told the doctor couldn't treat her kids because their SCHIP coverage had ended. She asked how much the cost of the consultation would be and was told $75 per child. As a widow who receives survivor's benefits and works several shifts to make ends meet for her family, Sarah knew that these fees were beyond her reach. She did not have the means to get her children the medical attention they needed in Texas. So she took her three U.S. citizen children to Mexico, where that evening they were diagnosed and treated for upper respiratory infections.

> Sarah later learned that SCHIP coverage had ended because she failed to pay an enrollment fee—a fee she had never been notified was due. She tried to resolve the problem with the call center. She called again and again, but customer service representatives would hang up on her, tell her that nothing could be done, or tell her that she would have to wait.

She didn't give up. For months Sarah unsuccessfully fought to have her children's coverage reinstated. During that time, her children's health began to suffer—particularly Damian's. Damian has a history of chronic ear infections, but while uninsured, the problem began to worsen. He began performing poorly in school and his grades dropped. His poor performance and incorrect pronunciation of words and phrases was so noticeable that his teachers suggested that he get help. Sarah had also noticed that at home he did not respond to her when she called for him and that he turned up the volume on the TV more and more each day.

It turned out that Damian wasn't suffering from an ear infection, but severe hearing loss. Sarah was told that Damian needed surgery in his left ear as soon as possible to correct his ear problem and prevent further hearing loss. Yet Sarah was forced to delay Damian's ear surgery until his coverage could be reinstated. She enlisted the help of a school nurse and local advocates and received a letter in November 2006— dated September 27, 2006— stating that her health plan had been activated in April 2006. The dates were unusual, but Sarah hoped her problems were resolved.

When Sarah took Damian in for a pre-op doctor's visit before the surgery in late November, she was told again that her child's coverage had not been reinstated. The health plan would not approve the surgery since the six-month coverage period noted on the letter had already expired.

Still, she didn't give up. Next, she turned to child advocates to join her in pleading her case. It wasn't until the advocates appealed to the highest levels of the Texas Health and Human Services Commission that Damian was successfully enrolled in SCHIP. In mid-December, Damian had surgery to alleviate his ear problem. While he still needs follow-up care and treatment to correct his hearing loss, Sarah is hopeful that his ear problem will no longer delay his progress in school and that in time he will be able to catch up with his classmates. She is also relieved that she can now take Damian and her other children to a doctor in Texas, instead of seeking medical attention in Mexico. Justice, at last.

Prayer

The parable of the widow and the judge, Luke tells us, is about the need to pray always and not to lose heart. It invites us to consider what it means to pray always, how many different ways we can pray throughout our day.

There are the silent prayers of our hearts, to be sure. Fervent prayers for the health of our child, for a troubled teen to find the right path, for the strength we need to continue being a voice for justice.

There are the spoken prayers of our lips. Prayers we murmur into the downy hair of a baby, giving thanks for their health or a plea for their healing. There are the prayers some sing around the dinner table: "For health and strength and daily food, we give you thanks O God."

There are the prayers of our hands and our feet. The Reverend Billy Graham is quoted as saying, "The most eloquent prayer is the prayer through hands that heal and bless. The highest form of worship is the worship of unselfish Christian service. The greatest form of praise is the sound of consecrated feet seeking out the lost and helpless." Rabbi Abraham Heschel once said, about participating in a Civil Rights march with Dr. Martin Luther King, Jr., "I felt as through my feet were praying." How might our hands and feet pray this day? Will they pray as you write a letter to an elected official calling for health care for all children? Will they pray as you package a health kit to donate to a family in need? Will your feet pray as you walk into a meeting with a legislator?

A Prayer to a Listening God

O God, we labor in the heat of the day,
and so often the labor feels hopeless, unproductive,
useless...

And yet, you hear our silent cries.
You give us one another
to speak that which we in our pain cannot speak.
You give us your Word
that utters those things we cannot find the words to say.

And not only do you give us the words to speak,
but you also turn your ear to us and hear us,
even when all we have strength to whisper is,
Lord, in your mercy, hear our prayer."

For you have promised to hear us.
You have promised to turn your face to shine upon us.
You have promised to be our shade
when the heat of the day saps our strength
and the well of hope runs dry.

And you have promised,
even in the silence,
to give us the sweet sound of peace.

—*John McCullough Bade*

From "A Prayer to a Listening God," in *Will I Sing Again?*
Listening for the Melody of Grace in the Silence of Illness and Loss
by John McCullough Bade (Minneapolis: Augsburg Fortress,
2003, p. 46)

Homily Notes on Children

The Rev. Walter J. Burghardt, S.J.
29th Sunday for the Year (C)

Our task as preachers this Sunday is a difficult one. The theme itself, suggested by the Children's Defense Fund is "My Boat Is So Small: Creating a Harbor of Hope and Health Care for All Children," so that no child is left behind in the grip of poverty and injustice. It is not our task to accomplish this through a homily; our task is to challenge and encourage our people to do so. Specifically by linking that theme to what God is saying to us in today's liturgical readings. Very simply, to relate God's Word to the practical problem. I suggest three states, three questions:

1) What is God's Word all about?
2) What are the social issues we confront?
3) What is our response to be?

I

First, God's Word: This time a parable from the lips of Jesus. The parable has two characters, two players: a judge and a widow. The judge is the symbol of power. And this particular judge is uncommonly powerful: Not only is he a judge in a patriarchal society, a culture in which males command and females obey; this judge is afraid of no one: neither God nor people. The widow is a symbol of powerlessness. With her husband dead, she has no male to defend her, protect her, plead her cause. Some unnamed male is taking advantage of her, she wants justice, and all she can do is appeal to a coldhearted, unfeeling male judge. Not surprisingly, the judge refuses.

What does she do? Retire to her home, re-enter her kitchen, submit the way women were supposed to submit? Not this widow. She keeps after the judge, keeps pounding away at him: "I want justice. I want justice. I want justice." So insistent is she that the judge finally gives in. Not because he is convinced by her arguments. No. What moves him is clear: "Because this widow keeps bothering me, I will grant her justice that she may not continue coming for ever and wear me out." (Luke 18:5)

The lesson? Perseverance; persistence. Suggested in the first reading (in the Catholic lectionary). When the Israelites were confronted by a fierce tribe, the Amalkites, they prevailed as long as Moses held his arm aloft, with the staff of God in his hand. "But Moses' hands grew weary, so (the Israelites) took a stone and put it under him, and he sat on it. Aaron and Hur held up his hands, one on one side, and the other on the other side; so his hands were steady until the sun set. And Joshua defeated Amalek and his people." (Exodus 17:12-13)

II

What are the social issues we confront? Child poverty and the injustice that leave behind millions of children in our nation. In this rich nation of ours, more than 12 million children remain in poverty. (Three out of four poor children live in families where someone worked in 2002, and one in three poor children lives with a full-time, year-round worker.) An American child is more likely to be poor today than 25 or 30 years ago; more likely to be poor than an American adult; and more likely to be poor than a child living in Canada, Germany, or France.

Not only are our children more likely than others to be poor, but they are standing on the precipice of an ever-widening canyon between rich and poor, left behind as injustice separates them from more privileged peers. The richest one-fifth of households made 10.7 times as much in median income as the poorest one-fifth in 2002, the widest gap on record, according to Census Bureau figures. Poor children are also being left behind by the tax cut package passed in 2003. The 2003 tax cut package raised the Child Tax Credit to a $1,000 maximum per child in 2003 and 2004 but at the last minute left out help for millions of children of hardworking parents with incomes between $10,500 and roughly $26,000.

The impact of that gulf between rich and poor is measured not in dollars alone, but in the damage it does to children, in the denial of the things that make life joyful and nurturing. As CDF notes, "Children need adequate family income if they are to have their most basic needs met, from diapers to doctor, to healthy food and safe housing. Whether a child will flounder or flourish can hinge on many things that money buys: good quality child care, eyeglasses for reading the chalkboard, a Little League fee, a musical instrument—or simply the peace of mind that lets parents create a warm and nurturing family life free from worries about eviction or hunger." Every child is a child of God. Every child is intended by God to flourish and not flounder.

III

A Catholic response? A sympathetic Protestant once said to a Catholic, "If you Catholics could get your act together, you'd be dangerous." We would indeed. The potential for effective organized activity is there. I am told that there are more Catholic parishes in the United States than there are post offices. How do we get our act together to ensure justice and care for all of God's children? Bishops' pastorals are important, but not enough—if only because it is the rare Catholic who ever reads a pastoral document in its totality. What then?

Start with the family. Let each family, each "little church," become aware of, realize, some of those disturbing facts—that more than 12 million children of our little sisters and brothers are crushed by poverty in this rich nation. (Nine million children don't have health insurance.) Let our more advantaged teenagers actually feed the hungry, actually clothe the naked, actually visit the sick and imprisoned.

In line with the widow of our Gospel, put pressure on the powerful, trouble your legislators. Tell them, "We want justice! Justice! Justice!" Tell them, time and again, that for $157,552, the amount that permanent Bush and Congress tax cuts would eventually give to **each** individual millionaire on average in one year, America could insure 112 currently uninsured children with comprehensive health and mental health packages. "We want justice!" Every year the Children's Defense Fund tracks how your members of Congress vote on children's concerns. If you're dissatisfied, organize to cry, "We want justice!" Get the

CDF annual report card on how well your state is investing in your children, protecting your children; shake a bad report in the face of your elected and appointed officials: "We want justice!" Is your area a killing field for guns and drugs? In hundreds and thousands cry aloud, "We want justice!" If you can, persuade them; if you can't, wear them down: "We want justice! We want justice! We want justice!"

Some years ago, at a women's protest rally, an imaginative banner read, EVE WAS FRAMED! I tend to agree. If not the original Eve, surely her daughters. Listen to these powerful words from Marian Wright Edelman, president of the Children's Defense Fund:

> "Although women constitute a majority of the population, of voters, of those in religious institutions, and of those who take primary care of children, we lack commensurate power. This must change now. Only when women, especially mothers and grandmothers, organize and stand up and say loudly to the men in power, "We will no longer look upon the killing of our children; we will stop the killing of children by guns and overcome the powerful NRA and its supporters." Only when enough mothers and grandmothers demand health care and child care and a safety net for poor women and children and stand up with our votes and voices to those in power will political leaders of all parties do right by our children. Every federal and state Senator and Representative and governor should be adopted by a well-informed, well-organized group of determined women and their allies with a focused agenda for children…"

And so we end where we began—with a woman seeking justice. But not quite the same woman. Today's woman can and must "bring a new moral dimension drawn from the insight of (her) struggles and marginality." And if the Equal Rights Amendment has not made for utter equality of male and female, today's American woman is also not isolated in a primeval garden or dominated by the male of the species. Today's American woman plays hardball with her male counterparts in Congress. Today's American woman is a CEO, a diplomat, a bank president, a chancellor of a diocese, governor of a state, president of a university. And since 1920, American women have enjoyed (if not always employed) a powerful weapon: the power of the ballot, the right to vote. Yes, beloved sisters, 52 percent of the voting population, if you could get your act together, you'd be dangerous. It's time, for the sake of America's children—your children.

This is not simply an important political issue. Here we touch the heart of a Catholic spirituality, what we call biblical justice, *God's* sense of justice. I mean fidelity to relationships, to responsibilities, that stem from our covenant with God but in the blood of Christ. One of these relationships is our responsibility to the more vulnerable in our society. The more vulnerable, the greater the demand on the rest of us. Time and

again the Hebrew Testament summarized this responsibility to "the widow, the orphan, and the stranger." For "the orphan" substitute "the child," specifically the poor child, and you begin to understand what God expects of us today. And what is that? Never cease clamoring for justice. With your votes and your voices. In the privacy of the ballot box and through whatever means of modern communication. With the Gospel widow, one ceaseless cry to the powerful: "Justice! Give me, give our children, justice!" Not charity, out of the goodness of powerful hearts. No. Justice—what our children have a right, human and divine, to demand. "Give me justice… justice…justice!"

Sermon Notes

Heading Downstream with Moses
Exodus 2:1-10
Rev. Eileen W. Lindner, Ph.D.

Understanding the Text

This familiar story sets the stage for all that we will come to know about Moses and his important role in leading his people from slavery to freedom. Here we learn that Moses is descended within the Levite tribe of Israel. The Levites are those who are devoted to the worship of God; priests to the people. In this passage we are not told his sister's name but elsewhere we learn that it is Miriam. Later, in the first spontaneous prayer in Hebrew scripture, Moses will pray for the restoration of Miriam's health. Along with their brother Aaron, these three siblings provide remarkable leadership to the children of Israel in their long trek through the wilderness with their backs toward Egypt and its slavery and toward Caanan and the promised land.

Because of the deadly edict of Pharaoh to kill every Hebrew baby boy, Moses' birth is not greeted with joy and thanksgiving but with dread and fear. If the child is discovered he will be killed. His mother, no doubt in fear for her own life as well as the child's, hides the baby for three months and then devises an ingenious plan to preserve her son. She makes a basket—here the word for "basket" is the same Hebrew word that is used to describe Noah's ark—another vessel of safety on the water! Placing her beloved son in the basket, she places the basket in the reeds near where the royal women are bathing and posts his older sister Miriam to watch what happens to him. When Pharaoh's daughter takes notice of the child, Miriam offers to go get one of the Hebrew women to care for him, and of course she selects her own mother, the baby's mother. Pharaoh's deadly menace is thwarted, the child has the protection of the court, and the mother gives care to her baby. An ironic and just outcome in the face of unspeakable injustice and cruelty.

Identifying the Theme

Verse 3 sounds a note of desperation when it says, "…when she could hide him no more…" Nine million American children lack the health care coverage that they require to stay well and grow to adulthood and the lives their parents dream of for them. They are in danger because they live in a society that has not protected them. We can hide them no longer. Like Moses' loving mother we need to find an ingenious response to enable our children to live the lives for which they were created. We need to place their cause symbolically in a sturdy boat and float it into the midst of the governmental sea in such a manner that the society as a whole will take responsibility for assuring the health care for all our children.

Sermon Outline

- Read the Scripture.
- Retell the story providing details about how the mother felt, how the older sister watched, how Pharaoh's daughter saw in the one child what she could not see when she (and her whole nation) ignored the well-being of all the Hebrew boy children.
- Make a point that it was when the situation could no longer be hidden that the people acted to find a better way.
- Speak about the worries and fears of parents of children you know of who lack health care.
- Point out that Moses' mother's desperate effort led the Pharaoh's daughter to do good.
- Imagine what gifts our children may have that will never be fully developed if they cannot obtain health care.
- Conclude with a strong emphasis on OUR CALLING to stop hiding the children and instead to trust God and to act boldly to obtain health care for all our children.

Children's Sermon: When Whining Is Wonderful

Have you ever had your mom or dad or another grown-up tell you to stop whining? Have they ever told you to stop asking for something after they said "no" the first time? Lots of times, when a kid wants a grown-up to give them something, or let them do something, they will keep asking and asking and asking, even if the answer the first time was "no." Sometimes the grown-up will say, "Stop whining. I said no and I meant no." Has anyone ever said something like that to you? Sometimes when kids are whining, a parent might even say, "I can't hear you when you use that voice." *[If you choose, you might invite the children to say "pleeeeeeease" in their most whining voice.]*

Now, the parents here might not like hearing this, but there is a story Jesus told in the Bible about how sometimes it is *good* to keep asking, good to keep trying even after being told "no." It is even good to whine!

Here's the story Jesus told:
There once was an unfair judge. He didn't care what God thought about him, and he didn't care what people thought about him. He was just mean and unfair. One time, a woman came to him. She was not powerful or important—she didn't have other people in her family to help her, she didn't have much money, and it seemed easy to ignore her. She asked the judge to give her justice, to make a fair decision to help her because someone had done something unfair to her. And the unfair judge said "NO!" Did she give up? Did she go away quietly? Nope! She came back. She asked him again and again to make the fair decision, to do the right thing, to help her. He said "no" but she kept coming back. It was almost like whining to get her way. And do you know what happened? Finally, the judge decided to do the right thing, to make the fair decision, to do what the woman asked because she wore him out! He didn't *want* to say "yes," but he did because he knew that she wasn't going to give up.

Now, Jesus didn't tell this story so that we would whine and complain about things that don't really matter. Jesus wasn't saying that if we aren't allowed to get something we want at the store, or stay up late, or have another piece of candy, or something like that that we should keep asking and whining and complaining to our parents. That's not the point of the story.

Jesus told this story so that his friends would know that it is important not to give up asking for things that really matter, and to trust that God will hear our prayers and help us to make things right. It's a story that reminds us when things are unfair, we should keep coming back, keep asking, keep complaining until the people in charge make the fair decision, the right decision.

Today, our church is celebrating the Children's Sabbath. It is a day when we remember the children who are having a really hard time. We are talking about children who can't see a doctor when they need to, children who are hungry and don't have enough food to eat. Families who don't earn enough money for the things they need. When children and families are in these hard, unfair circumstances, we can be like the woman in Jesus' story. We can keep working to make things better for them, we can keep praying to God to help us help them, and we can keep talking to people who can make things better until they do.

Let's have a prayer:

Dear God,
We know that you always hear our prayers and we know that you hear us now. Help us to keep asking people to help us make the world better for children and other people who are having a hard time. Even when the response is "no," remind us to keep trying, to keep asking, and to keep praying until things are more fair for everyone, especially the children. Amen.

(See page 156 for an alternative Children's Sermon based on the children's book, *Swimmy*.)

Daily Devotional Guide for Adults and Children's Activity Bulletins

Following are a daily devotional guide for adults and children's activity bulletins to photocopy and distribute to your members.

Daily Devotional Guide for Adults

Although the pages may look mixed up, follow these directions for photocopying to create a booklet. To do this, you need to use a photocopier that can make two-sided copies.

- Put the first sheet on the photocopier: the page that says "Saturday" on the upper left, and on the reverse side says "Sunday" on the upper left. Photocopy using the two-sided function so that you have one page with words on both sides.

- Put the second sheet on the photocopier: the page that says "Thursday" on the upper left on one side, and "Monday" on the upper left of the other side. Again, make a two-sided copy.

- Put the third sheet on the photocopier: the page that says "Wednesday" on the upper left of one side, and "Tuesday" on the upper left of the other side.

- Now, stack the three double-sided pages in the order they were created, and fold in the middle. The cover should appear on the front. Sunday should be the first page inside the cover, the rest of the days of the week should follow in order, concluding with Saturday on the back cover.

Make as many copies as you need and stack and fold each set. Distribute the devotional guides the Sunday before the Children's Sabbath to help adults prepare their hearts and minds for the Children's Sabbath, or distribute them on the Sunday of the Children's Sabbath to continue their prayerful reflection following the Children's Sabbath.

Children's Activity Bulletins

To create the two children's activity bulletins, you will again need to use a photocopier that can make two-sided copies.

- Activity Bulletin for Younger Children: Take the first page and make a two-sided photocopy. Fold in the middle to make a bulletin insert that says "Activity Bulletin for Younger Children" on the front.

- Activity Bulletin for Older Children: Take the page that says "Activity Bulletin for Older Children" on the upper right corner and make a two-sided photocopy. Fold in the middle so that "Activity Bulletin for Older Children" appears on the front.

My Boat Is So Small

Daily Devotional Guide
For the Children's Sabbath

By Shannon Daley-Harris

DEAR LORD BE GOOD TO ME THE SEA IS SO WIDE AND MY BOAT IS SO SMALL

Saturday: Walking on Water

Scripture Reading: John 6:16-21

The sea became rough because a strong wind was blowing. When they had rowed about three or four miles, they saw Jesus walking on the sea and coming near the boat, and they were terrified. But he said to them, "It is I; do not be afraid." Then they wanted to take him into the boat, and immediately the boat reached the land toward which they were going. (John 6:18-21)

Reflection

"Mommy, I have a drawing," my five-year-old daughter, Sophie, announced. I looked at the sheet in her hand. There was a large heart, colored with pink crayon, emblazoned with PEACE and surrounded by doves of various sizes. Next to it she had written: "The Lord we pray loves us for our wisdom and coruge [courage] no matter how small."

I immediately thought of how God loves each one of us, no matter how small, and was deeply grateful that Sophie knew that God loved all 42 pounds of her as much as any towering adult. Only later did I recognize the ambiguity: What was "no matter how small" describing—people or our courage and wisdom? I haven't pressed her to clarify what she intended, because I believe both are profoundly true. God does love every one of us—adult and child, teen and toddler—no matter our size. And yes, God does love us even when our courage and wisdom are less grand than we might hope.

As we venture out into rough waters, our courage and our wisdom are bound to fail. But when we listen to Jesus' voice, telling us not to be afraid, we can welcome him into our lives anew that we may get where we need to go. It is a message to share with children in our lives. It is a message to demonstrate by our deeds to children in our communities. Yes, even working faithfully to embody God's love of justice and care for the little ones throughout the nation will convey to them the truth that God goes with us; we don't need to be afraid.

Prayer

God of all comfort, when life is rough, open my eyes to your presence. When I'm scared, open my ears to your voice, telling me not to be afraid. When I'm exhausted from rowing against a strong wind, reach out my hand to welcome you into my boat. If I stay close to you, I know I will get where I need to go. Amen.

Sunday: The Sea Is So Wide

Scripture Reading: Psalm 107

Then they cried to the Lord in their trouble, and he brought them out from their distress; he made the storm be still, and the waves of the sea were hushed. Then they were glad because they had quiet and he brought them to their desired haven. Let them thank the Lord for his steadfast love, for his wonderful works to humankind. (Psalm 107:28-31)

Reflection

"Dear Lord, be good to me. The sea is so wide and my boat is so small," is a traditional fisherman's prayer from Breton. Even if you only saw the preview for "The Perfect Storm," a movie based on a true story that came out a few years ago, you got a pretty good idea of why this prayer might be on a fisherman's lips and in his heart. Hollywood's special effects did a great job of recreating the reality of swells that could capsize a small craft, waves of towering height and crushing power, winds that could snap a mast, tear a sail, damage a boat. Lives, indeed, were lost.

The prayer, accompanied by a child's drawing, has served as the Children's Defense Fund's logo for more than 30 years now. It is a prayer that we can imagine in the hearts of children...12 million American children overwhelmed in an ocean of poverty, xx children crushed by abuse and other violence, and nine million children without health coverage who are at the mercy of illness and injury that damage their small bodies.

It is a prayer that is on our own lips and in our hearts when we look at the sea of injustice swamping the lives of so many little ones in our nation and world. We may feel overwhelmed at the prospect of taking on child advocacy as a mission and calling. We may feel crushed by towering heights of systems and the status quo, by the crushing power of the wealthy and well-positioned. We may fear the criticism or skepticism that could damage our standing, reputation, or efforts.

In those moments, and in the week ahead as we prepare our hearts and minds for the National Observance of Children's Sabbaths, let us remember that the sea of injustice is wide, but God's mercy and justice is wider. We may be small, our efforts may feel inadequate, but God makes great things grow from even the smallest mustard seeds of service and values contributions even as tiny as the widow's mite.

Prayer

Dear Lord, the sea is so wide but my boat is so small. Help me to trust in your mercy and justice that is broader than the widest sea, your love that is deeper than any ocean. Keep me on the course you have for my life, steady me as I chart my way ahead and seek to protect the children. Amen.

Friday: In Danger of Drowning

Scripture Reading: Matthew 18:6-7

If any of you put a stumbling block before one of these little ones who believe in me, it would be better for you if a great millstone were fastened around your neck and you were drowned in the depth of the sea. Woe to the world because of stumbling blocks! Occasions for stumbling are bound to come, but woe to the one by whom the stumbling block comes!

Reflection

So what happened to "Jesus is our Friend"? This doesn't sound very friendly, does it? Such vehemence on the lips of Jesus ought to make us sit up and pay attention. What are the stumbling blocks in front of our children? In what ways are we responsible for them? Most importantly, how can we remove them?

There are stumbling blocks that tell children, by our actions and the circumstances we permit, that they don't matter, that they aren't beloved by God. Stumbling blocks that tell children that violence is entertaining, that their worth is measured in the brand of their sneakers, the size of their flat screen TV, and in the size of our salaries. Stumbling blocks that shunt some children toward failure and prison while others are put on pedestals. Stumbling blocks that hinder some children through poverty, inadequate education, and lack of health care. Stumbling blocks that trip some children while we look away or busy ourselves hoisting only our "own" children over them.

Can you imagine harsher words from Jesus? For us to put a stumbling block in the way of our children is so terrible, so cruel that it would be better if we were *dead*. It would be better if we had an enormous rock around our neck and drowned in the sea. We who do know Jesus as our Friend know that he does not wish for any of us to be dead. But he does want us to wake up to the seriousness, the evil, the enormity of the sin of putting stumbling blocks before our children. He wishes for us to keep our children from stumbling—to be part of the solution, not the problem.

Woe to the world because of stumbling blocks! Where do you see the woe that results from the stumbling blocks that are in our children's way?

Prayer

This prayer is found on the door of St. Stephen's in London. Use it as a prayer for yourself—your home and your heart. Use it as a prayer for your church and community, for our nation.

O God, make the door of this house wide enough to receive all who need human love and fellowship, narrow enough to shut out all envy, pride, and strife. Make its threshold smooth enough to be no stumbling block to children, nor to straying feet, but rugged and strong enough to turn back the tempter's power. God, make the door of this house the gateway to Thine eternal kingdom.

Monday: Fishing for People

Scripture Reading: Matthew 4:18-25

As he walked by the Sea of Galilee, he saw two brothers, Simon, who is called Peter, and Andrew his brother, casting a net into the sea—for they were fishermen. And he said to them, "Follow me, and I will make you fish for people." Immediately they left their nets and followed him. (Matt. 4:18-20)

Reflection

The phone rang. It was the frantic babysitter of my daughter's friend, three-year-old Margaret who had hurt herself on the playground and the babysitter hadn't been able to reach Margaret's mother yet. I called my two children and we headed out the door. I wasn't prepared—I happened to be barefoot and was too distracted to put on shoes—but I was certain that by the time we got there, all would be well. Margaret would be recovered from a superficial bump and her mother would be there tending her. As I neared the park, however, I could see it wasn't at all what I had expected. Margaret lay limply in the sitter's arms, her forehead gashed open, a hideous, deep, fleshy, bloody wound. This wasn't the quick in-and-out moment of offering a few words of comfort that I had imagined. Nevertheless, I summoned a friend who happened to be on the playground and asked her to care for my children and lend me her shoes. I scooped up Margaret and headed to the hospital, in shoes that felt too large, praying the whole time.

Wouldn't you love to know what Peter and Andrew were expecting? What did they think it was going to mean, to fish for people? What kind of people did they think they'd be fishing for? When we read the verses just following this passage, we discover what they were in for: Jesus was teaching, proclaiming the good news, and curing every disease and every sickness among the people. "All the sick, those who were afflicted with various diseases and pains, demoniacs, epileptics, and paralytics," those were their catch.

At first, those disciples must have felt like they were being asked to walk in shoes too large. Nevertheless…

If Jesus is calling us today to follow him and fish for people, who will we catch up and bring to healing and hope? All the sick, including the nine million children without health coverage, who are afflicted with various diseases and pains. The children tormented by the demons of mental illness without treatment. Those families paralyzed by mountains of medical debt.

Fishing is a messy business. It's not a keep-your-hands-clean-and-look-holy occupation. Maybe that's why Jesus called the fishermen. He knew what they would be doing as his disciples. We will misunderstand Jesus' call if we think fishing for people means just to offer some pious prayers, or try to convert them, or get them to church. If we really want to fish for people, we'd better put on our hip boots and get ready to wade into the sea of suffering, disease, and illness afflicting children in our nation and world, and find real ways to bring them to the healing they need.

Prayer

Dear God, I am caught up in the net of your love and for that I give you thanks. Touch my heart so that I respond immediately to your call to fish for people. Help me to engage in the messy business of bringing real healing and new hope to the lives of all who suffer, especially the children. Amen.

Thursday: Where Is Your Faith?

Scripture Reading: Luke 8:22-25

One day he got into a boat with his disciples, and he said to them, "Let us go across to the other side of the lake." So they put out, and while they were sailing he fell asleep. A windstorm swept down on the lake and the boat was filling with water, and they were in danger. They went to him and woke him up, shouting "Master, Master, we are perishing!" And he woke up and rebuked the wind and the raging waves; they ceased, and there was a calm. He said to them, "Where is your faith?" They were afraid and amazed, and said to one another, "Who is this, that he commands even the winds and the water, and they obey him?"

Reflection

When have you feared that you were perishing? Has there been a time when you felt so buffeted by the winds of life that you were in danger of going under? When have you cried out to God in terror? Has there been a time that you both turned to God for help, but then found yourself actually amazed that God had the capacity to restore calm?

The disciples are a lot like us. On a lovely, sunny day, when Jesus invites us to accompany him—even if it is to the unknown other side—we think, why not? Sounds like fun. Then, when things get a whole lot scarier than we imagined, when the storms come up, we are in a state of terror. Jesus invites us to trust him, not only in the easy times, but in the challenging ones. Jesus invites us to trust him as our friend no matter what life brings our way. He is not a fair weather friend, but a friend through it all.

When we set out, with Jesus, to make our communities, and our nation, and our world a better place for children, we need to be prepared for a bumpy ride. It won't always be easy, it won't be sunshine and warm breezes. Tackling problems facing children will lead us into stormy weather, when we are buffeted by others who disagree with us, by fears of speaking up, by a barrage of "no" and "it can't be done" and "it costs too much." Will we panic? Or will we trust that Jesus is our Friend through it all? Where is your faith? And who do you believe Jesus is?

Prayer

Dear God, when life is stormy and I feel buffeted by hard winds, it is easy to panic. Help me to trust in you, and know who you are, that you are my friend through it all, and that you have a power over all of life. Steady and calm me so that I can stay the course with you. Amen.

Tuesday: Heading Upstream

Scripture Reading: Exodus 2:1-10

When she could hide [the baby] no longer, she got a papyrus basket for him and plastered it with bitumen and pitch; she put the child in it and placed it among the reeds on the bank of the river. His sister stood at a distance to see what would happen to him. The daughter of Pharaoh came down to bathe at the river. She saw the basket among the reeds and sent her maid to bring it. When she opened it, she saw the child. He was crying, and she took pity on him.

Reflection

Have you heard the story about three people standing by the side a river when they see a child being swept along, crying out for help? One person starts to scold her for her carelessness falling in. Another offers coupons for swimming lessons. A third pulls her out. No sooner have they pulled her out than they hear the cry of another child being swept along, and then another and another. Several hours later, exhausted, frustrated, and deeply concerned, they realize they will not be able to keep up, and even if they could, some of those being pulled out are suffering from lack of oxygen or hypothermia. It finally occurs to one of them to head upstream and figure out why people are falling in to begin with.

Baby Moses afloat in the basket wasn't the beginning and the end of the problem. He was just one part of a broader, systemic problem that started with an order to kill all of the baby boys born to the Hebrews. In fact, his mother and sister placing him there was perhaps the best short-term solution they could find to a deadly situation. Pharaoh's daughter pulling Moses out of the water solved the immediate threat to his life and health but it wasn't the same as heading upstream to discover and solve the source of the problem that led to his watery berth. In fact, she knew the probable cause for him having been hidden there, but she didn't do anything to solve it for that would have challenged her father's political system.

As it happened, Moses himself took on the broader advocacy challenge of changing the systems that put children and families like his in such danger. Will we? Today, nine million children don't have comprehensive, affordable health coverage. We can pull some of them out of the water, one by one, with inadequate solutions, or we can head upstream and solve the problem once and for all.

Prayer

Dear God, thank you for the compassion you have instilled in my heart that responds to the cries of those in the water. Don't let me hesitate to offer the help I can. But don't let me stop there. Instill in me a commitment to justice. Push me upstream to discover what I can do to solve problems before they start and protect your children from harm. Amen.

Wednesday: The Other Side

Scripture Reading: Mark 4:35-41

On that day, when evening had come, he said to them, "Let us go across to the other side." And leaving the crowd behind, they took him with them in the boat, just as he was. Other boats were with him. (Mark 4:35-36)

Reflection

The "other side" became a more concrete reality when I lived in Belfast, Northern Ireland, a land long divided by the "Troubles." The community was divided by seen and unseen barriers of concrete, metal, and barbed wire, by neighborhood, school, and faith tradition. I'll never forget seeing a small child, as he was leaving school, cross the street to approach a uniformed soldier "from the other side" who was crouched and gripping his weapon. The child held out his crayoned drawing, a little shy, a little proud. As the small boy continued on his way, the soldier turned to his patrol mate and said, "I can't bloody stand this." The hesitant touch of a small boy had pierced his adult armor, and he felt the pain and poignancy of the division and separation.

The other side of the tracks. The other side of town. Most of the time, when we talk about "the other side," we use it to differentiate ourselves from "the others." It's a phrase used to talk about where to stay away from, who is unlike us.

Not with Jesus. Jesus' entire ministry was about going across to the other side, to those whom others would shut out, ignore, condemn. "What do you mean, let's go to the other side?" his followers wondered. That's where the crazy people are, those as good as dead who dwell in the graveyards, at their wit's end, that's where the Gentiles are, the tax collectors, the Samaritans, the unworthy, the unlike-us.

That's where the poor kids are, the sick kids are, the struggling families are, the in-debt parents are. That's where the tough kids are, the drop-outs are. That's where people of a different religion or political party or race or ethnicity are. Go over there? Seriously?

When Jesus invites us to go over to the other side, he is inviting us to cross all the boundaries we used to think were important to meet others up close and not view them at a distance.

When we go over to the other side, we realize that we can't remain comfortable with some children having health care, but not all; with some children having enough to eat and others going hungry. We can't enjoy the successful schools in our community and ignore the failing schools in others. We can't just focus on our children's success and look away from the forces that set other youths on a path to prison. We won't be able to stand it. When we go over to the other side, we realize that Jesus would have us all minister to each other, just as he came for all and not just for some. Let's go.

Prayer

Dear God, it is so easy to stay within my comfort zone, to draw boundaries that make me feel safe. Open my heart and eyes and move me to accompany you to the other side, to reach out to the broadest community you call us to serve, to embody the unified community you call us to be. Amen.

Activity Bulletin for Younger Children
(Ages 3-6)

Jesus told a story to remind us to pray and not to give up trying to make things fair.

Find the hearts hidden in this picture.

Jesus says to pray always and not to lose heart. "Do not lose heart" means don't give up.

On another piece of paper, draw a picture of something you pray for.

Connect the dots below.

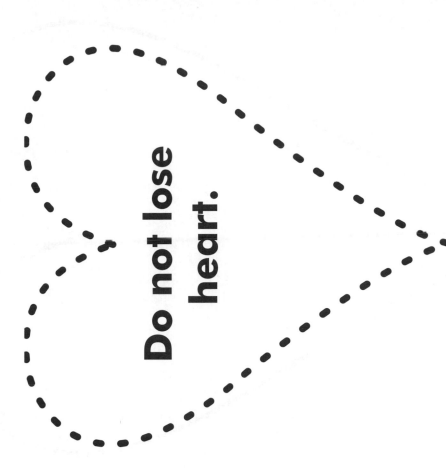

Do not lose heart.

It's Not Fair!

There are things all children **need**, like good food, a home, love, and a doctor when they are sick. Then there are things some children **want**, like a new toy, dessert, or a pet.

When children don't have the things they NEED, it's not fair. God wants grownups and kids to work together to help children who don't have the things they need.

Draw a CIRCLE around things all children NEED.

Put an X on those things children might WANT but do not need.

Activity Bulletin for Older Children
(ages 7-11)

A story about demanding justice:
The Widow and the Unjust Judge

Jesus told this parable in Luke 18:1-8 about the need to pray always and not to lose heart. Can you find it in your Bible?

"In a certain city there was a judge who neither feared God nor had respect for people. In that city there was a widow who kept coming to him and saying, 'Grant me justice against my opponent.' For a while he refused; but later he said to himself, 'Though I have no fear of God and no respect for anyone, yet because this widow keeps bothering me, I will grant her justice, so that she may not wear me out by continually coming."

After he told this parable, Jesus asked his followers, "Won't God grant justice to those who cry to God day and night? Will God wait a long time before helping?" Then Jesus said, "I tell you, God will quickly grant justice to them!"

Think about it....

If a mean, unfair judge will finally give justice, do you think we can count on God, who is never mean or unfair, to give justice? Will we work and pray faithfully, every day, for things to be fair, for justice for children who need it?

A **widow** is a woman whose husband has died. In Jesus' time, widows were usually poor and they didn't have any power. People ignored them and treated them like they didn't matter. Who are some of the people today who are poor or don't have any power? Who are some of the people that are ignored and treated like they don't matter?

Justice is a lot like fairness, but in the Bible it means something even more. For instance, it may be "fair" if two people have the exact same amount of something. Or it may be "fair" if someone who has a whole lot gets to keep it all because it belongs to them. But "justice" can mean that if someone has a greater need than someone else, they should have more. Or if someone has a lot and someone else has nothing, the person with a lot shouldn't keep it all. Justice in the Bible usually means making sure that the people who are having the hardest time, those who are poorest or weakest, come first. .

Pray always and don't lose heart!
Write a prayer for other children here:

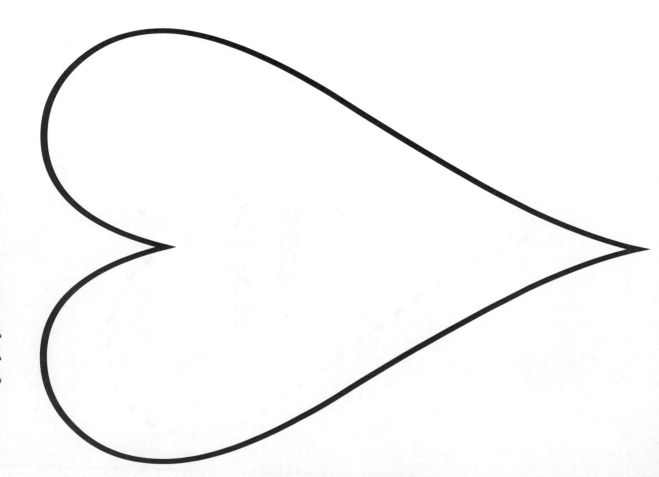

What do you think justice means? *Write your ideas to finish the sentences.*

Justice is…
Justice is….
Justice is….

God wants us to be people of justice—in what we say and what we do.

What can you do at school to help children?

What can you do at church to help children?

What can you do in your community to help children?

What can you do with your family to help children?

You can also make your voice heard by telling someone in government what you think. Ask an adult to help you find the name and address of leaders like Senators or the President. Write them a letter and tell them what you think is not fair. Ask for their help to bring justice to all children.

It's Not Fair!

Did you know…
One out of every 5 children in the United States lives in poverty.
Circle one of the children in the drawing to show this fact.
Do you think this is fair?

One out of every 9 children in the United States doesn't have health insurance and may not be able to see a doctor when they need to.
Circle one of the children in the drawing to show this fact.
Do you think this is fair?

Give me justice!

What do you think all children need? *Write some of your ideas here or on another piece of paper.*

_____

Talk about them with your family and other people.

Section 5

This section provides a range of resources for your Children's Shabbat:

- Suggestions for the services
- Passages related to children and health from Jewish sources
- Readings, reflections, and prayers for the services
- Suggested music for the services
- Sermon notes by Marc Katz, Religious Action Center for Reform Judaism
- Educational materials for use in Sunday or weekday religious school classes, youth groups, and adult groups such as sisterhood and men's club meetings, or one-time gatherings, are available for download at www.childrensdefense.org/childrenssabbaths.

Suggestions for the Services

Services on the Children's Shabbat are an excellent opportunity to help focus the congregation on the links between Torah readings, Jewish tradition, and advocating for children so that we create a harbor of hope and health care for all children. Children's Shabbat services also serve as a time to affirm the work of your congregation on behalf of children and to challenge members to continue and expand their responses to the needs of children locally and nationally.

The following suggestions may assist you in planning your own unique Children's Shabbat service or supplementing your congregation's weekly prayer and discussion.

- **There are several options for the services:** 1) Use or adapt the service readings provided in this section; 2) develop your own Children's Shabbat that reflects the theme of children and the need for action; or 3) use readings from the prayer books that include a social action theme. (Reform congregations may want to select a service with social action themes from Gates of Prayer, such as service #4.)

- **Determine ways in which the children of your congregation can participate in the various services on this Shabbat.** Involve children attending religious school, members of youth groups, and children who attend the day school. For example, religious school classes and youth groups could read prayers or Torah and Haftorah readings, lead songs or responsive readings, greet people as they arrive, or design and print the bulletin. Keep in mind, however, that this is a family event and should not be "given over" to children as "performers."

- **Focus the sermon, D'var Torah, or Torah discussion on children.** Emphasize working for justice so that no child is left behind and we create a harbor of hope and health care for all children.

- **Invite a professional from the congregation or the community who works with or on behalf of children to give the sermon.** For example, this might be a health care professional, a child care or Head Start provider, or staff from an organization or agency serving low-income families.

- **Bless the children.** On Friday night, incorporate the parental blessing for children into the service. Alternatively, incorporate the need to bless all children into the Shabbat morning blessing of Bar/Bat Mitzvah children.

- **Honor congregation members who are working to nurture and protect children.** This year, invite people who are working for children's health and well-being, such as pediatricians. Ask them to lead certain prayers or give them Aliyot during the Torah reading.

- **Collect Tzedakah in religious school to benefit a program serving children**, such as a community health clinic, Head Start program, mentoring or tutoring program, shelter for homeless families, or after-school program.

- **Distribute or insert the bulletin inserts** which can be found beginning on page 40.

- With the help of your Cantor, **prepare some new music to be sung by the children** at the service.

- **Encourage families to invite grandparents and other relatives to join them for the service.** If you wish, plan a special recognition of grandparents during the service.

- **Arrange for a special kiddush/oneg Shabbat/luncheon/s'udah shlishit in honor of the occasion.** As a resource, see "Planning a Shabbat or Holiday Family Meal" and "A Family Shabbaton," both from the Youth/School Liaison Department of the Women's League for Conservative Judaism.

- **Continue the celebration of Children's Shabbat with a M'laveh Malkah during the Saturday evening or the Sunday morning minyan/religious school sessions.**

Creating a Safe Harbor of Hope and Health Care for *All* Children: Passages from Jewish Sources

A cry is heard in Ramah
Wailing, bitter weeping
Rachael weeping for her children
She refuses to be comforted
For her children who are gone (*Jeremiah 31:15*)

Danger to life and health is of greater religious concern than other matters. (*Hullin 9b*)

A person should see to it that the body is kept healthy and strong, in order that they may be upright to know God. For it is impossible to understand and comprehend wisdom when one is hungry and ailing or if one's limbs ache. (*Maimonides, Hilkhot Deot 3:3*)

God created food and water; we must use them in starving off hunger and thirst. God created drugs and compounds and gave us the intelligence necessary to discover their medicinal properties; we must use them in warding off illness and disease. (Moses Maimonide's *Commentary on Mishnah Pesachim 4:9*)

Doctors are required to reduce their fees for the poor. Where that is still not sufficient the community should subsidize the patient. (Shulkan Aruch, *Yoreh Deah, 249*)

I, the Eternal, am your healer. (*Exodus 15:26*)

Why did God begin creation with one person? To teach that one who saves a single life—it is as if he has saved the world. (*Mishna Sanhedrin 5:1*)

One violates Shabbat for the sake of a one-day-old baby, but not for the corpse of David, King of Israel. (*Shabbat 151b*)

Neither shall you stand idly by the blood of your neighbor. (*Leviticus 19:16*)

If one person is able to save another and does not save him he transgresses the commandment, "Neither shall you stand idly by the blood of your neighbor." (*Leviticus 19:16*) Similarly, if one person sees another drowning in the sea, or being attacked by bandits, or being attacked by wild animals, and, although able to rescue him either alone or by hiring others, does not rescue him; or if one hears heathens or informers plotting evil against another or laying a trap for him and does not call it to the other's attention and let him know; or if one knows that a heathen or violent person is going to attack another and although able to appease him on behalf of the other and make him change his mind, he does not do so; or if one acts in any similar way—he transgresses in each case the injunction "Neither shall you stand idly by the blood of your neighbor." (Maimonides, *Code, "Laws Concerning Murder and the Preservation of Life," Chapter 1, Sections 14 and 16*)

A small bit of bread may be life to the poor; one who deprives them of it sheds blood. (*Ben Sira 34:21*)

"Therefore, man was created singularly to teach you that a) whoever destroys a single soul of Israel, is considered as if he destroys an entire world, and one who saves one soul of Israel, it is considered as if he saves an entire world; b) no one could say to their fellow that my father is better than your father; c) none of the heretics could say "There are many powers in Heaven"; d) again, to declare the greatness of the Holy One of Blessing, for man stamps out many coins with one die, and they are all alike. But the Ruler of all Rulers, the Holy One of Blessing, stamped each person with the seal of Adam, and not one of them is like his fellow. Therefore, each and every one is obliged to say, "For my sake the world was created." (*Mishna Sanhedrin 4:5*)

Medicine is prayer in the form of a deed… The body is a sanctuary, the doctor is a priest… The act of healing is the highest form of imitation of God. (Abraham Joshua Heschel)

Thou art the physician, not me. I am but clay in the Potter's hand, in the hand of Creator of all things, and as the instrument through which You cure your creatures. (Rabbi Jacob Zahalon – 17th century)

The true healer must have true spiritual depth and not be a "mechanic of the body." (Rab Nachman of Breslov)

"We cannot speak about the patient as a person unless we also probe the meaning of the doctor as a person. You can only sense a person if you are a person. Being a person depends upon being alive to the wonder and mystery that surrounds us, upon the realization that there is no ordinary man. Every man is an extraordinary man… The doctor is not only a healer of disease; he is also a source of emanation of the spirit of concern and compassion. The doctor may be a saint without knowing it and without pretending to be one. (Abraham Joshua Heschel)

Anyone who withholds what is due to the poor blasphemes against the Maker of all, but one who is gracious unto the needy honors God. (*Proverbs 14:31*)

You have not strengthened the weak or healed the sick or bound up the injured. You have not brought back the strays or searched for the lost. (*Ezekiel 34:4*) (condemnation for ignoring sickness)

The Torah grants physicians permission to heal. Healing is, in fact, a religious duty that falls under the rules for saving a life. If a physician withholds treatment when he is able to give it, he is regarded as a murderer, even if here is someone else who can heal a patient, because it may be in this case it is the special merit of this physician to provide the healing for this patient. (Joseph Cara, *Code of Jewish Law, Chapter 336, Section 1*)

Since when the body is healthy and sound [one treads in] the ways of God, it being impossible to understand or know anything of the knowledge of the Creator when one is sick, it is obligatory upon man to avoid things which are detrimental to the body and acclimate himself to things which heal and fortify it. (Maimonides, *Mishneh Torah, Hilkhot Deot 4:1*)

It is forbidden to live in a city where there is no physician. (*Kiddushin 66a*)

Whosoever is in pain, let him go to a physician. (*Bava Kama 46b*)

The great Rabbi Israel Salanter was missing from his synagogue on the Eve of Atonement, the Kol Nidre, the holiest night of the Jewish calendar. The elders of the synagogue went out searching for him and they found him. There are two versions: one, he was taking care of a wounded calf, the other, he was helping some sick child. And they said to him, "Rabbi, why aren't you in the synagogue?" He said, "Do you see what I'm doing?" "But, Rabbi, it's your duty to be in the synagogue praying." He said, "I am praying. Every act of kindness is a prayer—a prayer that walks, moves, breathes and lives." (Rabbi William B. Silverman from *Moments of Transcendance: Inspirational Readings for Yom Kippur,* edited by Rabbi Dov Peretz Elkins, p. 15.)

Do not neglect the children of the poor, for from them will go forth the law. (*Nedarim 81a*)

[Why was there violence in Gilead?] Because they made what is primary secondary and what is secondary primary. How so? Because they loved their possessions more than their own children. (*Midrash Tanhuma, Mattot*)

Touch not my Messiahs, namely my anointed ones, the children at school. (*Shabbat 119b*)

Train children in the way they should go, and when they are old, they will not depart from it. (*Proverbs 22:6*)

Teachers and schoolchildren are society's most beautiful ornaments. (*Shir Ha-shirim Rabbah 1:10:2*)

Raba said: Under the ordinance of Joshua ben Gamala, children are not to be sent every day to school from one town to another (for fear they may come to harm on the way) but any parent can compel the community of his town to appoint a teacher. (*Baba Batra 21a*)

If a city has made no provision for the education of the young, its inhabitants are placed under a ban, until teachers have been engaged. If they persistently neglect this duty, the city is excommunicated, for the world only survives in the merit of the breath of schoolchildren. (*Rambam Hilchot Talmud Torah, Chapter 2, Halachah 1*)

Defend the poor and the orphan; do justice to the afflicted and needy. (*Midrash Tehillim 82:3*)

Speak up, judge righteously, champion the poor and the needy. (*Proverbs 31:9*)

You shall not subvert the rights of the stranger or the fatherless; you shall not take a widow's garment in pawn. Remember that you were a slave in Egypt and that the Lord your God redeemed you from there; therefore I enjoin you to observe this commandment…when you gather the grapes of your vineyard, do not pick it over again; that shall go to the stranger, the fatherless, and the widow. (*Deuteronomy 24:17-18, 21*)

Rabbi Abba said in the name of Rabbi Simeon ben Lakish: "He who lends money [to a poor person] is greater than he who gives charity; and he who throws money into a common purpose [to form a partnership with the poor person] is greater than either." (*Babylonian Talmud, Shabbat 63b*)

If I am not for myself who will be for me
If I am only for myself what am I
If not now when (*Pirket Avot*)

Readings, Reflections, and Prayers for the Services

The following readings, reflections, and prayers may be incorporated into your services to focus attention on creating a harbor of hope and health care for all children, exploring the needs of all our nation's children for a healthy and hopeful future, and on Judaism's deep commitment to health and justice for all. Choose as many or as few as is appropriate for your congregation. Each reading suggests a particular point in the service for which it may be especially appropriate (in some instances, several options are offered), but there are, of course, many ways to incorporate these resources and you should do what works best for your service.

Sample Opening I

Maimonides wrote, "If one person is able to save another and does not save him he transgresses the commandment, 'Neither shall you stand idly by the blood of your neighbor' (*Leviticus 19:16*). Similarly, if one person sees another drowning in the sea, or being attacked by bandits, or being attacked by wild animals, and, although able to rescue him either alone or by hiring others, does not rescue him; or if one hears heathens or informers plotting evil against another or laying a trap for him and does not call it to the other's attention and let him know; or if one knows that a heathen or violent person is going to attack another and although able to appease him on behalf of the other and make him change his mind, he does not do so; or if one acts in any similar way—he transgresses in each case the injunction, 'Neither shall you stand idly by the blood of your neighbor.' (Maimonides, *Code, "Laws Concerning Murder and the Preservation of Life," Chapter 1, Sections 14 and 16*)

As we gather this evening, on the weekend celebrated as Children's Shabbat by congregations nationwide, let us renew our determination to save the children who are drowning in the stormy seas of illness and injury without the protection of health care coverage. Let us commit to provide a harbor of hope and health care for every child. We will not stand idly by the blood of our nation's nine million uninsured children who wait for health care and our caring.

Sample Opening II

Maimonides once wrote, "To what age are they to be regarded in these respects as orphans? Till they reach the age when they no longer need an adult on whom they depend to train them and care for them, and when each of them can provide for all his wants, like other grown-up persons." (From Maimonides, *Code, "Laws Concerning Moral Dispositions and Ethical Conduct," Chapter 6, Section 10*)

Childhood is a very special time. It is also a time of great vulnerability and dependence. Children are dependent on their parents, siblings, extended families, other child care providers, teachers, and mentors. It is a time of growth and development, when health care is essential. With the proper supports in place, childhood can be a time of wonder, great joy, exploration, and growth. Without them, a child bears seen and unseen scars. As wisely stated by Rashi, one of our greatest commentators,

"Do not let him slip down until he falls completely, for then it will be difficult to raise him; rather strengthen him as he begins to fall. To what is this comparable? To a burden upon an ass: While it is still on the ass, one person can hold it and set it in place; if it falls to the earth, even five people cannot set it back."

Rashi recognized that a person must be secure, protected, and supported. If they are, they will never fall completely. If we fail to provide support and help, in time, it becomes much more difficult—even impossible—to set things right later. A child needs adults who will train and care for them, as Maimonides recognized, in order for them to grow to responsible and self-sufficient adulthood.

Protection, security, and support are the ideal virtues imparted by family with the support of the community. Those who provide them to children act as family. They provide refuge and care so badly needed by children and young people. On this Shabbat, the one day of the week when we most appreciate and celebrate home and family, let us think about what those things mean, what they should be, and how we can work to create a harbor of hope and health care for all children, to ensure all children the protection, security, and support that home and family and community can provide.

Reflection Before the Candle Lighting

This Shabbat let us light candles of hope for all of our children, wherever they may live. Let us light them especially for children in the dark shadow of poverty and poor health and for those who have lost their way. May each one of them feel cared for, loved, protected, and safe. As we enter this sacred time of Shabbat, may each child feel the light of your and our love.

A Rebbi's Proverb (from the Yiddish)

If you always assume that the person sitting next to you is the messiah just waiting for some simple human kindness— You will soon come to weigh your words and watch your hands and attend to your responsibilities— And, if he so chooses not to reveal himself in your time— It will not matter.

The Wonder of Life

Sing a new song to God,
Give thanks for the wonders God has performed.
When we are trapped in narrow places,
Yet find strength to move forward
With confidence and trust;
When we could look the other way,
Yet take a chance to reach out to one another
With openness and compassion;
When we experience great pain or sorrow,
Yet find light in the midst of darkness;
When we recognize the Wonder of Life,
Ordinary moments become sacred.

(Mark Frydenberg, from *Havurah*, p. 6)

Introduction to the Lecha Dodi

Traditionally during the last verse of "Lecha Dodi," the congregation turns around and faces the door to welcome the Shabbat spirit into the room. Tonight, as we join with congregations throughout the nation, celebrating the National Observance of Children's Sabbaths, let us also turn and symbolically welcome all of those who work for every child to ensure justice, care, and well-being.

Responsive Reading (before the Bar'chu)

Leader: We come before the Eternal in a nation that is fractured by income, age, race, ethnicity, religion, and gender.

Congregation: Praise the One who heals divisions and binds us together.

Leader: We come before the Eternal with hearts broken by the wounds of children and families we advocate for and serve.

Congregation: Praise the One who binds up the broken-hearted.

Leader: We come before the Eternal with visions of justice that have been shattered, carrying in our hearts children whose hopes have been broken.

Congregation: Praise the One who restores our hopes and dreams.

Leader: Come, let us celebrate the Eternal's gift of children, and renew our commitment to cherish and protect them as we rise to be summoned and respond.

Reflection (following the Maariv Aravim)

God of the generations, God of new beginnings, children are Your promise of tomorrow made in Your image, a reflection of Your divine love. Teach us to raise our children worthy of this sacred trust of life. Sustain us and our children in health and love. We are thankful for the beauty of our lives and the ability to bring new life. We are thankful to all those who help us to raise our children in love.

(Adapted the Reconstructionist Rabbinical Association *Rabbi's Manual*)

Reflection (following the Maariv, before the Ahavat Olam)

The problem of our youth is not youth. The problem is the spirit of our age: denial of transcendence, the vapidity of values, emptiness in the heart, the decreased sensitivity to the imponderable quality of the spirit, the collapse of communication between the realm of tradition and the inner world of the individual. The central problem is that we do not know how to think, how to pray, how to cry, how to resist the deceptions of too many persuaders.

The problem is why my child should revere me. Unless my child will sense in my personal existence acts and attitudes that evoke reverence—the ability to delay satisfactions, to overcome prejudices, to sense the holy, to strive for the noble— why should he/she revere me?

(Abraham Joshua Heschel, exerpts from *The Wisdom of Heschel*, selected by Ruth Marcus. New York: Goodhill, Farrar, Strauss and Giroux, 1975)

Reflection (following the Ahavat Olam)

When justice burns within us like a flaming fire, when love evokes willing sacrifice from us, when, to the last full measure of selfless devotion, we demonstrate our belief in the ultimate triumph of truth and righteousness, then Your goodness enters our lives and we can begin to change the world; and then you live within our hearts, and we through righteousness behold your presence.

(*Gates of Prayer*)

Reflection (following the Ahavat Olam)

A loving parent does not show genuine love by telling a child, "Do whatever you want." That would not indicate love, but lack of concern and abdication of responsibility. The truly loving parent says to the child, "I care very much about you, and although I cannot live your life for you, I want you to have the benefit of my experience."

The Jew understood from the beginning that Judaism was a religion of love because it did not leave an individual to find the way through life alone and unaided. It offered advice, insight, and experience. It was out of God's love and concern for Israel that the Eternal gave them the Torah, so that instead of stumbling blindly, they might be aided by its principles, take heed of its warnings, and draw closer to the Holy One, who loves the people of Israel.

(Harold Kushner, *Likrat Shabbat*)

Reflection on the Sh'ma

Reader 1:   You shall love the Eternal your God with all your mind, with all your strength, with all your being.

Reader 2:   The path to the love of God is through the love of others; we do not love God until we love our neighbors as ourselves.

Reader 1:   Set these words, which I command you this day, upon your heart.

Reader 3:   Faith unites mind and heart. Even as our minds seek to understand life's meaning, so may our lives show love for all created things.

Reader 1:   Teach them faithfully to your children; speak of them in your home and on your way, when you lie down and when you rise up.

Reader 4:   We do not teach our children by words alone: May we make our lives and actions into good teachings.

Reader 1:   Bind them as a sign upon your hand; let them be a symbol before your eyes; inscribe them on the doorposts of your house and on your gates.

Reader 5:   Let our homes glow with the beauty of our faith in God. Let our doors be opened wide to wisdom and righteousness.

Reader 1:   Be mindful of all My Mitzvot and do them: So shall you consecrate yourselves to Your God.

Reader 6:   Each righteous act of loving kindness is a way to holiness. Righteous acts elevate our humanity. Let us learn to use them to magnify the divine in ourselves and in the world.

(Adapted from *Gates of Prayer*)

Geulah

Leader: Those who raise children in their home are considered by Scripture as the ones who gave birth to them.

Congregation: In loving and protecting them, those who raise them, bless them with the shelter of their deeds and their name. Call their name beloved, for they are our inheritors.

Leader: The ones who teach children Torah are considered as the ones who gave birth to them.

Congregation: Call their name beloved, for they are our inheritors. By them we have been blessed and upon their lives we have laid our blessing.

(From the Reconstructionist Rabbinical Association's *Rabbi's Manual*)

Reflection

Wherever we live, it is probably Egypt. There is, there really is, a better place, a promised land. And there is, there really is, a promised time. And there is no way to get from here to there, from now to then, except by joining together and marching— and sometimes stumbling—through the wilderness, watching, this time, not for signs and wonders, but for an opportunity to act.

(Adapted from Michael Walzer, *Exodus Revolution* RAC *L'taken* Seminar Shabbat morning service)

A Prayer

O God, we give thanks to You for the gift of our child, who has entered into the Covenant of Abraham. Keep this child from harm, and grant that our child will be a source of joy to us and all who love him/her. Be with us and give us health and length of days. Teach us so to raise our child with care and affection, with wisdom and understanding, to be a faithful child of our people and a blessing to the world. We give thanks to You, O God, the Source of life.

(From *Rabbi's Manual*, Central Conference of American Rabbis, 1988, p. 40)

G'vurot

Eternal God, the power of Your spirit pervades all creation. When we open our hearts to You, we are filled with Your strength: the strength to bear our afflictions, the strength to refuse them victory, the strength to overcome them. And then our will is renewed: to lift up the fallen, to set free the captive, to heal the sick, to bring light to all who dwell in darkness. Add your strength to ours, O God, so that when death casts its shadow, we shall yet be able to say: O source of blessing, You are with us in death as in life!

(*Gates of Prayer*, p. 356)

A Prayer for the Health of Young and Old

May the One who blesses all Life, bless and heal those people, children and adults alike, who struggle against illness.

May those afflicted with disease be blessed with faith, courage, loving, and caring. May they know much support and sustenance from their friends, their loving companions, and their communities.

May those children who live without proper health care be blessed with a government that ensures their safety. May they be blessed with a community that advocates on their behalf. And may the day come soon when all children everywhere will live without fear of illness or need for medical care.

May all sick children, and all the ill everywhere, be granted a full and complete healing of body and soul.

May those who seek ways of healing through increased medical knowledge and those who care for sick people, both young and old, be blessed with courage and stamina, governmental and community support. May they continually discover the joy of working as God's partner in the act of healing sick children.

May all, the sick and the well, the young and the old, the caregiver and the needy, be granted courage and hope. And let us say Amen.

(Adapted from a prayer by Leila Gal Berner in *Kol Haneshama*)

Mi she'bei'rach

May the One who blessed our fathers
Abraham, Isaac, and Jacob,
And our mothers Sarah, Rebecca, Rachel, and Leah,
Bless and heal the ailing
_____, the son/daughter of _____.
May the Blessed Holy One show him mercy,
Heal him and make him well,
Strengthen him, and give him life,
And send him speedily a complete healing,
Healing of soul, health of body,
Soon and in the near future,
And let us say Amen.

Song: Mi she'bei'rach

Mi she-bei'rach avoteinu
M'kor hab'rachah l'imoteinu
May the Source of Strength
Who blessed the ones before us
Help us find the courage
To make our lives a blessing
And let us say Amen.
Mi shebeirach imoteinu
M'kor hab'rachah l'avoteinu

Bless those in need of healing
With r'fuah sh'leimah
Renewal of body,
Renewal of spirit,
And let us say Amen.

(song by Debbie Freidman and Drorah Setel)

Avodah

We cannot merely pray to You, O God, to end war;
For we know that You have made the world in a way
So that all of us must find our own path to peace,
Within ourselves and with our neighbors.

We cannot merely pray to You, O God, to end hunger;
For you have already given us the resources
With which to feed the entire world,
If we would only use them wisely.

We cannot merely pray to You, O God,
To root out our prejudice;
For You have already given us eyes
With which to see the good in all people,
If we would only use them rightly.

We cannot merely pray to you, O God, to end despair;
For You have already given us the power
To clear away slums and to give hope,
If we would only use our power justly.

We cannot merely pray to You, O God, to end disease;
For You have already given us great minds
With which to search out cures and healing,
If we could only use them constructively.

Therefore, we pray to You instead, O God,
For strength, determination, and courage,
To do instead of just to pray,
To become instead of merely to wish.

Praised are You, O God,
You bless our people of Israel,
And all peoples, with peace.

(Adapted from Rabbi Jack Riemer)

Reflection (following the Shalom Rav)

True, we are often too weak to stop injustices; but the least we can do is protest against them.
True, we are too poor to eliminate hunger; but in feeding one child, we protest against hunger.
True, we are too timid and powerless to take on all the guards of all the political prisons in the world; but in offering our solidarity to one prisoner, we denounce all the tormentors.
True, we are powerless against death; but as long as we help one man, one woman, one child live one hour longer in safety and dignity, we affirm a human's right to live.

(Elie Wiesel, *Sages and Dreamers*)

Alternative Aleinu: It Is Up To Us

And then all that has divided us will merge
And then compassion will be wedded to power
And then softness will come to a world that is harsh and unkind
And then both men and women will be gentle
And then both women and men will be strong
And then no person will be subject to another's will
And then all will be rich and free and varied
And then the greed of some will give way to the needs of many
And then all will share equally in the Earth's abundance
And then all will care for the sick and the weak and the old
And then all will nourish the young
And then all will cherish life's creatures
And then all will live in harmony with each other and the Earth
And then everywhere will be called Eden once again.

(Alternative "Aleinu" by Judy Chicago as cited in *Kol Haneshamah: Shabbat Eve*, Wyncote, Pa: The Reconstructionist Press, 1989, p. 137)

Blessing of the Children

(Children and health care providers may be called up to the bimah.)

As we reach out to bless the children in our midst, let us also reach out with our hearts to bless the children we cannot see and do not know but whom the Eternal knows and loves, as they wait and long for care, protection, and guidance.

May you live to see your world fulfilled,
May your destiny be for worlds still to come,
And may you trust in generations past and yet to be.
May your heart be filled with intuition
And may your words be filled with insights.
May songs of praise ever be on your tongue,
And may your wisdom be on a straight path before you.
May your eyes shine with the light of holy words
And your face reflect the brightness of the heavens.
May your lips ever speak wisdom
And your fulfillment be in righteousness even as you yearn
To hear the words of the Holy Ancient One of Old.

(*Berachot 17a*)

Final Blessing

May we go forth to celebrate the gifts of each child.
May we go forth to heal the hurts of each child.
May we go forth to seek justice for each child.
This we ask as ones who are claimed as God's children. Amen.

(Shannon Daley-Harris)

Suggested Music for the Services

The following pieces of music are suggested by the Religious Action Center for Reform Judaism for incorporation into social action-focused services because of their social justice themes. Several are based on liturgical or other Jewish texts. Many of the songs are available in *Gates of Song* or *The Complete Shireinu*, both available from Transcontinental Music (www.etranscon.com). They also have included music from new, well-known and less well-known Jewish songwriters and have given information about how to acquire their music directly from the composer.

1) And the Youth Shall See Visions – Friedman, *Shireinu* p. 20

2) *Ani v'Atah* – Arik Einstein and Miki Gavrielov, *Shireinu* p. 28

3) *Bayom Hahu* – Lisa Silverstein Tzur, *Shir* p. 32, Barry Kanarek, *Shireinu* p. 33

4) Blessing for Social Justice: *Lirdof Tzedek* – Jeff Klepper, sheet music in pdf available for download at http://www.totshabbat.com /kleppersocialjustice.pdf

5) *B'makom* – Michael Isaacson, *Shireinu* p. 39

6) Down by the Riverside – spiritual, *Shireinu* p. 56

7) Dreamer – Lorre Wyatt, *Shireinu* p. 57

8) *Hinei Mah Tov* – folksong, *Shireinu* p. 89, Steve and Marni Dropkin, *Shireinu* p. 89, M. Jacobson-Drozi, *Shireinu* p. 90, folksong, *Shireinu* p. 91

9) Hold Fast to Dreams – music by Jeff Klepper, lyrics by A.B. Yehoshua, Langston Hughes, *Shireinu* p. 99

10) If I Had a Hammer – Lee Hays and Pete Seeger

11) *Im Ein Ani Li Mi Li* – folksong, arr. Davidson, Gates of Song #146, Debbie Friedman, *Shireinu* p. 106

12) *Kehillah Kedoshah* – Dan Nichols, from his CD, *My Heart is in the East*, sound clip and ordering information available at www.jewishrock.com

13) Last Night I Had the Strangest Dream – Ed McCurdy

14) Laugh at All My Dreams –Friedman, M. Samuels on Sachki, *Shireinu* p. 122

15) Let Peace Shine – Lynn Metrik, available for purchase by contacting the composer at lrmetrik@yahoo.com

16) *Lo Alecha* – Klepper and Freelander, *Shireinu* p. 135

17) *Lo Yarei'u/V'chit'tu* – William Sharlin and Ezri Gabbai, *Shireinu* p. 136

18) *Lo Yisa Goi* – folksong, arr. Davidson, *Gates of Song* #149, folksong *Shireinu* p. 137, Shalom Altman, *Shireinu* p. 138

19) Make Those Waters Part – Doug Mishkin, *Shireinu* p. 144

20) *Nefesh Achat* – Jon Gold, Natalie Hutner, Leslie Kane, Alicia Katzman, *Shireinu* p. 154

21) One People – Debbie Friedman, sheet music available for purchase at www.debbiefriedman.com

22) Open Your Hand – Karen Daniel, sound clip and ordering information available at http://www.cdbaby.com/cd/karendaniel

23) Peace & Love & Understanding – Lynn Metrik, available for purchase by contacting the composer at lrmetrik@yahoo.com

24) *Pit'chu Li* – Shlomo Carlebach, *Gates of Song* #156 or *Shireinu* p. 166, Steve Dropkin, *Shireinu* p. 167

25) Joe Black on his CD *Leave a Little Bit Undone*, sound clip and ordering information available at www.rabbijoeblack.com

26) The Prophet You – Julie Silver, *Shireinu* p. 168

27) *Shir LaShalom* – music by Yair Rosenblum, lyrics by Ya'akov Rotblitt, *Shireinu* p. 183

28) *V'yashvu Ish* – Jeff Klepper and Dan Freelander, *Shireinu* p. 213

29) *Yad b'Yad* – Craig Taubman, *Shireinu* p. 216

30) *Yih'yeh Shalom* – Rick Recht, *Shireinu* p. 222

31) We Choose Peace – Tracy Friend, available for purchase by contacting the composer at tracy.friend@acnielsen.com

Sermon Notes for Children's Shabbat

Prepared by Marc Katz, Religious Action Center for Reform Judaism, Washington, D.C.

Learning from Abraham

Jewish tradition emphasizes that we should learn from our forefathers and foremothers and work to emulate their virtues. This week's portion, *Lech L'cha* introduces us to Abraham, the father of modern monotheism and the embodiment of many of these merits. According to Midrash, Abraham actively sought out the poor in his community, inviting them into his tent and showing them hospitality. Furthermore, Abraham built "spacious mansions along the highways, and stocked them with food and drink, so that whoever entered ate, drank, and blessed Heaven" without ever needing to ask for help directly. (*Avot 1:5; Avot d'Rabbi Natan 7*)

By embodying these virtues in his everyday interactions, Abraham was able to gain the respect of his community. "The prices he quoted in his business dealings were always fair, people came to him for advice in times of trouble, and when he was told that someone was sick, he would not just offer a prayer but would visit and make the person feel better because of his concern and interest. (Genesis Rabbah Lech-Lecha, 11, found in *A Torah Commentary for Our Times*, Harvey J. Fields) For these reason's Abraham was viewed as a moral giant of his time.

Today, we have the ability to emulate Abraham and embody many of these virtues. Like Abraham, we can be compassionate, honest, and open. We can be hospitable, fair, and concerned. And like Abraham, we can act on these merits and strive to be a respected leader in our own generation.

If we are to be truly fair, how can we deny one child medical care while another receives it? If we are truly compassionate, how can we refuse any child the preventative care that would keep him or her out of the emergency room?

Abraham the Mediator

While Abraham conveys dozens of impressive virtues over the course of his life, few are spelled out as clearly as his ability to calmly mediate disputes. After leaving Egypt, Abraham and his nephew Lot stop in Bethel where their herdsmen begin to quarrel over grazing land for their cattle. In response, Abraham mediates a plan to divide the land between them, Lot choosing the southern Plain of Jordan, and Abraham continuing north to the land of Canaan. (*Genesis 13*)

Today, another dispute has arisen, yet instead of quarreling over nomadic grazing lands, we are fighting over our limited health care resources. These disputes come with a cost. There are still 46 million uninsured Americans, nine million of whom are children. Despite the fact that we are the wealthiest nation in the world, Americans are not getting the quality of care that they need; we currently rank 23rd for infant mortality and 20th for life expectancy worldwide.

Insurance companies, doctors, patients, and pharmaceutical businesses all resemble in their own way the biblical herdsmen in this story. While each has an individual stake in the successes and failures of this system, few are willing to give up their interests in order to compromise and find a solution.

What lessons can we learn from Abraham that will help us mediate this problem? How can we develop solutions that will benefit all parties involved? How can we learn to share our health care resources and provide quality care to those millions of Americans who cannot access it?

Freeing the Captive

Jewish tradition teaches us that *pidyon shevuyin*, freeing the captives, is one of the most important commandments in Judaism. Rabbi Moses Ben Maimonides expresses this sentiment when he writes, "One who ignores the responsibility to redeem a captive is transgressing the following Biblical commandments: 1) 'Do not harden your heart and shut your hand'; 2) 'Do not stand idly by the blood of your neighbor'; and 3) 'Do not rule over your laborer ruthlessly,' also goes against the commandments to 'open your hand to the poor' and the commandment to 'let your brethren live by your side,' the commandment to 'love your neighbor as yourself' and to 'not refrain from rescuing those taken off to death,' and many similar commandments. There is no greater mitzvah than redeeming the captive."

Abraham clearly understands the importance of this commandment. When his nephew Lot is captured by foreign kings, Abraham amasses a set of troops and rescues him. When he returns victorious, he is offered a reward for his work, but refuses, knowing that the merit of his deed is enough of a reward.

Today, millions of children are prisoners of poverty. Children from lower-income families are less likely to have insurance coverage. Children without insurance are 13 times less likely to have a relationship with a primary care doctor or clinic and twice less likely to have seen a doctor for a well visit than children with insurance. They get seriously ill more often, leading to more school absences, poorer grades, and lower graduation rates. Because of this, they have a harder time finding jobs that pay well and include benefits.

Hearing the Cries

When Abraham's wife Sarah is unable to conceive, Abraham turns to Hagar, Sarah's maidservant. However, when she becomes pregnant, Sarah grows jealous and abuses her so that Hager is forced to flee. In the wilderness, an angel of God finds Hagar and convinces her to return to Sarah, acknowledging that her child will grow up to father a nation. Perhaps the most powerful revelation of this passage, though, is the naming of Hager's unborn child, *Ishmael*, literally, He [God] will hear.

Judaism teaches us that we are all created B'tzelem Elohim, in the image of God, and for this reason we have both ability and the obligation to mimic God's actions. The sentiment is expressed in the Talmud when it is written, "R. Hama son of R. Hanina said: What means the text: You shall walk after Adonai your G-d?... The meaning is to walk after the attributes of the Holy One, blessed is G-d. As G-d clothes the naked, for it is written: And Adonai, God made for Adam and for his wife coats of skin, and clothed them; so should you clothe the naked. The Holy One, who is blessed, visited the sick... so do you also visit the sick." (*Sotah 14a*)

Just as we should clothe the naked and visit the sick as way of fulfilling our inherent divinity, so should we hear the cries of Hagar that still resonate. These are the cries of the 13 million children who go hungry everyday. These are the cries of doctors, frustrated by the choice to treat uninsured families for free or turn them away. And these are the cries of pregnant women like Hagar, one in six who have no prenatal care in their first trimester.

A major theme in this week's portion is the power of naming. Avram becomes Abraham, Sarai becomes Sarah, Hagar's unborn child becomes Ishmael. Even God receives a new name. After hearing her calls in the desert, Hagar renames God, *El-roi*, God that sees.

Like God we should all strive to receive the name *El-roi*. Zelda, a famous Israeli poet, once wrote, "Each of us has a name given by our celebrations and given by our work." It is our job to do the holy work of listening to the oppressed so we too can gain the distinctions of one who hears, sees, and acts.

Establishing a Covenant

The portion, *Lech L'cha*, ends with the establishment of a covenant between Abraham and God. If Abraham remains faithful to God and shows this faithfulness through the act of circumcision, God will make him the "father of a great nation." (*Genesis 17:5*) With this one act, God and Abraham set the framework of Judaism uniting future generations around the concept of faith.

Today we must renew this covenant and play the role of both Abraham and God. As Abraham, we must have faith that we can make good moral choices for our children's future. Furthermore, our sign of this covenant must be physical. Just as Abraham ensured that all children born to him and his children would be circumcised, we must ensure that all children born today get their physical as well as spiritual needs met. Meeting the needs of all our nation's children is an opportunity to act out the lessons of Abraham, showing the justice and compassion that can make us a great nation.

Section 6

In this section you will find suggested activities to engage your mosque, Islamic center, school, or group in the National Observance of Children's Sabbaths; materials for khutbahs and discussions; a dua, and a list of prgrams and clinics providing free subsidized health care for the community.

As well, with this year's focus on health care, a variety of materials from Islamic sources that deal with issues of health and sickness are available for download at www.childrendefense.org/childrenssabbaths. It is hoped these new materials will be used as a basis for engaging children in a variety of contexts—school, community, and home. We hope the materials will inspire reflection, discussion, research, presentations, activities, and community action around the theme of health care. We encourage mosques and community centers to introduce and maintain regular "Healthy Bodies, Healthy Minds" campaigns that include Friday khutbahs, halaqahs and regular seminars that address the issues of health care on a practical and activist level.

These materials were prepared by Nusaybah Ritchie, Peace Leaders Program Coordinator at Al Fatih Academy and Afeefa Syeed, Director of Al Fatih Academy in Herndon, Virginia. Special thanks to Ms. Sommieh Uddin from Crescent Academy in Canton, Michigan, whose activities from a unit on Healthy Living: A Balance of Mind, Body and Spirit, were used (from "Modeling Methods for Integrated Curriculum—Three Teaching Units" by Susan Douglass, Ann El-Moslimany, and Sommieh Uddin, a presentation at the Islamic Society of North America Education Forum, April 2005).

Suggested Activities

1. A Friday sermon on the vulnerability of children and the urgent need to care for them. Materials provided here in addition to other materials from the Qur'an, Sunnah, Islamic law, and the biography of early Muslim generations can be used to illustrate the care given to children.

2. An evening or weekend congregational event where parents and children who lack proper care, health insurance, or adequate education can speak to the community in order to raise awareness among members of the Muslim community.

3. A public and community-wide forum organized by the Islamic center or the Muslim community in which experts on the lack of health care coverage, child poverty, and other concerns, as well as public officials, can attend to provide information on existing resources and, at the same time, direct the public on productive ways of activism to change existing public policies and commit themselves to helping in these noble tasks.

4. A gathering of various ethnic and religious groups to raise awareness and commit themselves to producing the necessary and desirable change. The Muslim representative can read the Islamic-based prayer written by Afeefa Syeed in this section.

Materials for the Sermons and Discussions

From the holy Qur'an and the Sunnah of the Prophet (p.b.u.h.):

Use verses that assert the honor and dignity which Allah assigned to the human race, equality among all people, the essentiality of justice and standing for justice, the obligation to cooperate with everyone—Muslim or non-Muslim—on issues of justice and mutual good, the mercy of Islam and the kind treatment Muslims are required to give to the vulnerable and weak. Some illustrations are included below. Muslim leaders are encouraged to utilize the abundant sources in the Qur'an and Prophetic tradition to support the activities related to this program.

a. The nobility and honor bestowed on human beings

وَلَقَدْ كَرَّمْنَا بَنِي ءَادَمَ وَحَمَلْنَهُمْ فِى ٱلْبَرِّ وَٱلْبَحْرِ وَرَزَقْنَهُم مِّنَ ٱلطَّيِّبَتِ وَفَضَّلْنَهُمْ عَلَىٰ كَثِيرٍ مِّمَّنْ خَلَقْنَا تَفْضِيلًا ۝

We have honored the children of Adam; provided them with transport on land and sea; given them for sustenance things good and pure; and conferred on them special favors, above a great part of Our creation.

(*Qur'an 17:70*)

b. Justice

يَتأَيُّهَا ٱلَّذِينَ ءَامَنُوا كُونُوا قَوَّٰمِينَ لِلَّهِ شُهَدَآءَ بِٱلْقِسْطِ وَلَا يَجْرِمَنَّكُمْ شَنَئَانُ قَوْمٍ عَلَىٰ أَلَّا تَعْدِلُوا ٱعْدِلُوا هُوَ أَقْرَبُ لِلتَّقْوَىٰ وَٱتَّقُوا ٱللَّهَ إِنَّ ٱللَّهَ خَبِيرٌۢ بِمَا تَعْمَلُونَ ۝

O ye who believe! Stand out firmly for Allah, as witnesses to justice, and let not the hatred of others to you make you swerve to wrong and depart from justice. Be just, that is next to piety; and fear Allah. For Allah is well-acquainted with all that ye do.

(*Qur'an 5:8*)

c. The Islamic obligation to support just causes regardless of religious affiliation

لَّا يَنْهَىٰكُمُ ٱللَّهُ عَنِ ٱلَّذِينَ لَمْ يُقَٰتِلُوكُمْ فِى ٱلدِّينِ وَلَمْ يُخْرِجُوكُم مِّن دِيَٰرِكُمْ أَن تَبَرُّوهُمْ وَتُقْسِطُوا إِلَيْهِمْ إِنَّ ٱللَّهَ يُحِبُّ ٱلْمُقْسِطِينَ ۝

Allah forbids you not, with regards to those who fight you not for your faith nor drive you out of your homes, from dealing kindly and justly with them: for Allah loveth those who are just.

(*Qur'an 60:8*)

d. The mercy of Islam and kind treatment required

إِنَّ ٱللَّهَ يَأْمُرُ بِٱلْعَدْلِ وَٱلْإِحْسَٰنِ وَإِيتَآئِ ذِى ٱلْقُرْبَىٰ وَيَنْهَىٰ عَنِ ٱلْفَحْشَآءِ وَٱلْمُنكَرِ وَٱلْبَغْىِ يَعِظُكُمْ لَعَلَّكُمْ تَذَكَّرُونَ ۝

Allah truly enjoins justice and Ihsan (kind and excellent treatment). Prophet Muhammad (p.b.u.h.) states that which means: "The creatures of Allah (i.e., humans) are the children (i.e., liability and responsibility) of Allah and the most beloved to Allah are those who show kind and excellent treatment to His children."

The following dua was written and spoken by Afeefa Syeed at the Interfaith Service for Justice for Children and the Poor sponsored by the Children's Defense Fund at the Washington National Cathedral on October 28, 2004.

Our Prayer for Children: A Muslim Call to Justice

I begin with the name of God. The God of Abraham, Moses, Jesus and Muhammad. The God whose everlasting compassion and never ending mercy are the saving grace of all humanity. God who is the source of Peace and Perfection. God who is the Protector.

Our nation has been blessed with abundance. At this moment, Dear God, help us to remember and reflect on Your words:

There will be a time We will test you with affluence—avoid arrogance and practice justice and equality.

Oh Lord, Oh God! To every life afflicted with senseless, mean acts, grant your everlasting Mercy. We are comforted in the thought that innocent children whose lives were ended are safe now in Your embrace.

Your Prophet, Muhammad, said,

The best community will be known because of its kindness to children.

In this time of such suffering of the children, help us to remember that our children are a trust from You. We are their guardians and You will be the judge of how we guide and protect them. Guide us to teach them how to be better than we.

Help us to teach our children that a true believer's success is how close he is to God, how relevant and beneficial he is to mankind. The more pain we inflict on fellow human beings the more distance we put between us and God.

As parents in this nation, Lord, help us to sense and know that our children are born in a state of purity and innocence. They are gifts from You.

Remind us, oh Lord, of the story when a man came to Your prophet, Muhammad, and asked "Do you kiss your children? I have ten and have never kissed them." The Prophet replied with a sorrowful tone and a clenched jaw, "That shows you have no mercy or tenderness at all. Those who do not show mercy to others will not have God's mercy on them."

Our Prophet drew great joy and happiness even in times of despair and loss at the sight of children. His supplication should be our supplication:

I commend you, oh children of this world, to the protection of God's perfect words from every evil.

Help us to raise children who are gentle and polite, not timid, afraid, or cowed down. Help us to raise children who are helpful and considerate, not arrogant and loutish.

Help us teach our children to know Your prophet's words:

The strong person is not the one who is best at wrestling; but the one who controls himself in anger.

Help us as parents to be tolerant, kind, understanding, truthful, reverent so our children will be tolerant, kind, understanding, truthful, reverent. Help us, Oh Lord, to utter often the verse from the Qur'an:

God truly enjoins justice and kind and excellent treatment.

Oh Lord, those of us who carry Your trust now in our wombs pray to you. Help us to dedicate our offspring to the founding of justice. Let us take the example of Hanna, mother of Mary, who beseeched her Lord to protect and guide her child who was not yet born. Make us conscientious and steadfast parents, not accidental or incidental ones.

Lord, help us to know that Justice is Your Attribute. Justice is a balance. Most importantly, we know from Your words, Justice is a call to action.

Oh Lord, as children of this country, help us to grow as citizens who work for the betterment of our brothers and sisters—no matter how small the action.

As children of this country, guide us to be leaders who will not be blinded to the injustices of this world.

As children of this country, grant us the wisdom to know what our country must do to seek Your Pleasure.

Our nation is great. Our nation is vast. America is beautiful. Guide us, Oh Lord, to know that justice for all is not a luxury or a choice. Help us to remember You give all children the right to a good name, shelter, good health, and an education. We will work for these rights for those who are without—help us be passionate and proactive in the preservation and practice of justice.

Our children are the future, Lord. Do not let us forsake our future by harming the trust You have bestowed on us. We are ready as children and as parents of this country, as Americans all, to pass this test together.

Oh Lord! Guard our children with Your never slumbering eyes. Hold them fast with your embrace of mercy. Shower them whereever they go with love from Your bottomless well of compassion.

Let us remember the mission of all Your prophets from Adam, to Jesus, Moses, and through to Muhammad who said:
If any of you witness an injustice, he should change it with his hand, and if he is not able, then with his tongue, and if he is not able, then detest it with his heart. But that shows the weakest of faith.

Finally, we remember Your words to us:
Oh ye who believe! Seek help with patient perseverance and prayer. For God is with those who patiently persevere.

Amen.

Muslim Resources for the Children's Sabbath

In this section, we refer to "Allah" and "Prophet Muhammad." Allah is the Arabic word that means God. Like Muslims, Arab Christians call God by the name "Allah." Muslims believe that Allah is One, without partner, and that He has no son.

Allah has many beautiful attributes. Allah is our Creator. He is Most Kind, Generous, and Wise. He is All-Powerful and completely Just. He is the First and the Last. He does not need anything, but every single thing in the heavens and the earth needs Him.

Human beings need Allah. Muslims believe that Allah has sent His guidance to human beings throughout time. He has sent this guidance to chosen messengers, called prophets, to give people divine messages about what we should believe in, how we should worship Allah, and how we should behave towards one another.

Among his prophets are the prophets well-known in the Jewish and Christian traditions, like Noah, Moses, Abraham, and Jesus. May Allah send peace and blessings on them.

Muslims believe the last and final messenger sent by Allah was Prophet Muhammad. Prophet Muhammad was a very trustworthy, humble, and kind man, who loved Allah more than anything else. He was respected by all who knew him. He is beloved by Allah.

Muslims believe that Allah revealed the Qur'an as a divine guidance to the Prophet over a period of 23 years. Prophet Muhammad's sayings and actions are called hadeeth. His whole life is a model for action and emulation for Muslims. Whenever Prophet Muhammad's name is mentioned, Muslims ask Allah to send peace and blessings upon him.

Good Health Is a Blessing from Allah

Good health is a blessing from Allah, our Creator. Allah created human beings in a beautiful, balanced form. He created us with different colors, shapes, and abilities. The human body is amazing. It is a gift from Allah as well as a responsibility.

A great Muslim scholar, Ibn ul Qayyim, said:

> Health and well-being are among Allah's greatest favors and most bountiful gifts to His servants. Indeed, absolute well-being is unconditionally the greatest favor. Thus, it is the responsibility of him who has been granted a portion of well-being to preserve it and protect it from all harm. (*Zad ul-Ma'ad, Vol. 4, p. 167*)

We have to take good care of our bodies. We also have to ask Allah's help in keeping us healthy and safe. We must eat right, exercise, and avoid harming our bodies in any way.

Prophet Muhammad said:

> There are two blessings which many people are deprived of: health and free time. (*Bukhari*)

This might be because they cannot afford to stay healthy with good food or medical attention. Also, perhaps they cannot stop working so hard during the day to allow themselves to have time to relax and enjoy all that is around them.

Prophet Muhammad also said:

> Take advantage of five things before five other things: your youth before your old age, your health before your sickness, your richness before your poverty, your free time before you become occupied, and your life before your death. (*al-Hakim*)

Our good health is a great treasure. All too often we take it for granted. We must use our bodies to do good things while we are healthy and before sickness strikes—things like praying to Allah, working hard, helping our parents, and giving charity to the poor.

My Body, My Amana

Our body, our mind, and our hearts are a trust from Allah. A trust is an amana. This means that He has asked us to take care of these and do the best for them. We cannot do anything to hurt ourselves, and we must help others from going through any hurt as well.

Draw a picture of your body and show how and why the different parts function. How can you care for them and what are all the good things you can do with them? For example: What can you use your eyes for? What do you use to eat healthy foods? How can your feet and legs help you to do good for others?

Sickness Is a Test from Allah

Everyone knows what a test is. During a test, we are asked many questions about what we know and how we think, we are put under pressure to come up with the right answers, and how we do on a test depends on how well we have prepared and how focused we remain while under the pressure of the test situation.

Taking tests can be scary because we are never quite sure how we will do. Did we study hard enough? What questions will be on the test? Will we have time to answer? What if we don't know the answer? What if we don't do well on the test? Will we stay focused?

Doing poorly on a test leads to feelings of disappointment. We regret that we didn't study harder. We feel sad that others learned more and we didn't. Maybe we remember not really listening in class or hanging out with friends instead of doing our homework. We don't have to give up though—we can find ways to improve our study habits and push ourselves to do better next time.

Doing well on a test always brings some sort of a reward. Sometimes our reward is something we can see, touch, and hold: We may get a good grade, a trophy, a certificate, or a gift. Our reward could also be something we can only feel: a sense of relief and accomplishment, feelings of confidence and self-respect. We feel good about ourselves. Our teachers and our parents feel proud of us.

When we do well on a test, we show that we have learned what we were expected to learn, and we feel ready to move up to the next level, try even harder, and learn more.

Allah puts all human beings through tests. He tests us to see how well we behave when we are under pressure. He tests us to see how we will handle a difficult situation. In His tests, Allah asks us to answer many questions about our beliefs and character, such as:

- Will we turn to Allah for help and guidance?
- Will we be patient?
- Will we be kind to others even though we are having a tough time?
- Will we trust that Allah will reward us for passing the test?

Sickness is a test. By allowing us to become sick, Allah tests us to see how we behave. What will we do to show our faith in Allah?

Sickness is not only a test for the person who is sick. It is a test for the person's family, friends, community, and society. Allah is testing all these people to see how they will treat the sick person. Will they pray for the sick person? Will they visit and comfort the sick? Will they help pay the medical costs if the person cannot afford the costs of treatment? Will they discriminate against the sick? Will they think together about the best ways to handle sickness in their communities? Will they support all members of their society in gaining access to the means of staying healthy and curing sickness—medical treatment, medications, diagnostic tests, and preventive medicine?

Make Up a Sickness Test

Write up a "test" with questions that are being asked of sick people and of society. Then write up the answers to the questions according to what Islam says about these issues.

Prophetic Examples

Muslims believe that Allah sent prophets as good examples for people to copy in their own every day lives. Even though none of us is a prophet, we can try our best to imitate the prophets and practice the good beliefs and behaviors shown in their examples.

We can take comfort in knowing that sickness was faced by prophets. This helps us to know that Allah is not trying to hurt us unnecessarily, but instead Allah is trying to give us a way to remember Him, to be patient, and to gain spiritual rewards.

Prophet Muhammad said:

> We (prophets) are like this. Affliction is intensified for us, and our reward is multiplied. (*Reported on the authority of Abu Sa'id al-Khudri*)

Aishah, Prophet Muhammad's wife, said:

> I never saw anyone afflicted with as severe an illness as Allah's Messenger. (*Bukhari and Muslim*)

The prophet named Ayyub (or Job) is famous for withstanding the test of severe sickness. To have the "patience of Job" is a well-known saying, referring to this prophet's great patience with all the diseases and misfortunes that afflicted him.

The Prophet Ayyub was a wealthy man with a large family. Allah tested Ayyub severely for 18 years with sickness, poverty, loneliness, and discrimination. It is said that Ayyub was afflicted physically with so many different kinds of diseases that no part or limb of his body remained intact and healthy except for his heart and tongue. With these two healthy organs, Ayyub continued to remember and worship Allah.

At a certain point in his test, Ayyub's friends and family deserted him and he lost some family members. He was taken out of the town he lived in and was thrown onto a trash dump. Only Ayyub's wife felt loyalty and compassion for him and she continued to try to hold the family together by working. However, she and Ayyub soon became destitute, with no money or a home. People no longer wanted to hire Ayyub's wife because they feared they might become infected with Ayyub's illnesses through their contact with her.

Ayyub's faith in Allah only strengthened. He stayed patient with his sufferings and affliction, relying only upon Allah and continuing to praise and worship Him.

It is said that two men came near Ayyub one day, staying at a distance because of his bad smell. One of them said to the other: "If Allah knew any good in Ayyub, He would not have put him through this test." When Ayyub heard this, he became very angry because he knew that was not true.

Ayyub is said to have prayed:

> "O Allah! If You have known that I never spent a night satisfied if I had known someone hungry in that night, then prove me true."

A voice came from the heaven confirming this truth and the men heard it. Then Ayyub said:

> "O Allah! If You have known that I never had two shirts while I knew of a place where people were without clothes, then prove me true."

So a voice came from the heaven confirming this truth, and they heard it. Then Ayyub said:

> "O Allah! By Your Honor, I will never lift my head from prostrating to you until You release me from my suffering."

And he did not lift his head until he was cured by Allah.

Allah cured Ayyub with cool water, restoring his body to a beautiful shape, reuniting him with his faithful wife, and returning to him his wealth and family in abundance. Ayyub had passed his test through patience, good works, prayer, and reliance on Allah. And Allah knew that he had always been a good person, helping those in need and standing up for those who were oppressed.
(*From "Stories of the Prophets" by Ibn Kathir*)

And (remember) Ayyub, when he cried to his Lord, "Truly distress has seized me, but You are the Most Merciful of all those who show mercy." So We answered his call, and We removed the distress that was on him, and We restored his family to him, and increased their number as a mercy from Ourselves and as a reminder for all who worship Us. (*Qur'an, 21:83-84*)

> *Discuss the story of Prophet Ayyub. What can we learn from this prophet's story about sickness? What does this story have to say about discrimination against the sick and suffering? Ayyub's brothers thought that Allah must not like Ayyub to have made him suffer so much. Was this thinking wrong or right?*

The Medicine of the Prophet

Prophet Muhammad gave us many recommendations for keeping our bodies healthy and helping our bodies recover from sickness.

Prophet Muhammad said:

> Every disease has a medication: If the medication for a particular disease is found, the disease will be cured with Allah's permission. (*Muslim*)

And he said:

> Allah has not sent down a disease but that He has also sent down a cure for it. (*Bukhari*)

In this way, it seems that every disease and illness has a corresponding cure. Matching up the illness with its corresponding cure is like matching up pieces of a puzzle. When the two right pieces match up and make a fit, Allah allows the healing to occur.

The Prophet draws our attention to the fact that both illness and cure have been created by Allah. He has made one the cause to eradicate another. Both illness and cure work by His will, and it is His will that made the rule of cause and effect.

Muslims are encouraged to become doctors to find and apply cures for every illness. This is an encouragement to conduct every possible test and undertake any research in the hope of discovering cures of illnesses that have remained so far incurable.

People of different religions sometimes mistakenly think that they should not take any medicine as it might be a challenge to Allah's will. This notion is alien to Islam, which views illness and cure as aspects of Allah's creation.

Finding a Cure

Research a list of diseases and the medications used in their treatment. What major diseases or illnesses are there for which humans have not yet found the cure? What can we do to try to find a cure?

How We Eat and Our Health

Islam is a religion of balance. Muslims try to be moderate in all things. Being moderate means not doing too much of something good and not doing too little of something good. Muslims try to stay in the middle—between too much and too little. Muslims always try to avoid doing things we know are bad.

What do we mean by not having too much of something good? Can you think of examples of how having too much of a good thing can be harmful?

A good example of having too much of a good thing is overeating. Eating is not only good, it is necessary. If we don't eat enough, we could starve. But eating too much is harmful too. We can get a stomach ache, become obese, or suffer other harms.

Prophet Muhammad warned us about over-eating. He said:

A human being can't fill a worse container than his stomach.

It's enough for a person to eat a few morsels to give him the strength to support his back. But if he insists on eating more, then let him keep a third of his stomach for food, a third for water, and a third for the air he gets from breathing. (*Ahmad, Tirmidhi*)

Practice the "rule of thirds" in eating—measure out a certain quantity of food (for example, a cup of cooked rice), measure out the same quantity of water, and guess how many intakes of breath would make up the same quantity of air. Rotate eating, drinking, and breathing until you are finished with the food and water.

How do you feel after this "meal"? Think about your usual eating and drinking habits. Do you think you eat about the same amount as your intake of liquid and air? If not, do you eat more? How does the "rule of thirds" in eating reflect the idea of moderation?

Healing with the Qur'an

Muslims believe that the words of the Qur'an constitute a treatment for physical and spiritual sickness.

We set down stage by stage in the Qur'an that which is a healing and a mercy to those who believe… (*Qur'an, 17:82*)

The meanings, beliefs, feelings, and experiences engendered by the recitation of the Qur'an heal the hearts, minds, and bodies of Muslims.

Ibn ul-Qayyim said:

One of the important conditions for a sick person to benefit from a medicine is that he should accept it and believe that it will benefit him. His system will then accept it and employ it in opposing the illness…. Indeed, there is no medication for curing the heart more beneficent than the Qur'an. It carries a complete remedy that would not leave any illness uncured. It would preserve the heart's well-being and protect it completely from all harms. (*Zad ul-Ma'ad, Vol. 4, pp.79-80*)

Healing with the Qur'an is an approved treatment. Prophet Muhammad recommended curing physical, mental, and spiritual sickness with the Qur'an.

One of the most important *surahs*, or chapters, from the Qur'an used in the treatment of illness is the opening chapter, Surat al-Fatihah.

Al-Fatihah (Opening chapter of the Qur'an)

In the Name of Allah, the Most Gracious, Most Merciful.
All praises and thanks be to Allah, Lord of the worlds,
The Most Gracious, Most Merciful, the Master of the Day of Judgment.
You Alone do we worship, and You Alone do we ask for help.
Guide us to the Straight Way—
The Way of those on whom You have bestowed Your Grace,
Not of those who have earned Your anger,
Nor of those who have gone astray.

Allah Is the True Healer

Muslims are encouraged to seek out the treatments and cures for sickness and to use the known means for regaining health and well-being, whether through medication, healing foods, reciting Qur'an, doctor's visits, surgery, and so on.

Prophet Muhammad said:

For every sickness Allah has created, He has created its cure—except for old age. (*an-Nasai, al-Hakim*)

Nevertheless, Muslims must remember that Allah is the only true Healer and that treatments for sickness are only the means for cure that Allah has provided out of His great mercy.

Prophet Ibrahim said:

…(Allah) who created me, and it is He who guides me. It is He who feeds me and gives me drink. And when I am ill, it is He who cures me… (*Qur'an, 26:78-80*)

It is important for us to ask Allah on a regular basis to cure us of our ailments, both physical and spiritual. Many of our sicknesses are spiritual in nature and the only real cure for these is found in establishing a strong bond with our Creator and maintaining a good relationship with Him at all times in our lives, during sickness and health.

A good relationship requires believing in Allah as He is, worshipping Allah as He wants, trusting in Allah as we must, and loving Allah as only He deserves.

One of the standard supplications for good health is:

O Allah! Preserve for me my health. O Allah! Preserve for me my hearing. O Allah! Preserve for me my sight. There is no god or deity whatsoever except You. (*Bukhari*)

ALL of Us Must Be Healthy: Responsibility of the Community

Who should be healthy? Just the people who have money to buy good food, have clean water, and time to exercise? The Qur'an and our Prophet teach us that everyone should be given the chance to be healthy and strong. All children—girls and boys, in all situations, always and everywhere—have the right to live and thrive, to reach their full potential.

The *sharia*, law of Islam, guides Muslims to provide ways that help make sure that there is family environment, health, education, leisure and cultural activities, special protection, civil rights and freedoms. Adults of all societies have to make laws that work for these important things, as well as make sure that everyone follows these laws, and if they do not help everyone get the care they need, the prophet has told us to stand up and make a change.

The Qur'an and sunnah of the Prophet tell us that we have to honor and practice certain things:

Zat al bain – the essential bonds within our community—those things that make us know one another

Fard al kifaya – collective duty to care about others

Duty to help others and ourselves be self-sufficient, so we do not always depend on everyone else.

Responsibility of professionals, like doctors and scientists, to apply their knowledge to improve the health and well-being of us all.

How can we help families, communities, and governments make sure that EVERYONE is able to see a doctor, get medicine, eat properly, and be taken care of? What would you say to the person in charge of your masjid to help them know that some people are not able to get these things?

> *Write a letter to your newspaper, your imam, your teacher, or another adult and let them know how you feel about children not being able to live in a healthy way.*
>
> *Read the Amman Declaration on Health Promotion. It was signed by leaders of many Muslim countries. Do you agree with all the points? What else could be included, as a number 10 or 11?*

The Amman Declaration on Health Promotion*

First: Health is a blessing from God, which many people do not appreciate, as is mentioned in the hadith.

Second: Health is but one element of life, and cannot be complete unless the other major elements are provided, including: freedom, security, justice, education, work, self-sufficiency, food, water, clothing, housing, marriage and environmental health.

Third: People can preserve their health, as enjoined in the Qur'an, by maintaining a moderate health balance in a state of dynamic equilibrium, neither exceeding the bounds, nor falling short in that balance.

Fourth: Every human being is in possession of a certain health potential, which they must develop in order to enjoy complete well-being and ward off disease, as is mentioned in the hadith.

Fifth: The lifestyles followed by human beings have a major impact on their health and well-being.

Sixth: Islamic lifestyles embrace numerous positive patterns promoting health and rejecting any behavior that is contradictory to health.

Seventh: Islam, as defined in the Qur'an, is the natural course of life which God has bestowed on humanity. Hence, adhering to Islamic lifestyles is, in itself, a realization of the true nature of the human being, and ensures harmony with the laws of God in body and soul, in the individual, the family and community, and between human beings and their environment.

Eighth: The document appended to this Declaration comprises a list of the Islamic lifestyles derived from the Qur'an and the sunna of the Prophet, Peace Be Upon Him, and affecting health development and human development in general. It comprises an integral part of this Declaration.

Ninth: The Consultation calls upon all international organizations, governments, voluntary and nongovernmental organizations to promote health by encouraging positive lifestyles.

* The Consultation on Islamic Lifestyles and their Impact on Health Development and Human Development in General, held in Amman, Jordan, June 23-26, 1989, with a view to achieving Health for All by the Year 2000.

Programs and Clinics Providing Free/Subsidized Health Care for the Community

The Umma Clinic
Los Angeles, California
http://www.ummaclinic.org/

Our Mission:

To promote the well-being of the underserved by providing access to high quality healthcare for all, regardless of ability to pay.

Islamic Health and Human Services
Detroit, Michigan
http://www.hammoude.com/Ihhs.html

Houston Shifa Services Center
Houston, Texas
http://isgh.org/Medical.cfm

Islamic Society of Greater Lansing
Lansing, Michigan
http://www.lansingislam.com/fcds.htm

Inner-city Muslim Action Network (IMAN)
Chicago, Illinois
http://www.imancentral.org/

Section 7

Bahá'í Faith: Community Activities, Devotional Materials and Educational Resources

This section provides suggestions for learning activities for children, youth and adults, devotional and fellowship activities for the Nineteen Day Feast for the Month of 'Ilm (Knowledge), selections from the Bahá'í Writings on the importance of the care of children, and resources for continuing the community's involvement in the themes of the Children's Sabbath beyond the event itself. Please utilize these as appropriate for your community. A brief glossary is provided at the end of this section to acquaint the reader with terms that may be unfamiliar.

Suggestions for Observances and Related Activities

- **Nineteen Day Feast:** Consider using the program described and/or including the readings and prayers about faith in action reprinted in this section for the devotional, consultative and fellowship portions of Feast. Include a diversity of readers, including children and youth. Consider inviting others to serve refreshments to the children and youth, and/or to those who work to fill the needs of children and youth, such as teachers, parents, grandparents, social workers and health care providers. During the administrative portion of Feast, encourage consultation about specific needs and hopes of children and youth in your community and what opportunities and resources exist for Social and Economic Development (SED) projects to assist these.

- **Devotional meetings:** Encourage community and individual devotional meetings during the Children's Sabbath weekend to focus on the themes of Congregations Standing for Healthy Children or Service to Humanity, perhaps including some of the readings and prayers reprinted in this section. Consider inviting children and youth to be involved in planning and presenting a devotional meeting on the subject of service to humanity.

- **Children's and youth classes:** Encourage children's and youth classes in the community to utilize the materials in this manual for their participation in observing the Children's Sabbath.

- **Ongoing community learning through local study groups or weekend workshops:** Consider beginning study circles in your community that help develop strong, vibrant communities and families, in which children and youth can thrive. Many Bahá'í curricula support the themes of health and hope for children and youth, as well as the connection between physical health and spiritual well-being, since these are essential aspects of Bahá'í individual and community life.

- **Arrange for an Assembly Development Module Workshop to be presented to the adults in your community**, especially: "Fostering a Climate of Love and Unity," "Developing a Strong, Vibrant Community," "Domestic Violence and the Bahá'í Community," or "Advanced Practice in Administration of Justice: Focus on Domestic Violence." For information on these workshops and to download materials, visit http://www.louhelen.org/ncerc/downloads/Assembly_Development/moduleoverview.htm.

Use video as a means of enhancing community awareness, discussion and action, including at the 19 Day Feast or Cluster Reflection Meetings. Arrange for a showing of "*Family: Seeds of World Peace*" or "*What Role Do the Youth Play?*" Both are available for purchase from the Bahá'í Distribution Service (BDS) at www.bahaibookstore.com or 1 (800) 999-9019. Consider conducting a Fireside workshop on *Family: Seeds of World Peace* to promote discussion and further exploration of the video. Manuals for this and other workshops, designed for individuals to use as resources when planning intimate meetings in their homes, are available from BDS, or may be downloaded at http://www.education.usbnc.org/fireside_manuals.htm.

Other relevant videos available through Bahá'í Distribution Service (BDS) online at http://www.bahaibookstore.com/catalog.cfm?CatPos=409 include:

Arise: Bahá'í Youth
Bahá'í Faith: Through the Eyes of Young Bahá'ís
Bahá'í Faith: Unity in Diversity
I Am a Bahá'í
Power of Prayer
Power of Race Unity
Reflections on the Nexus: Science, Religion and
*   Development*
What If Children Were Born Without Prejudice?

- **Encourage the growth of child-development centered communities:** Take individual initiative to include the needs of children and youth in community consultation, and to consider the needs, interests and talents of children and youth when planning community events and activities. Encourage junior youth and youth to participate in study circles and devotional gatherings, and to serve on Bahá'í committees and task forces.

- **Consider Social and Economic Development (SED) projects that benefit children:** Visit "The Bahá'í World" at http://www.bahai.org. Click on "Social Action," then "Social and Economic Development" to see and read about Bahá'í-sponsored projects around the world that support development of spiritually and physically healthy communities to give you ideas for your own community. There are numerous other publications available through BDS, most recently an 18-page 2005 full-color publication: "In Service to the Common Good: Bahá'í Youth in Their Own Words" by the National Spiritual Assembly of the Bahá'ís of the U.S. This is a sequel to the original 56-page 2004 full-color publication: "In Service to the Common Good. Also available is the full-color 32-page "For the Betterment of the World" by the Bahá'í International Community, 2002. Also contact child welfare agencies to explore the needs of children in your community. Plan and implement your own project, or pledge support to an already-established initiative that strives to improve the lives and opportunities for young people in your community, and/or the nation and world. Then report to your community during the consultative portion of the Nineteen Day Feast.

- **Support young people through starting or assisting with a "Youth Workshop"** dance/drama program. Encourage and assist youth to plan for a Youth Year of Service. Visit www.bahaiyouth.com for information on programs specifically for youth.

- **Encourage every family in your community to subscribe to (and read with their child), _Brilliant Star,_** the Bahá'í children's magazine. Included in this section are many activities and articles from past issues. For subscription information contact BDS at www.bahaibookstore.com, call 1 (800) 999-9019 or visit www.brilliantstarmagazine.org. For a subject index of articles and activities by age group since 1991, see http://www.education.usbnc.org/child_spir_ed/bril_star.htm. Back issues featuring topics of "faith in action" (i.e., "service") are: Sep-Oct 94; May-June 95; Sep-Oct 95; May-June 96; Sep-Oct 97; May-June 99; Jan-Feb 00; Jan-Feb 02 and Jan-Feb 03.

- **Deepen your personal understanding of our role in improving the health, safety, and futures of children and their families by perusing the Bahá'í Writings** and books by Bahá'ís, including the following. All are available from Bahá'í Distribution Service: 1 (800) 999-9019 or http://www.bahaibookstore.com/index.cfm:

  - _Bahá'í Focus on Development,_ by Dr. Moojan Momen, Bahá'í Publishing Trust UK
  - _Foundations for a Spiritual Education, Research of the Bahá'í Writings_
  - _Family Life_ and _Bahá'í Education,_ compiled by the Research Department of the Universal House of Justice

- _Healing Racism: Education's Role,_ Editors: Nathan Rutstein and Michael Morgan, Whitcomb Publishing
- _On the Front Lines: Bahá'í Youth in Their Own Words,_ Editors: Heather Brandon and Aaron Emmel, George Ronald Press
- _Health and Healing,_ compiled by the Universal House of Justice Research Dept., Bahá'í Publishing Trust, India
- _Health for All: The Challenge of the New Millennium,_ by Dr. Robert J. Kim-Farley, M.D., M.P.H. Bahá'í Publications, Australia
- _ONE Magazine: Wealth & Poverty, Vol. 2.5,_ Editor: The Bahá'ís of Eliot, Maine
- _The Brilliant Stars: The Bahá'í Faith and the Education of Children_ by H.T.D. Rost, George Ronald Press
- _To Be a Mother_ and _To Be a Father,_ both compiled by Wendi Momen, George Ronald Press
- _When We Grow Up_ by Bahíyyih Nakhjavani, George Ronald Press
- _Virtues Project Educator's Guide, The: Simple Ways to Create a Culture of Character,_ Jalmar Press
- _Youth: Channels for Change: A Compilation of Extracts from the Writings of the Báb, Baháá'u'lláh, 'Abdu'l-Baháá, Shoghi Effendi and the Universal House of Justice Relating to Youth_

Glossary of some Bahá'í terms

'Abdu'l-Bahá: (1844-1921) Son of Bahá'u'lláh, designated His successor and authorized interpreter of His writings. Named Abbás after His grandfather, 'Abdu'l-Bahá was known to the general public as Abbás Effendi. Bahá'u'lláh gave Him such titles as "the Most Great Branch," "the Mystery of God," and "the Master." After Bahá'u'lláh's passing, He chose the name 'Abdu'l-Bahá, meaning "Servant of Bahá'u'lláh." 'Abdu'l-Bahá visited the United States, on an extensive speaking tour, in 1912.

Báb, the: The title, meaning "Gate," assumed by Siyyid 'Ali-Muhammad, who was the Prophet-Founder of the Bábi Faith and the Forerunner of Bahá'u'lláh. Born 20 October 1819, the Báb proclaimed Himself to be the Promised One of Islam and announced that His mission was to alert the people to the imminent advent of "Him Whom God shall make manifest," namely, Bahá'u'lláh. Because of these claims, the Báb was executed by order of Náziri'd-Dín Sháh on 9 July 1850.

Bahá'í Writings: The Writings of Bahá'u'lláh, the Báb and 'Abdu'l-Bahá constitute Bahá'í Sacred Scripture.

Bahá'u'lláh: Title assumed by Mírzá Husayn-Ali, Founder of the Bahá'í Faith. Born on 12 November 1817, He declared His mission as the Promised One of all Ages in April 1863 and passed away in Akká, Palestine, on 29 May 1892 after 40 years of imprisonment, banishment, and house arrest. Bahá'u'lláh's Writings are considered by Bahá'ís to be direct revelation from God.

Local Spiritual Assembly: The local administrative body in the Bahá'í Faith, ordained in the Kitáb-i-Aqdas. The nine members are directly elected by secret ballot each year at Ridván from among the adult believers in a community.

Nineteen Day Feast: The principal gathering in each local Bahá'í community, every Bahá'í month, for the threefold purpose of worship, consultation, and fellowship. The Bahá'í calendar is composed of 19 months of 19 days each. The names of the months are attributes of God, such as Glory, Mercy, Knowledge, etc. The months are referred to by both their Arabic names and the English translation.

Social and Economic Development (SED) Project: An initiative designed to upraise the quality of human life. For Bahá'ís, this involves efforts to develop the capacity of the community to address its own needs and ensure the well-being of all its members through the application of spiritual principles including education, consultation, and reflection.

Universal House of Justice: Supreme administrative body of the Bahá'í Faith, ordained by Bahá'u'lláh in the *Kitáb-i-Aqdas*. The Universal House of Justice is elected every five years by the members of the National Spiritual Assemblies who gather at an International Convention for the purpose.

Passages and Prayers from the Bahá'í Writings Related to the Care of Children

O God! Educate these children. These children are the plants of Thine orchard, the flowers of Thy meadow, the roses of Thy garden. Let Thy rain fall upon them; let the Sun of Reality shine upon them with Thy love. Let Thy breeze refresh them in order that they may be trained, grow and develop, and appear in the utmost beauty. Thou art the Giver. Thou art the Compassionate.

'Abdu'l-Bahá, *Bahá'í Prayers*, pp. 34-35

I give you my advice, and it is this: Train these children with divine exhortations. From their childhood instill in their hearts the love of God so they may manifest in their lives the fear of God and have confidence in the bestowals of God. Teach them to free themselves from human imperfections and to acquire the divine perfections latent in the heart of man... Therefore, make ye an effort in order that these children may be rightly trained and educated and that each one of them may attain perfection in the world of humanity. Know ye the value of these children, for they are all my children.

'Abdu'l-Bahá, *The Promulgation of Universal Peace*, pp. 53-54

O Thou kind Lord! These lovely children are the handiwork of the fingers of Thy might and the wondrous signs of Thy greatness. O God! Protect these children, graciously assist them to be educated and enable them to render service to the world of humanity. O God! These children are pearls, cause them to be nurtured within the shell of Thy loving-kindness. Thou art the Bountiful, the All-Loving.

'Abdu'l-Bahá, *Bahá'í Prayers*, p. 34

Utilize every means to make this School a garden of the All-Merciful, from which the lights of learning will cast their beams, and wherein the children, whether Bahá'í or other, will be educated to such a degree as to become God's gifts to man, and the pride of the human race.

'Abdu'l-Bahá, *The Compilations of Compilations, Vol. 1*, p. 277

O Peerless Lord! Be Thou a shelter for this poor child and a kind and forgiving Master unto this erring and unhappy soul. O Lord! Though we are but worthless plants, yet we belong to Thy garden of roses. Though saplings without leaves and blossoms, yet we are a part of Thine orchard. Nurture this plant then through the outpourings of the clouds of Thy tender mercy and quicken and refresh this sapling through the reviving breath of Thy spiritual springtime. Suffer him to become heedful, discerning and noble, and grant that he may attain eternal life and abide in Thy Kingdom for evermore.

'Abdu'l-Bahá, *Bahá'í Prayers*, p. 36

They [children] must be constantly encouraged and made eager to gain all the summits of human accomplishment, so that from their earliest years they will be taught to have high aims, to conduct themselves well, to be chaste, pure, and undefiled, and will learn to be of powerful resolve and firm of purpose in all things. Let them not jest and trifle, but earnestly advance unto their goals, so that in every situation they will be found resolute and firm.

'Abdu'l-Bahá, *Selections from the Writings of 'Abdu'l-Bahá*, p. 135

I supplicate God that thou mayest become a kind parent to orphaned children, quickening them with the fragrances of the Holy Spirit, so that they will attain the age of maturity as true servants of the world of humanity and as bright candles in the assemblage of mankind.

'Abdu'l-Bahá, *Selections from the Writings of 'Abdu'l-Bahá*, p. 138

O Lord! Make this youth radiant, and confer Thy bounty upon this poor creature. Bestow upon him knowledge, grant him added strength at the break of every morn and guard him within the shelter of Thy protection so that he may be freed from error, may devote himself to the service of Thy Cause, may guide the wayward, lead the hapless, free the captives and awaken the heedless, that all may be blessed with Thy remembrance and praise. Thou art the Mighty and the Powerful.

'Abdu'l-Bahá, *Bahá'í Prayers*, p. 36

These children must be reared with infinite, loving care, and tenderly fostered in the embraces of mercy, so that they may taste the spiritual honey-sweetness of God's love; that they may become like unto candles shedding their beams across this darksome world, and may clearly perceive what blazing crowns of glory the Most Great Name, the Ancient Beauty, hath set on the brows of His beloved, what bounties He hath bestowed on the hearts of those He holdeth dear, what a love He hath cast into the breasts of humankind, and what treasures of friendship He hath made to appear amongst all men.

'Abdu'l-Bahá, *Selections from the Writings of 'Abdu'l-Bahá*, pp. 21-22

Wherefore, O ye illumined youth, strive by night and by day to unravel the mysteries of the mind and spirit, and to grasp the secrets of the Day of God. Inform yourselves of the evidences that the Most Great Name hath dawned. Open your lips in praise. Adduce convincing arguments and proofs. Lead those who thirst to the fountain of life; grant ye true health to the ailing. Be ye apprentices of God, be ye physicians directed by God, and heal ye the sick among humankind. Bring those who have been excluded into the circle of intimate friends. Make the despairing to be filled with hope. Waken them that slumber; make the heedless mindful. Such are the fruits of this earthly like. Such is the station of resplendent glory.

'Abdu'l-Bahá, *Bahá'í Education*, No. 97, p. 41

Nineteen Day Feast Children's Sabbath Program

(The Nineteen Day Feast is the principal gathering in each local Bahá'í community, every Bahá'í month, for the threefold purpose of worship, consultation, and fellowship. This activity also may be used at other community gatherings.)

Preparation:

- Prepare an environment that warmly welcomes friends of all ages. Consider adding color, through flowers or artwork; create inviting, comfortable areas and surfaces on which all ages can sit, including on the floor with pillows and throws. As the friends enter, have cheerful music playing, such as melodies from different cultures or children's songs.

- In advance, make several photocopies of the previous pages, "Passages and Prayers from the Bahá'í Writings Related to Hope and Healthcare."

- Review the "Building Communities" activity, make copies of the quotations squares, cutting them into sets and placing them in envelops.

- See "Fellowship Portion" for suggestions of refreshments tied to the theme, as well as stories and games to prepare.

Devotional Portion:

- Lovingly introduce the theme of the evening/day's devotions: standing for the health of children. Invite readers to intone selections from the photocopied "Passages and Prayers."

- Consider using music to help set the tone, such as "Songs of the Ancient Beauty" and Red Grammer CDs like "Teaching Peace" for the end of the program. (CDs available through the Bahá'í Distribution Service, www.bahaibookstore.com)

Consultative Portion:

- Open the consultative portion of Feast (or other gathering) by reading aloud the second selection on the first page of the selected writings (*The Promulgation of Universal Peace*, pp. 53-54) from 'Abdu'l-Bahá.

- Introduce the theme and purpose of the Children's Sabbath, and suggest that consultation be centered on the needs of our children and youth and how we may respond, standing for healthy children, in our daily acts of generosity and compassion for the poor, vulnerable and oppressed. According to the Writings, what is the station of children and youth in the community? What is their spiritual destiny? How can we as community members assist them to achieve this high destiny? How can we translate our understanding of these principles into action in light of current plans for community development?

- Refer to the Suggestions for the Observances and Related Activities (see first page of this section) for ideas and possible action steps or tools your community may wish to pursue after identifying issues.

- For larger gatherings, consider breaking into smaller (8-12 person) multi-age consultation groups to address the issues facing children and youth and how we might respond. Ask each group to appoint someone to record their findings and suggestions. Allow smaller groups sufficient time (about 30 minutes) for their consultation before returning to the large group for sharing ideas.

- Together, plan action steps that can be completed in three to six months. Decide how progress will be evaluated and who will communicate needs and encouragement to others. Celebrate your collective dedication to our children and youth!

Fellowship Portion:

- Refreshments: Consider making a "friendship soup" or "friendship salad," with many diverse vegetables or fruits representing how we each bring a special sweetness and flavor to the community. If possible, ask each person or family to bring one ingredient; these can be added to the simmering soup pot, or to the salad bowl or salad bar, as each arrives.

- Activities: Read or tell the folktale, *Stone Soup*, prior to serving the "friendship soup" or "friendship salad." You can download a simple version at: http://faculty.cmsu.edu/jrobins/ss_toon.htm or ask your children's librarian for a copy of this Swedish folktale.

- *"The Promise of Peace"* worksheet: Distribute copies of this worksheet (see following pages) to small groups of friends working together. Allow a few minutes to complete it, then take turns verbally sharing one answer at a time. (From the *Brilliant Star*, July/August 2003, p. 18)

- Make available copies of the document *The Promise of World Peace* so that those who are inspired by the worksheet may study it in its entirety. (*The Promise of World Peace*, Oct. 1985, sometimes referred to as the "Bahá'í Peace Statement," which may be downloaded from this site: http://www.bahai.org/article-1-7-2-1.html, or is also available for purchase in booklet form from the Bahá'í Distribution Service (BDS) at www.bahaibookstore.com or 1 (800) 999-9019.)

- Make and play the game, "Building Communities" (see following pages) from the *Brilliant Star*, Special Edition 1999, pp. 22-23.

- Go through the "True or False: Bullies Can be Stopped!" worksheet (from the *Brilliant Star* Nov./Dec. 2005 p. 11). Create an environment of sharing and safety. Encourage children and youth to share their experiences and determine healthy ways to deal with these challenges.

- Invite a Bahá'í Youth Workshop dance group to perform the "Poverty Dance" or another performance arts piece about overcoming social injustice.

The Promise of Peace

The Universal House of Justice guides Bahá'ís all over the world. It is the international governing body of the Bahá'í Faith. It helps us share Bahá'u'lláh's Teachings and live by His laws. In 1985, the Universal House of Justice wrote *The Promise of World Peace*. It tells all the people of the world that it is time for world peace. It describes problems that keep us from living in peace, like racism and poverty. People must work together and solve these problems.

Over the years, Bahá'ís have given *The Promise of World Peace* to more than 194 world leaders. Local Bahá'í communities have shared it with city leaders, neighbors, and friends. It has been translated into many languages.

Here are some quotations from *The Promise of World Peace*. Use the word list to fill in the blanks.

Words: **success • reach • world • peace • problem • possible • earth • oneness**

1. "The Great Peace . . . is now at long last within the r ___ ___ ___ ___ of the nations."

2. "World peace is not only ___ ___ s ___ ___ ___ ___ ___ ___ but inevitable."

3. "No serious attempt to set human affairs aright, to achieve ___ ___ ___ ___ d peace, can ignore religion."

4. "There are spiritual principles, or what some call human values, by which solutions can be found for every social ___ r ___ ___ ___ ___ ___ ___."

5. "World order can be founded only on an unshakable consciousness of the ___ ___ ___ ___ n ___ ___ ___ ___ of mankind, a spiritual truth which all the human sciences confirm."

6. "Disunity is a danger that the nations and peoples of the ___ ___ ___ t ___ can no longer endure; . . ."

7. "No nation can achieve ___ ___ ___ ___ ___ ___ ___ s unless education is accorded all its citizens."

8. ". . . unity and p ___ ___ ___ ___ ___ are the attainable goal towards which humanity is striving." ✳

Building Communities

Activity by Meg Andersen

Prepare

1 Copy the 5 quotation squares, one set of five for each group in your game.

2 Keeping sets separate, cut each square into three pieces on the dotted lines.

3 Put each set of 15 pieces into an envelope.

Play

1 Divide into groups of 5 (families or diverse intergenerational groups).

2 Each group receives one envelope containing 15 partial quotations.

3 Once the envelope is opened, there is to be **no talking or non-verbal communication**.

4 A group member opens the envelope and distributes the puzzle pieces in the following way:

> player 1 - 1 piece
> player 2 - 2 pieces
> player 3 - 3 pieces
> player 4 - 4 pieces
> player 5 - 5 pieces

5 Players may give and receive pieces, but no one may take a piece from another player.

6 Play is over when each of a team's 5 members is holding the 3 pieces of a single quotation.

7 Set a time limit of 20 to 30 minutes.

8 Discuss what happened during the game:

> How many pieces did you receive? How did that make you feel?
> What did you first do with your pieces?
> What did others do with their pieces?
> How did others react to what you were trying to do?
> How did you react to what others were trying to do?
> Did you see matches that others did not? How did that feel?
> Did you have any trouble getting pieces? How did that feel?
> How well did your group work together?
> What other way could it be done?
> What did you learn about how your group functions?
> What else did you learn from the game?
> What Bahá'í guidance would help this situation?

9 Within each group, discuss the 5 quotations. How can this guidance help us in building communities?

Copy and cut these squares

Cut along the dotted lines as indicated below.

Each square divides into 3 pieces. Total pieces = 15.

This constitutes one set which is placed in an envelope.

"Since Bahá'ís everywhere are at the very beginning of the process of community building, enormous effort must be devoted to the tasks at hand."

—The Universal House of Justice, Ridván 153

"His constant hope is that the believers will conduct themselves, individually and in their Bahá'í Community life, in such a manner as to attract the attention of others to the Cause."

— Shoghi Effendi, *The Compilation of Compilations*, v. 1, p. 382

"Consider the welfare of the community as one's own."

—'Abdu'l-Bahá, *The Secret of Divine Civilization*, p. 39

put into envelope

"It is essential to the spiritual life of the community that the friends hold regular devotional meetings."

— The Universal House of Justice, Ridván 153

"The flourishing of the community, especially at the local level, demands a significant enhancement in patterns of behaviour."

— The Universal House of Justice, Ridván 153

TRUE OR FALSE?
BULLIES CAN BE STOPPED!

Ever had to deal with a bully? Most people do. Why do bullies make you feel so bad? Because being treated with injustice always hurts. When you stand up for yourself or ask others to help you stop a bully, you bring justice to your school or neighborhood. And you'll feel safer and more confident. Test your knowledge about bullies. For each question, circle *all* the answers that are true.

QUESTIONS:

1. Which of these statements is right?
A. Bullying should not be accepted as normal.
B. Some people deserve to be bullied.
C. Bullying should not be kept secret.
D. Bullies can't help themselves.

2. Who is a bully?
A. Someone who spreads mean rumors about you.
B. Someone who kicks, punches, shoves, or trips you.
C. Someone who steals or breaks your things.
D. Someone who calls you names.
E. Someone who makes you feel scared.

3. Why do kids become bullies?
A. To feel as if they have power over others.
B. They have been bullied.
C. To get on the football team.
D. They have low self-esteem.

4. What can you do about bullying?
A. Walk or run away.
B. Look the bully in the eye and say, "STOP DOING THAT!"
C. Stick with friends so you're not alone.
D. Tell an adult.

ANSWERS:

1. A and C: No one should *ever* be bullied. Even if a bully makes you promise not to tell anyone, talk to someone who can help. Just like any action, a person can choose to bully others or not. Some kids need help learning that bullying is a choice.

2. A, B, C, D, and E: Someone who regularly does *any* of these is a bully. Whether bullies use words or actions, it hurts.

3. A, B, and D: Many bullies have been bullied themselves. To keep from feeling powerless, they find ways to have power over others.

4. A, B, C, and D: It takes courage to carry out any of these actions. Some kids don't want to tell an adult, but sometimes adults are the only ones who can stop a bully. Don't be afraid to talk to your parents or teachers.

Section 8

Buddhist Resources for the Children's Sabbath

We are pleased to offer Buddhist resources prepared specifically for Buddhist communities to participate in the Children's Sabbath (in addition to participation in community-wide interfaith services). We offer deep thanks to Vanessa Zuisei Goddard of the Zen Mountain Monastery in Mt. Tremper, New York, for preparing these materials.

Buddha's Birthday Celebration: Sample Service

Generally defined, liturgy is an affirmation or restatement of the common experience of a community. In theistic religions, liturgy reaffirms one's relationship with God. In Christianity this is expressed through an emphasis on one's relationship with Jesus, while in Judaism there is a focus on reconnecting the individual with the teachings of the Old Testament. In Zen the question of a divine being is not central and, instead, the emphasis is on the ground of being, the buddha nature, which is not separate from the nature of the self.

All of Zen's rites and rituals are constantly pointing to the same place, to the realization of no separation between the self and the ten thousand things. Zen liturgy is *upaya* (skillful means). Like *zazen* (seated meditation) and all the other areas of Zen training, it functions as a way of uncovering the truth that is the life of each one of us. Skillful means are necessary because each one of us, just as we are, is already perfect and complete. We lack nothing. What we seek is exactly where we stand, yet this truth has to be realized as the functioning of our lives. For liturgy to function, it must first be wholeheartedly engaged.

Buddha's Birthday, traditionally known as *Wesak*, offers an opportunity for Buddhist communities to not only include children in their service, but to have them be the main participants in the celebration of the founder's birthday. In the Mountains and Rivers Order, this service is celebrated at the same time as Easter.

Buddha's Birthday Service

Chants:

Heart Sutra

Avalokiteshvara Bodhisattva, doing deep Prajna Paramita,

clearly saw emptiness of all the five conditions,

thus completely relieving misfortune and pain.

Oh Shariputra, form is no other than emptiness,

emptiness no other than form.

Form is exactly emptiness, emptiness exactly form.

Sensation, conception, discrimination, awareness are likewise like this.

Oh Shariputra, all dharmas are forms of emptiness;

not born, not destroyed, not stained, not pure, without loss, without gain.

So in emptiness there is no form,

no sensation, conception, discrimination, awareness,

no eye, ear, nose, tongue, body, mind,

no color, sound, smell, taste, touch, phenomena,

no realm of sight, no realm of consciousness,

no ignorance and no end to ignorance,

no old age and death and no end to old age and death,

no suffering, no cause of suffering,

no extinguishing, no path, no wisdom, and no gain.

No gain and thus the bodhisattva lives Prajna Paramita,

with no hindrance in the mind; no hindrance, therefore no fear.

Far beyond deluded thoughts; this is Nirvana.

All past, present, and future buddhas live Prajna Paramita

and therefore attain anuttarasamyak-sambodhi.

Therefore know Prajna Paramita is the great mantra,

the vivid mantra, the best mantra, the unsurpassable mantra.

It completely clears all pain. This is the truth, not a lie.

So set forth the Prajna Paramita mantra,

set forth this mantra and say,

Gate! Gate! Paragate! Parasamgate! Bodhi Svaha! Prajna Heart Sutra.

Dedication (Liturgist):

Buddha nature pervades the whole universe, existing right here, now.

In reciting the Maha Prajna Paramita Heart Sutra

We dedicate its merits to:

The great master Shakyamuni Buddha Daiosho,

the all pervading and everlasting Three Treasures,

all arhats and bodhisattvas, mahasattvas

and their relations throughout the dharma worlds.

May our sincere vows to accomplish the buddha Way be realized together.

Echo:

All buddhas

throughout space and time,

all bodhisattvas mahasattvas

Maha Prajna Paramita.

Jizo Shingon Dharani

Jizo Bodhisattva is considered to be the protector of children. This chant is accessible for most children and young adults to do on their own or as part of the Buddha's Birthday Service.

OM KA KA KABI SAM MA E SOWA KA

(Chanted repeatedly until abbot and all children have poured water on baby Buddha and offered a flower in bowers set up especially for the service)

Dedication (Liturgist):

The pure Dharmakaya neither appears nor disappears.

The vows of great compassion seem to come and go.

On this anniversary of Shakyamuni Buddha's birth,

We respectfully call together the Sangha.

In reciting The Jizo Shingon Dharani,

And in offering flowers, candlelight, incense, sweet water, cake and tea,

We dedicate their merits to:

The birth of the great master

Shakyamuni Buddha

And appreciate the supreme wisdom

of the Tathagata;

May it endlessly pervade everywhere,

And may we maintain and carry forth the Dharma together.

Echo:

All buddhas

throughout space and time,

all bodhisattvas mahasattvas

Maha Prajna Paramita.

Entering the Fray

Adapted from John Daido Loori Roshi's commentary on "Guishan's 'Do Not Betray Others'"

Master Dogen's 300 Koan Shobogenzo,* Case 47

Note: A dharma discourse is a formal talk given on a koan (lit. "public case") in a Zen meditation hall or *zendo*. A koan is a seemingly paradoxical statement designed to short-circuit the intellectual process and point directly to our awakened or buddha nature. Because these talks are not meant to be understood intellectually, they are said to be "dark to the mind but radiant to the heart." In this case, the discourse was given by John Daido Loori Roshi, founder of the Mountains and Rivers Order of Zen Buddhism and abbot of Zen Mountain Monastery. Though this recorded dialogue is more than a thousand years old, Daido Roshi's commentary—elucidating the place of compassion and the importance of social action in Zen—is both timely and relevant.

The Main Case

One day Guishan, after sitting the whole day, gathered his feet in his hands, pointed to his straw sandals, and said to Yangshan, "All hours of the day we receive people's support. We should not betray them." Yangshan said, "Long ago, in Sudatta's garden, the Buddha expounded just this." Guishan said, "That's not enough. Say more." Yangshan said, "When it is cold, to wear socks for others is not prohibited."

The Commentary

All masters throughout time have always looked to guiding and aiding all living beings. They would set up their shops according to their capacities, and in response to the imperative of time, place, position, and degree. Appearing and disappearing in harmony with the occasion, they created countless kinds of expedient means to alleviate suffering.

We should understand that to wear socks for others is a very personal matter. It is the seamless dharma activity that is the ten thousand hands and eyes of great compassion itself. It is the spiritual light of four virtues of the bodhisattva manifesting in the ten directions. But tell me, right now, how do you manifest it in your life?

Capping Verse

Pure jewelled eyes, virtuous arms,
formless and selfless, they enter the fray.
The great function works in all ways,
these hands and eyes are the whole thing.

Every night millions of Buddhist practitioners all over this country chant the Four Bodhisattva Vows. Every night each one of us vows to save innumerable sentient beings; to manifest the ten thousand hands and eyes of Great Compassion, of Kannon Bodhisattva. For me, these hands and eyes are none other than the sangha, the community of dedicated practitioners who take up the challenge to address the endless list of problems we face today.

Right now we are prosperous as a nation and as a sangha. The dharma is growing in the United States. Buddhist centers continue to appear and new practitioners are engaging the practice. At the same time, millions of people are starving. World peace is still a dream. This Great Earth is dying. Overpopulation persists and diseases are rampant. Our children receive the greatest brunt of suffering. The imperative is clear. The burning question is: What will we do? What will *you* do? Right action, which is part of the Eightfold Path of the Buddha, means to guide and aid all living beings and respond to their cries for help. It means taking care of our fragile planet.

This koan addresses the issue of compassion within the context of our vows. The commentary begins, *All masters throughout time have always looked to guiding and aiding all living beings.* That's what our vow is; that's what our practice is. It's not a self-centered endeavor. Right from the outset, we should understand clearly that individual liberation is a contradiction in terms. Personal liberation is fulfilled only within the context of social liberation.

---

* *The Three Hundred Koan Shobogenzo* is a collection of koans gathered by 13th century Zen Master Eihei Dogen during his study in China. John Daido Loori Roshi's book, *True Dharma Eye: Zen Master Dogen's Three Hundred Koans* (Shambhala 2005), includes his and Kazuaki Tanahashi's translations of each case, as well as Daido Loori's commentary, capping verse, and notes.

Trying to achieve real freedom is impossible while approaching this practice with a self-centered point of view that excludes even a single speck of dust. Look at what is liberation and what it means to be free. To be liberated means to merge with the ten thousand things, with the whole catastrophe. Master Dogen, undoubtedly one of the greatest religious teachers and thinkers in the history of Buddhism, says, *To study the Buddha Way is to study the self, to study the self is to forget the self, and to forget the self is to be enlightened by the ten thousand things.* To be enlightened by the ten thousand things means to merge with the ten thousand things. It means to realize that there is no separation between self and other.

All masters throughout time have always looked to guiding and aiding all living beings. They would set up their shops according to their capacities, and in response to the imperative of time, place, position, and degree. "Setting up according to their capacities" is a critical line. We have a tendency to fall into extremes. We either wallow in hopelessness or hide from our problems like an ostrich with its head in the ground; or we run around in a frenzy, like a chicken without a head. Either way, we don't accomplish anything.

Look at Vincent Van Gogh. The man was all heart, but he was not very practical. Before he was an artist, he was the minister for a small coal mining town. There he witnessed unimaginable suffering and deprivation. Wanting to help, he immediately started giving away everything he owned: his clothes, food, furniture, his house. In two weeks he had nothing left and his ministry had ended. He became just another shivering soul. That was not very skillful of him at all. Granted, he was a great artist, but he was a lousy minister. "Setting up shop according to your capacity" means to know exactly what your capacity and power are. Each one of us has personal power, and it's different for different people. We need to know clearly what we are capable of—how to use our talents and energy for the benefit of others, responding appropriately to the imperative of time, place, position, and degree. That appropriate response is at the heart of practicing Right Action. It is also at the essence of skillful means. Skillful means change according to time. What was effective 20 year ago may no longer be effective today. What is skillful in one place may not be appropriate in another place. Your position in relationship to the problem determines what skillful means you can use.

While I was a research scientist working in a chemical plant, I found out that the company was polluting a local stream. I was in a position of authority at the time, so I used it. I went to the plant engineer and talked to him about the problem. At first he was resistant, but when I offered to help him figure out an alternative to get rid of our waste he agreed to cooperate. We worked together and the pollution stopped. In this case, my position allowed me to intervene directly. Five years later, when a different ecological crisis involved the same plant, I was no longer working there. All I could do was stand outside the fence with pickets and protest. My position changed so my way of dealing with the situation had to change, too.

Most important is the matter of degree. In any given situation, how do we know how much action is necessary and optimal? That's a very difficult question. Many of us engage a worthy cause with a vengeance, frequently fired by self-righteousness. We know unequivocally what's wrong and what's right, and from that kind of discrimination we obtain plenty of fuel to propel our anger. To be able to funnel that anger into effective and skillful action requires that we take all aspects of a situation into consideration.

The Buddha was a master of skillful means. Our Buddhist ancestors were too. *Appearing and disappearing in harmony with the occasion, they created countless kinds of expedient means to alleviate suffering.* Appearing and disappearing are important dimensions of compassionate action. Sometimes you need to be very present; sometimes you need to be invisible. Both can be equally effective.

We should understand that to wear socks for others is a very personal matter. It is the seamless dharma activity that is the ten thousand hands and eyes of great compassion itself. A bodhisattva is a being who postpones entering complete enlightenment until all beings are saved. Kannon, the Bodhisattva of Compassion, is often depicted with ten thousand hands and eyes. It is said that she responds to the cries of suffering in the world. She acts without a moment's hesitation, appearing in whatever form is needed in a particular situation.

It is the spiritual light of four virtues of the bodhisattva manifesting in the ten directions. These are four attributes of a bodhisattva. They are: giving, loving speech, service for the welfare of all beings, and identity with others. Dogen writes beautifully about them, saying:

Giving means non-greed. Non-greed means not to crave. It means to give freely and not expect receiving anything in return because of that giving. That is true giving. Let us offer flowers of the distant mountains to the Tathagata [the Buddha] or share the treasures with all sentient beings in spiritual things as well as material things. When the Way is surrendered to the Way, you attain the Way. Upon being enlightened you necessarily let the Way come through itself. The self gives the self for the sake of giving the self. The other gives the other for the sake of giving other.

This kind of giving is purposeless. There is no reward, no pay-off. Within this giving, we merge with each other.

Spiritual teachings are material wealth and, likewise, material wealth is spiritual teachings. If you study giving carefully, you realize living as well as dying are both giving. To be sure, to make a living and to regulate a business is none other than giving. Flowers are innocently fondled by the wind, and birds trust freely to time. These too are feats of giving. Indeed, by reason of being originally gifted with the power of giving, one's present self came into being.

There is no giver and no receiver.

About the second virtue, loving speech, he writes:

As you meet sentient beings, you arise the sense of compassion first in your mind, and treat them with consideration and affectionate words completely devoid of any violent or spiteful language. As you take delight in affectionate words, they will gradually flourish. Even those loving words which were before unknown and unperceived will show themselves. As long as your present life lasts, you should take pleasure in speaking compassionately. Generation after generation, let us exert ourselves unremittingly. Compassionate speech is fundamental to the pacification of enemies and the reconciliation of others. You should ponder that thoughtful words arise from the loving mind. The loving mind has compassion as its seed.

Compassionate action does not have to be grandiose. We don't have to be white knights in shining armor, galloping off to battle. Often, all that's required is simply some loving speech.

About the third virtue:

Working for the welfare of all beings means that you contrive ways to benefit all sentient beings, high and low. You think of various means that will be most congenial to their well-being. Commiserate with the turtle in trouble. Take care of the sparrow suffering from injury. When you see the distressed turtle, watch the sick sparrow, you do not expect any repayment for your favor. You are moved entirely by your desire to help. So serve enemies and friends equally. Assist self and other without discrimination. If you grasp this truth, you will see that this is the reason that even the grasses and trees, the wind and water are all naturally engaged in the activity of giving.

This is selfless giving. It is boundless giving.

Lastly, about identity with others:

Identity with others is non-difference. It applies equally to self and other. There is a truth that after the self assimilates others to itself, the self lets itself be assimilated by others. The relationship of self and other varies according to circumstances.

What does it mean to save all sentient beings? We must keep in mind that in order to save all sentient beings, we must be totally prepared to be saved by all sentient beings.

We should understand that to wear socks for others is a very personal matter. It is the seamless dharma activity that is the ten thousand hands and eyes of great compassion itself. "Wearing socks for others" means knowing personally the suffering of others and responding accordingly. It is always possible to become complacent, to take the easy route. The easy route is to realize yourself and then go off to enjoy your life. I am thankful that the Buddha did not take the easy way; that a countless number of Buddhist teachers did not saunter off into the sunset. The path of the bodhisattva is to not rest on your laurels until each and every living being has been saved. Again, liberation can only be fulfilled in the context of the liberation of all beings. This is called wisdom. When wisdom arises, compassion immediately arises with it. There is no way to hold it back. There is no way to limit it. There is just the spiritual light of the four virtues of the bodhisattva manifesting in the ten directions in all of our encounters.

This teaching has always been implicit in Mahayana Buddhism from its inception thousands of years ago. But it never had the opportunity to manifest itself freely. It flourished in countries where there were significant political constraints; where there was no religious freedom. Monasteries were isolated. They were not in direct contact with much of the pain and suffering surrounding them. But we do not have that problem. We live in an age of communication, knowing very well what is going on at the furthest corners of the earth. We have the potential to feed the world. We have the potential to heal the earth. We have the potential to take care of the waste that we produce, to take care of our impoverished children, to bring world peace. It is said that there are three million Buddhists in the United States. That is a formidable number of people who are vowing every day to save all sentient beings. Why isn't there more political and social action arising within Buddhist communities?

The commentary ends: *But tell me, right now, how do you manifest it in your life?* That is the ever-present challenge. There is a long list of things we can do as a community, and that list will continue to grow as long as we are practicing. But aside from that, as an individual, what will you do in your everyday activities? Each and every one of us has countless opportunities for manifesting true giving, loving speech, service for the welfare of all beings, and identity with others. Are you willing? Are you able? Do you have the power to manifest the ten thousands hands and eyes of great compassion? That is what Kannon is.

The capping verse: *Pure jewelled eyes, virtuous arms. Formless and selfless, they enter the fray.* Formlessness is not self-centered. A self-centered action is completely different from a selfless action. Doing good is not necessarily compassionate activity. Sometimes, on the surface, compassion may not seem like compassion at all. In compassion, there is no sense of separation between the doer and the doing. Someone falls, you pick them up. No one giving; no one receiving. "Formless and selfless, they enter the fray." It means taking a chance. It means practicing the edge.

The great function works in all ways. The Dharma Wheel turns in all directions. The great function is your life, the Buddha nature, your enlightened nature. *These hands and eyes are the whole thing.* What are these hands and eyes? They are not the hands and eyes of some mythical deity that was incorporated into the pantheon of Buddhism. The ten thousand hands and eyes of great compassion are *your* hands and eyes, *your* life. Every time that great heart of compassion comes to life inside your body, you give birth to the hands and eyes of Kannon Bodhisattva. That is where she exists—no other place. Our challenge as individuals and as a nation is to rise up to meet our vows to save all sentient beings. Please, take care of this.

John Daido Loori is the founder and spiritual leader of the Mountains and Rivers Order of Zen Buddhism and abbot of Zen Mountain Monastery, as well as a lineage holder in both the Rinzai and Soto Schools of Zen. Devoted to maintaining the authenticity of these traditions, Daido Roshi is known for his unique adaptation of traditional Buddhism into an American context, particularly with regard to the arts, the environment, social action, and the use of modern media as a vehicle of spiritual training and social change.

The Hare's Sacrifice

by Rafe Martin

Once, the Buddha was born as a tenderhearted hare. One day he and his friends—an otter, a monkey and a fox—decided that once a month they would observe a fast day. On this day they would give the food that they themselves might have eaten to someone else, someone hungry and in need.

A month passes quickly in the forest. Trees bend and shift in the wind. By day clouds drift across the sun, and at night they race across the moon. Clear streams rush, carrying leaves and twigs and bugs down over the rocks and on to heaven knows where. Soon another fast day had arrived.

"I will be good," said the otter to himself, scratching his stomach and fluffing up his wet fur. Slipping into the water, he swam across the shining lake. There, on the other shore, he found a fisherman's camp. Seven fish lay on the grass, strung in a row on a stick. "Is there anyone here?" called the otter quietly. There was no answer. "Well, these fish must have gotten lost," he decided. Taking the stick firmly between his teeth, he re-entered the water and swam home. Just before he reached the shore, he suddenly remembered the fast day. "Someone is going to have a fine feast," he thought sadly, "but alas, it's not going to be me!" And feeling very righteous, he waddled out of the water, shook himself vigorously, and sat down in the sun to dry his fur and rest.

The monkey too, swinging in the trees, thought of the fast and resolved to be good. He would give his own meal to another. Hunting around, he found beautiful bananas and mangoes. "Why couldn't I have only found these yesterday?" he couldn't help but think. "Well, today they shall be given to another." And setting them aside, he, too, rested in his tree feeling righteous indeed.

The fox was trotting along, her sharp nose to the wind. Catching the scent of cooked foods, she bounded through the bushes until she came to a farmer's hut. "Ho, ho!" she thought to herself, "What, no one around? Why, look here, someone's left a pot of yoghurt on the ground and some bread baking on a spit." Slipping her head through the cord attached to the yoghurt pot and taking the spit of bread between her teeth, she trotted off, the plume of her tail waving with delight as she thought of the fine meal that lay ahead. She had not gone far when she remembered the fast day. Her tail drooped. "Oh well," she sighed, "someone is going to eat well." Then, recovering her spirits, she trotted on feeling very righteous indeed.

The hare thought, "Today is the fast day. I'm tired of giving what grows of its own in the ground—carrots, cabbages, potatoes and such. I want to give more than that. But what do I have left to offer?" He thought and thought, then he leapt up with delight. "I have it! This very day I shall offer my own body to someone in need. I shall give myself, give all!"

Up in the heavens Shakra's marble throne grew hot, a sign that somewhere on the earth someone was about to undertake a noble deed. "Aha," said the King of the Gods, "a little hare is about to take a big leap. I shall test him."

In less than an instant, the high god appeared in the hare's forest. Taking the form of an old beggar, he hobbled off, leaning on a staff, to where the otter was resting by the lake shore.

"Friend," said Shakra, King of the Gods, his voice weak and trembling now, as if with age, "can you spare a little food for me?"

"Of course," said the otter, "sit down right here. Rest." Running to his den, he dragged out five of the fish and lay them at the beggar's calloused feet. "Eat well," said the otter.

"Thank you for your kindness," said Shakra, his voice again full of vigor and strength. "I may be back for these." And off he went, leaving the astonished otter alone by the shore.

Next he came to the monkey. "Have you some food for a weary traveler?" he asked, extending a shaky hand.

"Of course. Sit down," chattered the monkey as he scrambled up a tree. In a moment, he returned carrying several bananas and a mango. "These are for you. Eat and enjoy them. They are fresh and ripe."

"Thank you," said Shakra, "you are very generous. I may be back for these." Striding off, he left the monkey scratching his head in confusion.

Next he approached the fox. "Help me!" he piteously cried. "I am old and very hungry. Have you any food?"

"Of course!" yelped the fox. "Lucky man, I've got just the thing!" Racing off, she returned with the pot of yoghurt and the spit of bread. She threw herself down grinning and panting, delighted with her own goodness. But, to her amazement, the old beggar rose and marched off into the twilight saying, "Thank you. I may be back!"

Then the god Shakra came to the little hare just as the moon was rising. "Friend," he groaned, "I have not eaten for many days. The roads have been hard and I am faint. Have you anything that I might eat?"

"Yes," said the hare, "I do. Just seat yourself and be patient, for tonight you shall have such a meal as I have never offered before!"

Gathering leaves and twigs, the little hare started a small blaze on the rocks of the forest floor. When the fire was burning fiercely, he shook himself to save any fleas that might yet be in his coat. Then, leaping high, he jumped straight into the flames! But what was this? The fire was cool! It was like ice. Not a hair or pore of his body was even singed!

"Come out from the flames, brave little hare," said a noble voice. And leaping out from the fire again, the little hare found himself facing one of the radiant gods. It was Shakra himself! The old beggar had vanished.

"What! What has happened?" exclaimed the little hare in astonishment.

"You, yourself are the great event that has happened," answered Shakra, King of the Gods. "Your noble sacrifice shall be remembered for an entire eon. Look!" And reaching up with a finger, he drew the hare's picture on the shining disk of moon. "There, noble hare. You shall not be forgotten for as long as the moon shall shine in the sky. Now come with me. Let me show you my home."

Bending down, the mighty god lifted the little wide-eyed hare up into his arms. Then, soaring upward, they disappeared together into the vastness of the night sky.

The forest became very still. The flames of the fire died down. A glowing log popped, shooting up a vast burst of sparks. The sparks whirled up, rising higher and higher, until they too disappeared, lost at last against the brilliance of the moon and stars.

The three friends—the otter, the monkey and the fox—lived on in harmony. Seated together, they would look up at the moon and remember with amazement the day that the King of the Gods himself had walked among them. And they would recall their friend, the little hare, and his great sacrifice.

All that was long, long ago, but the hare in the moon shines just as brightly today as he did when Shakra first put him up there. If you don't believe me, why, just go out some night and look! There he is—a sign for all to see that compassion is the light that illumines our darkness.

Rafe Martin, a practitioner of Zen Buddhism for more than 25 years, is the author of numerous award-winning books and recordings for children and adults. His books and recordings have won him several prizes, and he has been featured at the National Storytelling Festival, as well as at schools and libraries, conferences and festivals throughout the United States and around the world.

Note: *The jataka tales are a collection of stories about the Buddha's previous births in the animal realm. A traditional part of the Buddhist canon found in both Pali and Mahayana texts, the jatakas are not merely folktales for children, but parables that can awaken adults to their own potential for compassion and selflessness.*

"The Hare's Sacrifice" from *The Hungry Tigress*
© 1999 by Rafe Martin, pp. 121-24

Yellow Moon Press, Cambridge, Massachusetts 02238
(617) 776-2230 or ymp@tiac.net

Section 9

The Children's Sabbath's power and inspiration comes, in large part, from the connections it makes across faith traditions, across our nation, across generations. It is an extraordinary opportunity to recognize and celebrate our shared commitment to assuring justice and care for children and to affirm the unifying message of our religious traditions that calls us to nurture and protect those who are young, poor, sick and vulnerable. Indeed, central to every great religious tradition is the mandate to protect the young, the weak, and the poor with justice and compassion. Over the past 16 years, many communities have come together to proclaim and respond to that mandate through *interfaith* Children's Sabbath celebrations. These community-wide Children's Sabbaths stand as an important example of the promise and power of interfaith partnership for a common cause.

If planned with care, sensitivity, and a commitment to inclusion, an interfaith Children's Sabbath can be a time of new understanding, of celebration, and most importantly, of uniting and strengthening your community to nurture and protect children with even greater justice and compassion.

In this section you will find resources for planning an interfaith Children's Sabbath:

- Planning suggestions for coordinating the practical aspects of an interfaith service
- Liturgical suggestions for planning the content and leadership of the service
- A sample interfaith Children's Sabbath service that you may use "as is" or adapt. The service includes readings and prayers from a variety of faith traditions. Feel free to add others to represent additional faith traditions in your community or to draw from the resources in other sections of this resource manual.

Planning an Interfaith Celebration

Organizing a community-wide interfaith service may sound like a daunting task, but it can be done successfully, and has been, with tremendous contributions to the communities. These are suggested ways to coordinate the event. Feel free to adapt this process to suit your needs.

❏ **Recruit a crew.** Connect with two, three, four, or more people to help you get started. Then convene an advisory committee of eight to fifteen members. Strive to build an advisory committee that represents the full range of religious bodies, races, and ethnicities of your community. Be sure to involve from the outset all of the faith groups you hope to include, so no one feels like an afterthought.

❏ **Chart your course.** Develop an efficient agenda for the initial meeting of the advisory committee. A productive meeting will generate energy, enthusiasm, and continued commitment. Key items to determine include the date, site, range of events, and point people to assume responsibility for aspects of the event. You may find it helpful to use one of the Children's Sabbath Power Point presentations to convey the purpose and power of the Children's Sabbath. (The Power Point presentation may be downloaded for free from www.childrensdefense.org/childrenssabbaths.)

❏ **Invite others on board.** Begin to contact as many congregations and community organizations as you can to get them on board. Be sure to invite congregations of all ethnic and racial groups. Network with ministerial, rabbinical, and interfaith associations, Islamic centers and associations of mosques, schools, social clubs, and organizations dealing with children,

health care, juvenile justice, poverty, violence, hunger, homelessness, education, and parenting. Contact them by letter and include a response form for those who wish to participate. Follow up with a phone call. Make a quick reference list of those who respond affirmatively that you can add to later.

❏ **Assign areas for coordination.** Areas to coordinate include site selection, administration and funding, worship planning, music, outreach/promotion/media, and activities to raise awareness and generate service and advocacy.

❏ **Choose a good day and time.** Schedule the interfaith service for a time that does not exclude any group's participation. For example, scheduling an interfaith service on Saturday afternoon, during the Jewish Shabbat, would prevent some Jews from attending. Similarly, Sunday morning scheduling is likely to conflict with most church services. Sunday afternoon or evening is usually the best time for an interfaith event. Be aware, however, that you will need to do lots of outreach and promotion to generate strong attendance for an interfaith service, whenever it is scheduled. See the promotion suggestions in Section 3.

Interfaith Worship Resources

❑ **Find a suitable location.** Seek advice from people who have done similar events, and choose a site as early as possible. Feasible sites for interfaith activities include auditoriums, hospitals, convention centers, atriums of public buildings, and schools. Of course, religious places of worship are also good sites. If you use a congregation's building, be sure the religious leader is involved in the planning, since he or she will know the logistics of the site.

Consider the following in selecting a site:

- **Size:** Make sure it is large enough to accommodate the crowd you expect, but not so large that when the congregation has arrived it looks half-empty and makes your turn-out appear small.

- **Staging:** Will it accommodate choirs and a procession? Is there a good sound and lighting system?

- **Location:** Is it centrally located and convenient for all segments of the community? If not, can you arrange for shuttle buses to transport groups from other areas of the community to encourage and enable them to attend?

- **Cost:** Try to find a site that will host the service without any charge.

- **Worship space:** Is it conducive to interfaith worship? Will it foster unity among persons who don't know each other? Consider temporary removal of symbols or objects that might cause others distress that can be easily removed. Also, consider the addition of banners and symbols or expressions of welcome that may make guests feel more at home.

- **Parking:** Is parking available or is public transportation nearby?

- **Accessibility:** Is it accessible to people with disabilities? (Remember to have a sign language interpreter for those who are deaf or hearing impaired.)

Liturgical Suggestions for Interfaith Services

If everyone will be speaking or singing it, be sure it is inclusive. If a part of the interfaith service, such as a prayer or song, will be spoken or sung by the congregation, be sure that it does not include language that feels exclusive (such as "Jesus Christ" or "Muhammad"). Instead, draw on the universal and unifying aspects of our various religious traditions. Appropriate ways of addressing God in an interfaith service are Creator, Source of All Life, Divine, Our God and Sustainer, Eternal, Holy One, and Source of Our Being. Some appropriate closing addresses include: "In Thy name we pray," "In the name of God," or simply "Amen."

Have representatives present readings or prayers specific to their traditions. If individual leaders will be presenting readings or offering prayers, they may include references specific to their own traditions (such as "Jesus Christ" or "Muhammad"). Similarly, a choir that is performing an anthem could sing music specific to its tradition. Just make sure that you invite representatives from a range of faith traditions and encourage them to select readings and prayers that are as inclusive as possible and do not denigrate other religious traditions. (If you won't have time to include readings from every single religious tradition represented, you may want to print additional readings in the service program.)

Be as broadly representative as possible. Try to include representatives from as many faith traditions as possible. Also be sure to balance gender, racial, and ethnic representation. You may not be able to give every representative a "speaking part" in the service. Invite those who will not be able to speak in the service to participate in an opening procession (with each processor wearing robes or other religious garb appropriate to their tradition) and sit in a special section, either on the stage with the speakers or at the front of the congregation. List the processors and their religious affiliation in the service program.

Know ahead of time what will be spoken and sung. An interfaith service is not the right time for surprises! It is important that the service have a unified message that lifts up children's needs and inspires people to action. While one would never constrain leaders from reading or praying what they feel is right in services entirely under their leadership, in a cooperative service like an interfaith Children's Sabbath, which aims to lift up particular concerns, it is entirely appropriate to exercise such oversight for the service.

- One possibility is to use a service that you, along with your planning team, write in advance. Then assign the pre-written parts to religious leaders. The only part that would not be pre-written would be the sermon. It is important to select a leader to give the sermon who you are confident will speak in terms appropriate for an interfaith gathering and also will address the children's concerns that are the focus of the service. The sample interfaith Children's Sabbath service in this section is one model that you could use.

- Another possibility is to have the invited religious leaders write their own "parts" or select their own readings. In this case, be sure that they give you a copy of their prayer or reading in advance. If the prayer or reading is not in keeping with the Children's Sabbath theme, give them more guidance about the Children's Sabbath theme and purpose and ask them to select another prayer or reading.

Be clear about timing. An interfaith service that strives to be representative runs the risk of being too long. Additionally, a sense of time and appropriate length for services varies by faith tradition. When you invite leaders, be sure they know how much time has been allotted for their part. Emphasize that everyone must keep to his or her allotted time. (This is another reason for having copies in advance of what each leader will be reading or praying.) Know in advance what you will do if the service begins to run too long and you need to shorten it. The least offensive place to cut is usually verses from a congregational song or an entire song. Be sure that the music director knows in advance that this is a possibility and decide who will make the decision and who will communicate it to the leaders and congregation, if necessary.

Brief the leadership in advance. Ask all of the participating religious leaders (both those with speaking parts and those who will be processing) to gather 30-60 minutes before the start of the service. At that time, give each a copy of the service program, allow time for them to robe or put on their religious garb, and brief them on the logistics of the service: who will process with whom, where they will sit, which podium they will speak from, and other such details. Remember that when leaders are in an unfamiliar place of worship of a tradition other than their own, they may not know the terminology and be reluctant to ask for clarification. (For example, the Christian term "narthex" or the Jewish term "bimah" may be unfamiliar to others.) Be sure that when you brief leaders that you take extra care to ensure that everyone understands the directions about where they are to gather, sit, speak, and so forth. You may want to designate one leader to be responsible for filling in if a leader doesn't show up or for handling unexpected occurrences.

Convene a special combined choir for the service. Invite a wide range of congregations' choirs to participate (children's, adults, or both). Then send the selected music to each choir director, who will teach the song to her or his choir during their own rehearsals. Schedule several combined rehearsals during which all of the choirs will sing together under the direction of one appointed director. Incidentally, this is a good way to build attendance, since many proud family members are likely to attend to hear their children sing.

Interfaith Service: My Boat Is So Small: Creating a Safe Harbor of Hope and Health Care for All Children

Prelude

Opening Procession of Religious Leaders and Children

> The Act of Commitment, below, includes a suggestion for incorporating origami boats into the Act. Alternatively, when you start planning for the service, invite children and adults to make origami boats. Either aim for as many as possible, or for a certain symbolic number, such as 76 to represent the number of children born each hour without health insurance. During the opening procession, bring the boats forward to display at the front. They could be carried in shallow baskets or on trays (so that they are visible to the congregation), strung on strings as mobiles and dangled from a dowel hung at the front, or in some other arrangement depending on your setting. Directions on folding a sample boat are available on pages 54-55.

Welcome

(The religious leader in whose place of worship the interfaith service is being held may offer a very brief welcome. If the service is not being held in a place of worship, one of the key leaders involved in planning the Children's Sabbath may give a brief welcome. Or the welcome may be omitted and the service may move directly from the Opening Procession to the Gathering Words.)

Gathering Words

[If desired, representatives of each tradition could pour a portion of water into a larger container before they read each line.]

People: **Like the water that comes down from the heavens and finds its home in many lakes and rivers, seas and oceans, so, too, we find our spiritual homes in many traditions.**

Jewish Leader: We come from a tradition whose people set out for a land of freedom and justice, through the waters of the Yam Suf, the Sea of Reeds.

Christian Leader: We come from a tradition whose people were baptized in the River Jordan and whom Jesus reminded that whoever gives even a cup of cold water to a little one will not lose their reward.

Hindu Leader: We come from a tradition whose people gathered by the River Ganges.

Muslim Leader: We come from a tradition whose people have seen the Zam Zam spring up in the dry desert because of the faithful prayers of Hagar, and this gift of water from the Most Merciful enabled a civilization of peace to be born.

Sikh Leader: We come from a tradition whose people drink the sweet water of Amrit.

Bahá'í Leader: We come from a tradition whose people recognize that we all "are as waves on the sea of spirit; although each individual is a distinct wave, the ocean is one, all are united in God." ('Abdu'l-Bahá, *Paris Talks*)

People: **We come together to praise the Eternal, source of life, who sustains us as water sustains the earth.**

We come together out of concern for children buffeted by a wide and stormy sea of need.

We come together with commitment to bring children into safe, sheltered waters, a harbor of hope and health care for all children.

> *You may wish to use the following Gathering Words in place of the Gathering Words above.*

Gathering Words

We come…
from east and west, north and south
from congregation and classroom, home and office
from churches and synagogues, mosques and temples.
We are young and old,
> hopeful and heartsick,
> drained and determined.

We come…
To praise the Eternal, source of love and justice;
To find strength in God and in each other
To share our stories
To amplify our voices
And to proclaim God's desire for
> community and caring,
> health and wholeness, and
> justice for every single child.

Congregational Hymn

Select a song with inclusive words, such as: Sing Out My Soul, the Goodness of the Lord, God Is So Good, Great Is Thy Faithfulness (change "Father" to "Creator" or "Eternal") or Immortal, Invisible, God Only Wise.

> *This Opening Prayer may be used in place of the Gathering Words or the Litany of Lament that follows, if desired.*

Opening Prayer

Dear Lord, be good to us. The sea is so wide and our boats are so small. We come together, O God, knowing that millions of your beloved children are adrift on the stormy sea without the protection they need. Children's small bodies are battered by illness and injury without the harbor of health and mental health coverage. Families are swamped by medical debt. Our voices crying for help can be drowned out by the howling winds of the wealthy and powerful, the rich and the well-positioned. Strengthen us, we pray, to join our voices to make them heard. Guide us, we pray, to bring all children home safely to a harbor of health care. Sustain us as we set our sights on the justice you intend. Embolden us, inspire us, that we never give up until *all* of your children can live the lives of health and wholeness for which they were created. Amen.

Litany of Lament *(read by several children and youths):*

Reader 1: Do you remember this song? "Row, row, row your boat, gently down the stream. Merrily, merrily, merrily, merrily, life is but a dream." Many of us wish it were so for all children, that they could easily move ahead through their own efforts in a gentle world, and that they experience life as a happy dream.

Reader 2: But for millions of children in our nation and world today, life is not a happy dream that brings a cheerful song to their lips. Instead, the hardships and fear they experience bring silent prayers better expressed in this fisherman's plea: "Dear Lord, be good to me. The sea is so wide and my boat is so small."

Reader 3: I stand for the nine million children in America who don't have health insurance. When I'm sick, I may not be able to see a doctor or may go late when I've gotten much worse. My family may face a mountain of debt from medical expenses. The sea is so wide and my boat is so small.

Reader 4: I stand for Devante Johnson, who struggled courageously against kidney cancer while his mother struggled with the health care system trying to renew his Medicaid coverage. For four months he went without health care. On March 1, he died at age 14 from complications of the disease. The sea is so wide and his boat was so small.

Reader 5: I stand for Gabriela Garcia, who survived Hurricane Rita but whose family lost health care coverage in the aftermath. So she missed 29 days of school as she endured untreated sinus infections, severe migraines, and other health problems. The sea is so wide and her boat is so small.

Reader 6: I stand for little Vivian, a toddler whose respiratory problems leave her struggling to breathe and who lost her health coverage because her parents' income put them just $37 above the income limit for the state Children's Health Insurance Program but is not nearly enough to afford private insurance. The sea is so wide and her boat is so small.

Readers Together: Will you stand with us? Will you take a stand so that all of America's children are guaranteed health care coverage they can count on in the storms of life?

Anthem: The Sea Is So Wide or Congregational Hymn such as **Stand by Me** (selected verses)

The Sea Is So Wide
Words and music by Mac Huff and John Jacobson. Available for SATB, SAB and 2-Part. Hall Leonard Concert Festival Choral Series, copyright 1991. To order, contact Hal Leonard Publishing Corporation, 777 West Bluemont Road, P.O. Box 13819, Milwaukee, Wisconsin 53213

Stand By Me (selected verses)

When the storms of life are raging, stand by me. (2x)
When the world is tossing me, like a ship upon the sea,
Thou who rulest wind and water, stand by me.

In the midst of tribulation, stand by me. (2x)
When the hosts of hell assail, and my strength begins to fail,
Thou who never lost a battle, stand by me.

In the midst of faults and failures, stand by me. (2x)
When I've done the best I can, and my friends misunderstand,
Thou who knowest all about me, stand by me.

Time with Children: *Swimmy*

In this special time of conversation directly with the children, if numbers and space permit, you can invite the younger children present to come forward for this story. Read Leo Lionni's children's book, Swimmy (New York: Dragonfly Books, 1963). If the numbers and space don't work for the children to come forward, consider instead projecting the pages of the story on a screen that all present could see.

Introduce it by saying something like, "We are going to hear a story about a little fish in a wide sea of big, dangerous fish. Even though he was small, he found a way to work with others so all of the small ones were safe.

Read the story, Swimmy.

After reading the story, say something like:

Today, we have all come together to talk about children who are in a big sea of trouble—like children who can't see a doctor when they need to, or children whose families don't have

enough money for food or homes or the things they need. Today, we have come together because we want to work together to keep all children safe. We know that even though the problems facing children are big, God is bigger. Even though each one of us is small, working together as God's family, we can help keep each other, especially all children, safe and sound.

Let's have a prayer: Dear God, we know that there are children who feel small and face great big problems. Help us work together to keep every child safe. Remind us that you are bigger than the biggest problem and love us with a love that is bigger than anything. Amen.

Readings, Prayers, and Reflections from Many Faiths

Depending on the religious traditions represented at your service, invite leaders to lead prayers or read brief passages from their sacred texts related to the theme and offer brief (1-3 minutes) reflections on their religious tradition's call to do justice and bring hope and health care to children.

If the readings are recited in another language, either have the readers also read the English translation or, to keep the service from becoming too lengthy, provide written translations into English in the service program.

Below are examples from a few religious traditions. Several options are provided for some traditions; it is recommended that you select just one from each tradition to limit length. Add readings from other traditions as appropriate. **Be sure to intersperse the Readings, Prayers, and Reflections with musical selections sung by the congregation or choirs. This will help to keep the service lively and to engage congregation members.**

Jewish Readings

Plucking one child, jeopardized by unjust policies in the land, from the water may have saved his life, but it didn't end the injustice. It took the child, grown to adulthood, to take on the challenge of advocating for freedom and justice for all:

Then Pharaoh commanded all his people, "Every boy that is born to the Hebrews you shall throw into the Nile, but you shall let every girl live." Now a man from the house of Levi went and married a Levite woman. The woman conceived and bore a son; and when she saw that he was a fine baby, she hid him three months. When she could hide him no longer, she got a papyrus basket for him and plastered it with bitumen and pitch; she put the child in it and placed it among the reeds on the bank of the river. His sister stood at a distance to see what would happen to him. The daughter of Pharaoh came down to bathe at the river.... She saw the basket among the reeds and sent her maid to bring it. When she opened it, she saw the child. He was crying, and she took pity on him. "This must be one of the Hebrews' children," she said. (*Exodus 2:1-10*)

If one person is able to save another and does not save him he transgresses the commandment, "Neither shall you stand idly by the blood of your neighbor." (*Leviticus 19:16*) Similarly, if one person sees another drowning in the sea, or being attacked by bandits, or being attacked by wild animals, and, although able to rescue him either alone or by hiring others, does not rescue him; or if one hears heathens or informers plotting evil against another or laying a trap for him and does not call it to the other's attention and let him know; or if one knows that a heathen or violent person is going to attack another and although able to appease him on behalf of the other and make him change his mind, he does not do so; or if one acts in any similar way—he transgresses in each case the injunction, "Neither shall you stand idly by the blood of your neighbor." (Maimonides, *Code, "Laws Concerning Murder and the Preservation of Life" Chapter 1, Section 14 and 16*)

Buddhist Readings

"Health is the greatest possession. Contentment is the greatest treasure. Confidence is the greatest friend. NIRVANA is the greatest joy." (*The Dhammapada, 204*)

"A mother, even at the risk of her own life, protects her child, her only child. In the same way should you cultivate love without measure toward all beings. You should cultivate toward the whole world—above, below, and around—a heart of love unstinted, unmixed with any sense of differing or opposing interests. You should maintain this mindfulness all the time you are awake. Such a state of heart is the best in the world." (Majjhima Nikaya in *The Buddha Speaks*)

Christian Readings

Could the brothers have imagined that "fishing for people" means not just teaching and preaching, but working to restore them to health?

As [Jesus] walked by the Sea of Galilee, he saw two brothers, Simon, who is called Peter, and Andrew his brother, casting a net into the sea—for they were fishermen. And he said to them, "Follow me, and I will make you fish for people." Immediately they left their nets and followed him. As he went from there, he saw two other brothers, James, son of Zebedee, and his brother John, in the boat with their father Zebedee, mending their nets, and he called them. Immediately they left the boat and their father, and followed him. Jesus went throughout Galilee, teaching in their synagogues and proclaiming the good news of the kingdom and curing every disease and every sickness among the people. So his fame spread throughout all Syria, and they brought to him all the sick, those who were afflicted with various diseases and pains, demoniacs, epileptics, and paralytics, and he cured them. (*Matthew 4:18-24*)

One day he got into a boat with his disciples, and he said to them, "Let us go across to the other side of the lake." So they put out, and while they were sailing he fell asleep. A windstorm swept down on the lake and the boat was filling with water, and they were in danger. They went to him and woke him up, shouting "Master, Master, we are perishing!" And he woke up and rebuked the wind and the raging waves; they ceased, and there was a calm. He said to them, "Where is your faith?" They were afraid and amazed and said to one another, "Who is this, that he commands even the winds and the water, and they obey him?" (*Luke 8:22-25*)

Bahá'í Prayers

"O God! Rear this little babe in the bosom of Thy love and give it milk from the breast of Thy Providence. Cultivate this fresh plant in the rose garden of Thy love and aid it to grow through the showers of Thy bounty. Make it a child of the kingdom, and lead it to Thy heavenly realm. Thou art powerful and kind, and Thou art the Bestower, the Generous, the Lord of surpassing bounty." ('Abdu'l-Baha from *Prayers for Young Bahá'ís*)

"Thy Name is my healing, O my God, and remembrance of Thee is my remedy. Nearness to Thee is my hope, and love for Thee is my companion. Thy mercy to me is my healing and my succour in both this world to come. Thou, verily, art the All-Bountiful, the All-Knowing, the All-Wise." (Baha'u'llah, *O Thou Kind Lord! Prayers and Readings for Children from the Bahá'í Writings*)

Muslim Readings

And why should ye not strive in the cause of God and of those who, being weak, are ill-treated and oppressed?—Men, women, and children, whose cry is: "Our Lord! Rescue us from this town whose people are oppressors, and raise for us from Thee one who will protect, and raise for us from Thee one who will help!" (*Qur'an 4:75*)

By the morning light,
By the night when it darkens and is still,
Your Lord has neither forsaken you, nor is he displeased.
And indeed, the Hereafter is better for you than the present life of this world.
And indeed, your Lord will give you all good so that you shall be well pleased.
Did He not find you an orphan and gave you shelter and care?
And he found you wandering and He gave you guidance.
He found you poor and in need and made you independent.

Therefore, treat not the orphan with harshness,
Nor repulse the petitioner unheard, and the bounty of thy Lord proclaim! (*Qur'an 93:1-11*)

It is not righteousness that ye turn your faces towards East or West; but it is righteousness to believe in God and the Last Day, and the Angels, and the Book, and the Messengers; to spend of your substance, out of love for Him, for your kin, for orphans, for the needy, for the wayfarer, for those who ask, and for the ransom of slaves; to be steadfast in prayer, and practice regular charity, to fulfill the contracts which ye have made; and to be firm and patient, in pain [or suffering] and adversity, and throughout all periods of panic. Such are the people of truth, the God-fearing. (*Qur'an 2:177*)

Sikh Hymn

The Lord is my Mother and Father. He it is who blesses me with sustenance,
And the Lord takes care of me. For, I am the child of God.
He abandons me never and feeds me steadily,
And minds not my demerits and hugs me to His bosom,
And He blesses me with all I seek; yea, He the Bliss-giving Father,
And He has blessed me with Words of Wisdom, yea, the riches of the Name,
And made me worthy of Himself.
And made me a partner (of His Grace) with the Guru, and now I possess all joys.
May my Lord forsake me not: Yea, He, who is my All powerful Lord. (*Hymn composed by Guru Arjan thanking the Lord for the gift of life*)

Hindu Prayer

May there be welfare to all beings;
May there be fullness and wholeness to all people;
May there be constant good and auspicious life to everyone;
May there be peace everywhere…
May all be full of happiness and abundance;
May everyone in the world enjoy complete health, free from diseases;
May all see and experience good things in their lives,
May not even a single person experience sorrow and misery.
Om!
Peace! Peace! Peace! (*Daily prayer of Hindus*)

Charge to the Congregation

(*Invite a dynamic speaker to present a charge to the congregation. Be very clear about the time allotted for this portion. Five minutes may be appropriate.*)

Act of Commitment

When planning the interfaith service, arrange for children and adults to make origami boats (see instructions on pages 54-55) ahead of time, so that there will be enough for the expected number of service attendees each to have one. If desired, write a brief prayer for children on the origami paper before folding the boat, even if the prayer is as brief as "for children in poverty."

At the beginning of the act of commitment, have children carrying baskets full of the origami boats distribute them to the seated participants. Introduce the act of commitment by saying something like, "The children will now distribute origami boats bearing the hopes and prayers for our children and of our children. Take one as a symbol of your commitment to create a harbor of hope and health care for all children."

Leader: Children pushed through the pipeline to prison, not set on paths of promise, need the guidance of adults, high expectations, good schools, and real opportunities. Will you help create a harbor of hope?

People: **We will create a harbor of hope.**

Leader: Uninsured children need affordable, accessible health insurance that all of them can count on for health and mental health care, prevention and treatment. Will you help create a harbor of health care for all children?

People: **We will create a harbor of health care for all children.**

Leader: Children who are abused and neglected, children who are jeopardized by violence in their schools, neighborhoods, and communities, need the protection of caring adults and responsive systems. Will you help create a harbor of safety for all children?

People: **We will create a harbor of safety.**

Leader: Children, who cannot vote, lobby, or make campaign contributions, are ignored in the political process in favor of the rich and the powerful. They need us to be their champions and call on our elected leaders to be their champions. Will you create a harbor of justice?

People: **We will create a harbor of justice.**

Leader: May the Eternal who harbors us in the safety of divine love strengthen us to fulfill our commitment to create a harbor of care for all children.

This Prayer of Commitment by Marian Wright Edelman may be used in place of the Act of Commitment.

Prayer of Commitment

O God, make our hearts bigger
Our love deeper
Our faith stronger
Our hope unwavering
Our strength greater
Our efforts unceasing
Our voices unflinching
Our vision Yours as we seek justice and care for every child.

Blessing

Go forth, knowing that you are harbored in the love of the Eternal.
Go forth, committed to bringing children into the shelter of your care.
Go forth, to be a beacon of light that shows our children the way to safety.
Go forth, to be a voice for justice that rises over the howling winds and cuts through the obscuring fog.
Go forth, trusting in the goodness of the Eternal.

Recessional

Section 10

The activities you plan for the weekend of your Children's Sabbath are an essential part of the experience. While the worship services and education programs help people pray, learn, and reflect on what their faith calls them to do in response to the urgent needs of children, the activities give them an opportunity to put their faith into action. With the inspiration of the worship and the deepened understanding from the education programs, people will be eager to get into action right away. Whether they assemble a kit of essential health care supplies, write a letter to their legislator, or participate in a site visit to see first-hand what is happening to children without health care, the activities on the Children's Sabbath weekend will be an unforgettable part of the experience.

This section provides suggestions for several kinds of activities:

Health Coverage Awareness, Outreach, and Enrollment Activities to connect eligible uninsured children with health care coverage;

Health Coverage Advocacy Activities to help congregation members be powerful voices for justice in the campaign to ensure that *all* children have health coverage; and

A Variety of Activities to Help Children that connect congregation members with numerous hands-on service, education, and advocacy opportunities.

1. Health Coverage Awareness, Outreach, and Enrollment

Make Health Coverage Information Available to Your Congregation

Every state has material about its SCHIP and Medicaid programs. This material provides information about how to apply for these programs, what benefits are included, and what, if any, cost is involved in enrollment and participation. Your SCHIP or Medicaid offices can provide your congregation with such things as flyers, informational brochures, posters, and applications. **Contact and eligibility information for your state can be found at www.insurekidsnow.gov.**

Before the Children's Sabbath, get copies of these materials. The state can also provide updates on changes in eligibility levels, documentation requirements, and contact information.

On the Children's Sabbath, have copies of materials that describe SCHIP and Medicaid as well as applications available wherever the congregation gathers (for instance, in the fellowship hall).

After the Children's Sabbath, continue to make these materials available in an appropriate location in your congregation's buildings, such as the library, main office, main meeting hall, or in the lobby area leading to the sanctuary. Provide your religious leaders and staff with a copy of these materials so they are familiar with them and can assist those who need help.

Gather Stories of Uninsured Children to Call Us to Justice and Community

As a community of faith, we know the power of story to reveal our brokenness, our injustice, our failure to live in community, as well as the capacity of sacred story to reveal God's intention for us to live in relationships of love, justice, and wholeness with each other and with God.

Invite congregation members to share their stories of children who have had trouble getting and keeping sufficient health insurance as a witness to our need to better embody God's desire for a community of love, justice, and wholeness. Stories might include problems with red tape, inadequate benefits, being slightly above the income eligibility limit, not having access to providers, etc. Also, what effect has being uninsured had on the families, their children, and on their ability to function? Determine the best way to do this in the context of your particular congregation. Possibilities include:

- Inviting congregation members to share their stories in writing (anonymously or not, as they prefer), which could be collected and shared with the congregation as an insert to raise awareness and invite prayer and action;

- Inviting several congregation members to share their stories aloud with the congregation during worship or education time; and

- Gathering stories for a wall of witness. Invite people to post their stories of being uninsured (anonymously or not, as they prefer) or prayers for uninsured children on the wall— open if for others to read, folded if not.

Distribute Informational Materials with the Newsletter or Bulletin

Before the Children's Sabbath, if possible, contact your state or local organization involved in SCHIP and Medicaid outreach and obtain quantities of informational flyers and applications for distribution.

On the Children's Sabbath or at a later time (or several times during the year!), place a note in the bulletin, newsletter, or other mailing to alert families to the availability of child health coverage materials at the congregation's building, or enclose the informational materials themselves. Or, mail the informational flyers to the congregational mailing list.

Help Your Congregation Connect Low-Income Families with Health Care and Other Benefits They Need

Before or on the Children's Sabbath weekend, organize a team to conduct community outreach for SCHIP and Medicaid and other benefits for children. Following the meeting, send the team out in pairs to distribute informational flyers, posters, and other materials.

On the Children's Sabbath, put up posters and make available flyers about the SCHIP and Medicaid programs in your place of worship and have extra copies that volunteers can place throughout the community.

Invite a Speaker on Children's Health and Mental Health Care

Invite someone from the community who is involved in children's health and mental health coverage outreach to talk about the importance of health insurance for all children and the availability of children's health coverage, either during the service or afterwards. Ask them to address as well the importance of coverage for children with special mental health needs and other disabilities. Good places to find a speaker include local child advocacy organizations, or health care providers who have experience giving care to uninsured populations, and your state's Medicaid or SCHIP offices.

Help Enroll Eligible Children in Children's Health Coverage Programs

Before the Children's Sabbath, contact your SCHIP or Medicaid office. Ask if a staff person or qualified volunteer could come to your Children's Sabbath to enroll any eligible families or if a volunteer from the congregation could be trained to help with the enrollment process. Publicize the availability of child health coverage enrollment assistance throughout the congregation and community, using posters, flyers, notices in community newspapers, and other channels.

On the Children's Sabbath, provide a location in one of your congregation's buildings that will provide privacy and confidentiality to increase congregation and community members' comfort in making use of this service. Have your enrollment volunteer or staff and enrollment materials available, and be sure people know when and where to go.

As you plan activities for the Children's Sabbath, keep the following tips in mind:

First, offer a range of activities focusing on raising awareness, hands-on service, and advocacy. Making a difference for children requires all three kinds of effort! It also enables people to choose activities based on their particular skills and interests.

Second, plan some activities that can be completed on the Children's Sabbath, such as assembling kits with health supplies to donate to organizations serving low-income families, and some that will lead people into long-term commitments, such as signing up volunteers to do outreach and enrollment for Medicaid and the State Children's Health Insurance Program or volunteer with a community health clinic once a month.

Third, plan activities that will engage all ages. For example, if there is a table to write letters to elected officials, provide crayons and markers so that young children can draw pictures to enclose or have them dictate their letters to an older child or adult.

Fourth, use the Children's Sabbath to reinforce existing congregational programs that serve children, particularly children's health (for example, highlighting accomplishments, recruiting new people to help, or soliciting donations), while introducing new opportunities to serve children and families and improve their health and well-being.

Finally, be sure you are prepared to guide people in the activities so that they understand the connection between the worship and the action. You may want to provide a preview of the activities on a bulletin insert or during the announcement time in worship. During the activity period, it works best to have several people at each activity who are prepared to explain and guide participation.

After the Children's Sabbath, make arrangements to provide this service again. Consider offering it on different days of the week and different times to be accessible to members of the community as well as the congregation. Share your experience with other congregations that may want to do the same, especially those that serve populations most likely to be uninsured (low-income and minority). If you notice members of your congregation are experiencing ongoing difficulties enrolling in child health insurance programs (for example, difficulty getting to an office to sign up), consider taking steps to overcome these barriers (for instance, asking for volunteers at the church to provide transportation).

2. Health Coverage Advocacy Activities

Gather Signatures in Support of Comprehensive Health Coverage for All Children

All children should be guaranteed access to comprehensive health benefits with easy enrollment and recertification procedures. Invite congregation members to sign CDF's petition to indicate their support for health coverage for all children. Sign up volunteers to circulate the petition in their neighborhoods, workplaces, and among friends. A copy of the petition may be downloaded from the Children's Sabbath action page at www.childrensdefense.org/childrenssabbaths.

Support a Child Advocacy Group

Invite a representative from a local or state coalition or organization that advocates on behalf of children, including advocacy for health coverage for all children. (Contact CDF for a list of state child advocacy groups.) Ask them to make a brief presentation about their group's work and how people can support it. If appropriate, have a sign-up sheet for new members, sample copies of newsletters or action alerts, and a means of making donations.

Be a Voice for Justice for Children

See the following pages for ways your congregation can speak out for justice on the Children's Sabbath weekend and throughout the year. Options include writing letters to members of Congress, writing letters to the editors of local newspapers, and planning visits to members of Congress.

Children's Sabbath Action Page! The status of the State Children's Health Insurance Program (SCHIP) and Medicaid coverage is expected to change in the months between the publication of this Children's Sabbath resource manual and the Children's Sabbath weekend in October. For the most up-to-date, effective actions you can take and resources to use in October, visit the Children's Sabbath Action Page at www.childrensdefense.org/childrenssabbaths any time after October 1st.

Tips on Writing Letters to Your Members of Congress

- Be brief. Address only one issue. A letter need not be longer than four or five sentences.

- Be specific. If you are writing about specific legislation, include its bill number or title.

- Write your own letter, adapting a sample letter as appropriate. Form letters do not receive the same attention as individually written letters.

- Be positive and constructive. Try to say something complimentary in the first paragraph. It is just as important to thank members of Congress for voting the right way as to criticize them for voting the wrong way.

- Say in your own words why the legislation matters to you and to children. Clearly state your reason for supporting or opposing the bill or issue you are writing about.

- If you have a personal story about your health or the health of your child, consider sharing it. These personal stories are the most effective way for your legislator to truly understand the issue and the impact it has on real lives.

- If you have particular knowledge or expertise, describe it. Relating the bill to local or state conditions is especially effective.

- If you wish, feel free to include a copy of a report, a newsletter story, or a local survey to support your arguments. Don't presume that the legislator is aware of such information, even if you think it is common knowledge.

- Be sure to sign your name legibly and include your address and telephone number so your Representative or Senator can respond.

- If possible, fax the letter (since postal mail may be delayed by screening procedures) or send the letter electronically. Your legislator will likely have a link on his or her Web site directing constituents to "contact us."

Step-by-Step Sample Letter

(Please note: This is written as an example only. Please feel free to write your letter in your own words to reflect your concerns, experience, and perspective.)

The Honorable _____   Or: The Honorable _____
United States Senate   United States House of Representatives
Washington, DC 20510   Washington, DC 20515

1. Introduce yourself. My name is *Janet Doe* and I am a member of *Mytown Congregation* in *Mytown*. I appreciate your commitment to public service and desire to do the right thing.

2. Share your concern for children. I am writing out of concern for uninsured children in our community and throughout America, most of whom live in working families.

3. Share your vision for children. As a person of faith, I believe providing health coverage for all of our nation's children is our moral obligation and the right thing to do. I believe every child needs and deserves health care coverage so they can get the health care they need when they are sick and for preventive care.

4. Talk about the solutions and urge action on them. Child health coverage under Medicaid and SCHIP should be simplified and consolidated into a single program that guarantees all children in America coverage for all medically necessary services. It should also improve children's access to health services by increasing the level of reimbursement to providers. I hope you will support proposals by the Children's Defense Fund that will provide health coverage for all our children. *[Visit the Children's Sabbath action page at www.childrensdefense.org/childrenssabbaths after October 1st for the latest information on legislation and needed action and an updated sample letter.]*

5. Thank the Member of Congress and ask for a reply. Thank you for your attention to our community's children and the nine million children who are uninsured. I look forward to your reply informing me of how you will address these concerns so that all children have the health coverage they need and deserve.

Sincerely,

Your name

Your address

Your telephone number

How to address your envelope:

The Honorable _____   Or: The Honorable _____
United States Senate   United States House of Representatives
Washington, DC 20510   Washington, DC 20515

Tips on Writing a Letter to the Editor

(Adapted from *Reclaiming Our Democracy: Healing the Break between People and Government* by Sam Daley-Harris)

1. Respond to a recent news story or editorial. A good letter might begin, "Your article on the new health statistics ('More Americans Are Uninsured,' Oct. 4) was excellent. Readers might want to know that of those 45 million uninsured Americans, nine million are children...." You don't have to agree with the article, editorial, or column. Say respectfully whether you think they got the story right or not and assert your views.

2. Make your letter short. Check your local paper for submission criteria; a letter should contain 200-300 words. Provide a few striking facts that might surprise an editor or a reader. ("One out of every nine children in the United States is uninsured. Most of them have parents who work.")

3. Use descriptive words that communicate your passion about the issue. Don't be dry. ("Imagine walking into a classroom of 27 second grade students. Could you look around and pick out three children in that room who don't deserve health insurance?")

4. Offer a solution to the problem. "The Children's Defense Fund's proposed plan would simplify and consolidate children's health coverage into a single federal program that guarantees all children in America access to health coverage for all medically necessary services. The proposal also improves children's access to health services by increasing the level of reimbursement to providers."

5. Review. Re-read your letter and check for any spelling or grammatical mistakes before you submit it. Include your address and day and evening phone numbers; editors usually verify the identity of the writer before they print the letter.

3. Various Activities for the Children's Sabbath Weekend

Host a "Hope and Health Care for Children" Community Forum

Invite a panel of speakers to address health and mental health care and what we can do to assure children get the health care they need. Possible speakers include the medical director or head of clinical staff from a community health clinic or neighborhood health center; the chief of obstetrics or pediatrics at a local public, community, or children's hospital; the agency head of the city or county health department; the head of the state maternal and child health agency; the director of the state Medicaid agency (usually part of the state's welfare or health agency) and the state Children's Health Insurance Program; pediatricians, a school nurse or parish nurse; or a staff person from a statewide health advocacy organization. Invite a member of your congregation who is a health professional to help coordinate and moderate the session. Include a panelist who can speak about relevant initiatives in Congress and the state legislature. Ask the speakers to describe the problems (causes and effects) as well as the solutions and how people can help. Have a question and answer session so members can learn how they can act for change.

In addition to hearing from professionals working in these areas, when possible and appropriate arrange to hear from the real "experts": those who are personally affected by the issue, such as parents, grandparents or other relatives raising children, or youths. Also consider inviting legislators or candidates for public office to serve as panelists or to respond to what the panelists present.

Invite members of the community to attend the forum in addition to your congregation's members. You may want to invite another area congregation to join you in sponsoring this forum. See the media tips in Section 3 for ideas about inviting the media to cover your forum.

Distribute "Bring Hope and Healing" Pledge Cards

Ahead of time, prepare social action pledge cards that list all of the opportunities to help children through your place of worship for the coming year, such as volunteering with the education program or after-school or summer programs, participating in

service projects (e.g., Habitat for Humanity), mentoring young people, leading youth retreats, preparing food for the soup kitchen, or any other efforts in which your congregation is engaged. Include one-time and weekly opportunities. By listing all of the service opportunities in one place, you will help the congregation get a better picture of all the ways your congregation is meeting children's needs and give them an opportunity to find the right place for them to help, notes *Lirdof Tzedek: A Guide to Synagogue Social Action.* Distributing pledge cards on the Children's Sabbath takes advantage of the increased attention and commitment that the weekend generates. Collect the completed cards so that the appropriate staff or volunteers can follow up with members to fulfill their pledges at the appropriate times throughout the year. (Congregations of traditions that would not write on the day of the activities can mail the cards in later.) **Harcourt Parish (Episcopal) in Gambier, Ohio**, included their pledge cards in the worship bulletins on the Children's Sabbath and collected and blessed them as part of the service.

Prepare a Health Care Map of Your Community

In the weeks before the Children's Sabbath, prepare a health care map of your community that shows the health services available to people in various neighborhoods. Alongside it place a chart that shows the health services that are available to people at various economic levels in your community. Display it on your Children's Sabbath. Distribute copies to other congregations and community groups.

Serve Healthy Snacks

During the coffee hour, oneg Shabbat, or other community gathering for snacks or a meal, instead of or in addition to the usual fare, provide healthy food such as cut-up fresh fruit, vegetables, water, and 100 percent fruit juice. Include children's favorites such as small containers of yogurt, small sandwich squares, and dried fruit snacks.

Organize a "Walk for Hope and Health Care for Children"

Plan a measured route (perhaps five miles or 10 kilometers) through your community. Arrange for stops at some of the sources of health care identified on your community health map (see above). Invite walkers to solicit pledges to be donated to a hospital or clinic serving children or to support children's health care through some other means. The route for the walk could include stops at the local hospital or health clinic or WIC site, with a brief prayer offered before continuing on the walk. Make and carry a banner or signs that will help educate the community and show your congregation's concern for children's health. Involve people who are not able to join in the walk to serve as sponsors making pledges, sign and banner makers, and in other roles. This would be a great activity to do together with other congregations in your community.

Make Cards to Thank People Who Help Children

Ahead of time, compile a list of people who are working for children's health and well-being. On the Children's Sabbath, involve all ages in writing and decorating cards of thanks to send to them, as did **Advent Lutheran Church in Anoka, Minnesota.** They distributed their cards to members of a group that makes quilts for children and to people who volunteer with the Family Table Meal Program each month to help feed hungry children.

Prepare Healthy Food for Hungry Children

Ahead of time, contact a program serving low-income or homeless children, such as a shelter, after-school program, or soup kitchen. Arrange to provide nutritious food on the day of your Children's Sabbath celebration or the next day. During the activity time, engage members of all ages in preparing the food to be served—either at your congregation to be delivered or at the shelter, soup kitchen, or other site.

Or, collect nutritious food donations (announced in advance) and engage people in packing bags to be distributed to hungry families through a food pantry or other organization. Children can color paper shopping bags to carry the food.

Sponsor a Faith in Action Fair

Arrange for a variety of organizations and programs to set up tables with information about opportunities to volunteer, donate, or advocate, as did **Christ United Methodist Church in Norfolk, Virginia.** Include both congregational programs and community-based organizations. Encourage those staffing the tables to bring photographs or other visuals to depict their work and copies of newsletters or brochures. Urge them to be specific about volunteer needs. When possible, encourage

them to offer a variety of options for ways individuals or congregations can support their organizations.

Help Working Families Keep More of What They Earn to Make Ends Meet

Before the Children's Sabbath, find out about Volunteer Income Tax Assistance (VITA) sites in your community or other places that are conducting outreach and enrollment efforts to help low-income families receive the benefits for which they are eligible. On the Children's Sabbath, sign up volunteers for these existing outreach projects. To find a nearby VITA site:

Call the IRS at 1 (800) TAX-1040 or 1 (800) 849-1040.

- Visit the Children's Defense Fund's Web site (www.childrensdefense.org/tbo) to find a list of free tax preparation sites and other information.

- Visit the AARP's Web site (www.aarp.org/money/taxaide) or call their toll-free hotline for information: 1 (888) 227-7669

- Visit the American Bar Association's Web site at www.abanet.org/tax/sites.html.

Ahead of time, arrange for a trainer to come and train members as VITA volunteers who will work at local VITA sites to assist eligible families in getting the Earned Income Tax Credits they are due. Call CDF at (202) 662-3542 for help arranging for a trainer.

Conduct a Site Visit to See First-Hand the Challenges and Solutions

Arrange a tour to raise awareness of children's needs and solutions (on the Children's Sabbath weekend or the following week). Have people sign up in advance to participate. Visit, for example, a neonatal intensive care unit or pediatric wing of a hospital, Head Start program, shelter or soup kitchen serving families, community health center, local clinic, or congregational program (your own or another's) for children. For each site, have the host provide a briefing about the children and/or families they serve, the kinds of need they see, the causes and the solutions. Have them discuss how people can work for positive solutions to prevent or address the needs. Where possible and appropriate, provide an opportunity to talk with the children and/or families being served, not just those who staff the programs. End with a debriefing that helps participants process what they have seen and heard and identify ways that they will respond.

Collect a Boatload of Items That Help Children Get the Start They Need

Check with organizations serving children in need in your community for specific needs, and consider items such as children's toothbrushes and children's toothpaste; first aid kit items such as adhesive bandages, children's pain reliever, thermometers, and a paperback copy of *Dr. Spock's Baby and Child Care*; or safety items such as cabinet locks and electrical outlet guards. These could be distributed through a food pantry, shelter serving homeless families, health clinic, or other avenue. You could also collect books, puzzles, and toys for the waiting room of a community health clinic, or Medicaid or WIC site. In advance, ask congregation members to bring in some of the items on the Children's Sabbath. Alternatively, purchase the items with approved congregational funds. On the Children's Sabbath, gather the items in a centrally located canoe, rowboat, inflatable boat, or cardboard box constructed to look like a boat. If appropriate for your tradition, on or near the boat post a sign that says, "Dear Lord, Be good to me. The sea is so wide and my boat is so small."

Section 11

The Children's Sabbath is about much more than one weekend a year; it is about energizing *year-round* efforts to improve the lives of children. It is important for your place of worship to continue working throughout the year to help meet the immediate needs of children without health care and to achieve justice for all children. This may mean re-energizing existing efforts for children in your place of worship, inspiring individuals to make new commitments to volunteer, donate, advocate, or help children in need in some other way, or it may mean that the congregation as a whole develops a new program or other effort to improve the lives of children and bring hope and health care to them.

Keeping the momentum going after your Children's Sabbath celebration is as important, or more important, than the event itself. This chapter offers suggestions and ideas for doing that. Program ideas are presented in three separate sections:

1) **Continue to Campaign for Comprehensive Child Health Coverage.** The first section describes follow-up ideas to create connections to assure children health care coverage—connections with other congregations, organizations, health care providers, families, and others;

2) **Every Voice and Vote Counts!** The second section provides ways you can give voice to children's concerns in this election season for the children who cannot vote for themselves; and

3) **Give It a Try!** Third are follow-up ideas that can be launched fairly easily without much planning or expense, as well as other ideas to reinforce and increase your congregation's efforts to serve and speak up for children.

Continue to Campaign for Comprehensive Child Health Coverage

We must not give up until every child in our rich nation has health coverage. God never gives up on us and never stops expecting us to pursue justice, show compassion, and live as a community that seeks the health and wholeness of all, especially for the youngest, poorest, excluded and most vulnerable members of our society. The Children's Defense Fund won't give up until all children have the health coverage they need and deserve, and we hope that you will be committed partners with us in that campaign to assure all children health care.

Designate congregational child health campaign liaisons: Designate two congregation members, or designate a staff member or committee, to be the liaison for your congregation to CDF's Healthy Child Campaign. Email their contact information to mrosen@childrensdefense.org and he will ensure that they are connected to the campaign and have the information and tools to help win health justice for all children. In addition, encourage individual members to sign up for CDF's monthly e-newsletter so they can stay informed of children's needs and what they can do. Individuals can sign up at www.childrensdefense.org/newsletter.

Partner with local community organizations to enroll eligible children in SCHIP and Medicaid programs: Identify an organization to meet with, and discuss with them how a partnership between your organizations could help to enroll more eligible children in SCHIP and Medicaid. Some potential collaborative partners can be your state's local *Covering Kids and Families* grantees. For more information, visit www.coveringkidsandfamilies.org. (If you meet prior to the Children's Sabbath, the following suggestions may take place on the Children's Sabbath itself. If you meet with the organization after the Children's Sabbath, select another date to launch your joint outreach.)

- Plan a time or times when families can get assistance in completing applications for the SCHIP or Medicaid programs.
- Publicize this through congregational communications as well as throughout the community. Place an announcement in the local newspaper and distribute flyers with the information to families who come in contact with your congregation. Encourage all families with uninsured children to apply for coverage.
- Provide space for staff or volunteers from a community organization involved in enrollment to assist families after the service, or arrange for a congregation member to be trained to assist with enrollment.

Designate a children's health insurance outreach coordinator: Designate or recruit a staff person or volunteer in the congregation to promote enrollment in SCHIP or Medicaid programs, to coordinate enrollment activities with local child advocates, and to provide members of the congregation with information about how to enroll their children. This person should learn about different ways people are eligible for these programs, and be aware that children of different ages in the same family may be eligible for coverage under different programs. Contact the state agency that operates the SCHIP and Medicaid programs to coordinate training for your children's health insurance outreach coordinator.

Display information in congregation buildings: Place SCHIP and Medicaid information and applications in your congregation's office, library, social hall or other gathering room, and near the classrooms for religious education or a weekday school or child care program. All faith-based organizations should display general information about the programs, including where families can go to get assistance.

Connect with other local child advocates and coalitions: Meet with local service providers, community groups, local organizations, other faith-based organizations, and neighborhood associations to promote enrollment among their members. Form or join a child health coalition with members from these groups. This will give your coordinator an opportunity to assess what outreach activities are currently underway and provide a better understanding of the role your organization can play in helping to assist the community with outreach and enrollment efforts.

Find out about children's mental health advocacy in your community and state: All states have active family groups that work to promote services and supports for children with emotional, behavioral or mental disorders and their families. Identify them and work in partnership with them and other advocates to promote help for children in need of mental health services. For local contacts, visit the Federation of Families for Children's Mental Health Web site at www.ffcmh.org.

Coordinate with state agencies: Your state's agency for SCHIP and Medicaid can provide your coordinator with information and materials for outreach, as well as information on resources available through the state to conduct outreach and educational activities. The state agency can also provide information to send out to your congregation mailing list. This information might include updates on enrollment levels, information on materials that are available from the state and how to order them, and information on other outreach campaigns or activities that have been successful in your state or region.

Engage the health care community: Talk to administrators in local hospitals, doctors, and staff in health clinics and invite them to partner with your congregation on outreach and enrollment activities. Many communities have health vans that go out to communities and provide immunizations and vision and hearing screenings. A health van could be included in a day of children's health and enrollment.

Sponsor a "Sign Them Up" enrollment booth at local congregation and community events: Talk to event planners for any events your congregation or community is planning and encourage them to add outreach and enrollment in SCHIP and Medicaid to their events. Local advocates from the local child health coalition may be able to staff these events.

Work with local business leaders: Send out a request asking local stores to display outreach information at checkout counters and put outreach flyers in shopping bags, on food tray liners, and on ticket stubs. Ask utility companies to include a flyer about SCHIP and Medicaid with the bills they send to customers. Encourage local businesses to provide good, affordable health coverage for their employees and families.

Recruit other faith-based organizations in your child health work: Ask these congregations or religious organizations to promote SCHIP and Medicaid in their weekly bulletins, newsletter, or as part of a sermon. Ask faith-based organizations to incorporate outreach and enrollment activities into their bazaars, child care centers, schools, food pantries, and community-based work with low- and moderate-income populations.

Build a diverse group representing children most likely to be uninsured—African American, Latino, and low-income families: It is essential to assemble a diverse group in your efforts to reach families. Diversity will enable you to identify cultural barriers that have kept families from enrolling in these programs. If your congregation doesn't include a significant number of members representing these key populations, think through how you can forge those connections. Contacting ministerial alliances, community cultural organizations, social service agencies, and other congregations are good ways to start.

Every Voice and Vote Counts!

Children can't vote so their needs are often ignored in the election process. In the coming year, your congregation can ensure that children's concerns aren't ignored in the campaigns for public office, that as many people as possible are registered to vote, and that we are all informed on what candidates have done and commit to do for children—especially those who are poor, uninsured, and facing other challenges.

Educate members about the role of congregations in elections: Some congregation members may be confused about what is or isn't legal or appropriate for congregations to do in an election year. Of course, it is never legal or appropriate for a religious congregation to endorse a particular candidate or political party. It is, however, legal and appropriate for congregations to encourage every eligible person to vote and to ask non-partisan questions about priorities and commitments to meet the needs of America's children. It is equally important to alert congregation members about upcoming local elections and make them aware of any issues affecting children and families that may be on the ballot. A good idea might be to hold a special session after services or at another time to inform members about upcoming elections and what is and isn't legal and appropriate congregational activity in an election year. In addition to the materials here, contact your denomination, movement, or faith tradition's national staff for any materials they might have on these topics.

Resources are available from several sources, including:

The Religious Action Center for Reform Judaism, www.rac.org, has a Voter Information Center with excellent resources including a comprehensive "Get Out the Vote Guide," "Some Thoughts on Citizenship, Responsibility, and Political Involvement," "The IRS, the Congregation, and the Election," and "Top Ten Ideas to Mobilize Voters." Visit www.rac.org/advocacy/specialresources/vote.

The Interfaith Alliance, www.interfaithalliance.org. Resources include *Religion and Politics: A Guide for Houses of Worship*, designed to "help religious leaders understand: the importance of encouraging members to vote but never telling them for whom to vote; that a partnership between religion and government can and should preserve the autonomy of houses of worship and ensure that religious institutions are not held

hostage to the priorities and interests of federal, state, or local governments; and that religion's powerful healing force in politics can be severely compromised when America's shared values are replaced by values that advance only particular sectarian interests"; and *Navigating Politics and the Pulpit*, a recorded phone seminar with the IRS that covers the guidelines for what are appropriate activities by houses of worship in an election year. Also included is a question and answer session with the IRS and various religious leaders around the country.

Sojourners, www.sojo.net, has a 20-page resource, *Voting God's Politics: Election Action Guide*, available for download at www.sojo.net/Action/Alerts/VGP_Election_Action_Guide.pdf. It includes helpful articles, prayers, tips, a summary of what is and isn't allowable for congregations to do in an election, and suggestions for what young people can do in an election year even though they are too young to vote.

The U.S. Conference of Catholic Bishops has a variety of resources available through the "Faithful Citizenship" section of their Web site at www.usccb.org/faithfulcitizenship.

Register voters: Help people in your congregation and community get registered to vote. It is never too soon to get started. Don't wait for a big election year, when deadlines loom. Make this an on-going effort in your congregation. Find ways to reach out to different kinds of constituents:

- **Congregation members**: Remind congregation members of the importance of registering to vote and voting. Send out letters or emails, and include information in the newsletter, bulletin, or during announcement time. Have a voter registration table and forms available in the congregation's gathering spot and during large congregational events. Include special outreach to members who are homebound or in nursing care facilities or retirement communities. Reach out to college students, too.

- **Community members:** Join with other congregations or community groups to conduct voter registration, especially in areas that are typically under-represented in voter registration and turn-out. Voter registration booths might be set up at public transportation terminals, grocery stores, near health clinics, food pantries, and other locations. Train volunteers, reminding them that they must not discuss for whom new registrants should vote. Equip them with necessary supplies (pens, forms, clipboards, and so forth), and make sure they know who will submit the collected forms at the end of each day. If appropriate, have someone with the necessary language skills for particular neighborhoods.

Sponsor a candidate forum: Join with other congregations in your community to host a candidate forum so that voters can become informed about the candidates' policy positions that will affect children and families, so they can make informed decisions in the voting booths. Here are planning tips for a candidate forum, excerpted and adapted from the Religious Action Center for Reform Judaism's "Get Out the Vote Guide":

- Invite candidates well in advance to ensure that they make time for the event in their campaign schedules; or for presidential elections, to allow the candidates' representatives to get it on their calendar ahead of time.

- Invite all of the candidates who are running for a particular office. (For details on the rules, download RAC's "Get Out the Vote Guide" at www.rac.org.)

- Choose moderators who are non-partisan and knowledgeable about a wide range of relevant issues.

- Publicize the candidate forum in the congregational/organizational community and/or in the community at large (local newspaper announcements, flyers, etc.).

- Prepare questions on a wide range of issues affecting children (For details on the rules, download RAC's "Get Out the Vote Guide" at www.rac.org.)

- When introducing the event, be sure to state that the organization does not endorse any of the candidates who appear and that their views are their own and do not represent the sponsoring organization.

- Give all candidates equal time for introductions, questions and answers, and concluding remarks.

- Do not allow candidates to distribute campaign materials at the event.

- It is permissible to invite all of the candidates to appear on separate evenings if the events are all equivalent (e.g., you cannot invite one candidate to speak to the congregation on Yom Kippur or Rally Day or Palm Sunday and another to speak on a regular weeknight).

Check out "Tips for Conducting Candidate Forums" from the U.S. Conference of Catholic Bishops at www.usccb.org/faithfulcitizenship/pdf/tips.pdf for additional helpful suggestions.

Host a "Children's Concerns in the Election" night: Your efforts to register and mobilize voters to be a voice for children should include education for voters on children's concerns. Invite speakers representing a variety of perspectives to present information and give the public an opportunity to make informed decisions about the kind of leaders our children need and deserve.

Here are planning guidelines, excerpted and adapted from the Religious Action Center for Reform Judaism's "Get Out the Vote Guide":

- Invite people to speak on both sides of an issue. Presenters may be non-profit professionals, academics, local, state, or federal lobbyists, or others with expertise in the policy area under discussion.

- Include an introduction by a religious leader to provide context about why these issues are important to the religious community, without endorsing one policy position over another.

- Present the issues objectively and fully.

- Just as a candidate forum cannot be focused on a single issue on which the views of the non-profit organization sponsoring the event are known, "issue nights" must cover multiple issues to avoid implicit endorsements of specific candidates (whether or not they are present). For example, hold an evening focused on poverty, health care, and education.

Ask questions: Distribute copies of the questions on page 176 to congregation and community members. In any encounter with a candidate for public office—whether at a town hall forum, call-in radio program, or "meet and greet" event—ask them these questions. Write to their campaign headquarters and ask for a response.

Questions to Ask Any Candidate Who Wants Your Vote

1. How will you ensure that America's nine million uninsured children are guaranteed health coverage with a comprehensive and equal benefit package and simple enrollment to get and keep children covered?

2. What will you do to reduce child poverty in our nation?

3. How will you break up the cradle to prison pipeline that is routing so many of our young people into jail and away from productive futures?

4. When faced with a choice to give tax breaks to the wealthy or to help children and working poor families, what will you do?

5. To what extent does our nation have a moral obligation to protect children from the worst ravages of hunger, homelessness, poverty, lack of health care, and violence? How will you lead our nation in meeting that obligation?

For additional questions that you might ask candidates, see the letter from Marian Wright Edelman on page 1.

Spread the word about the "Elect Susie" campaign: ElectSusie.com is the Web site for CDF's campaign to ensure that all children in the United States have health insurance. "Susie Flynn" is a symbolic candidate, a 10-year-old child running for President of the United States to help our nation's millions of uninsured children. As her Web site notes, "This is a crisis. These children have been let down, yet the people accountable are doing too little to solve it. By running for President, I intend to make everyone in America aware of the issue so that it will no longer be ignored. Under your next President, every child in America must get the health insurance he or she deserves."

Visit the Elect Susie Web site, www.electsusie.com, to find out how you can spread the word about this campaign to get children's health concerns addressed in the presidential election.

Give It a Try!

Consider the interests of your congregation, the needs of children in your community, and the resources your congregation has to offer. Find ways to strengthen what your congregation already does for children and new opportunities to serve and speak out for children.

Start a Child Advocacy Book Group

Select a book or other resource on children's concerns and child advocacy. The resource section in this book has many suggested titles. For churches an excellent book to start with is *Thus Far on the Way: Toward a Theology of Child Advocacy* by Eileen W. Lindner. Your faith tradition's Web site or publishing house may have additional resources. How you structure the book group can be tailored to suit the interests and availability of group members. You could meet weekly and discuss one chapter of the resource or monthly to discuss the entire resource.

Create a Child Advocacy Bulletin Board

Choose a public gathering place for your bulletin board to share news about children in need and initiatives taken by the local, state, and federal government on economic justice and children's concerns. Contact your faith group's public policy office or other body providing legislative and justice information and post that on the bulletin board as well. Use the bulletin board to highlight ways that your congregation is already meeting the needs of children and to highlight opportunities for members and visitors to also support those efforts.

Set up a Justice for Children Letter-Writing Table

Establish a Justice for Children letter-writing table that is available to congregation members every week or once a month. Supply it with paper, pens, envelopes, and action alerts or other advocacy information from your faith group's Washington or public policy office or a children's concerns group like the Children's Defense Fund. See pages 165-167 for a sample letter and tips.

Take a Comprehensive Look at Justice for Children in Your Place of Worship

Convene a group or work within an existing committee to take a comprehensive look at the place of children and child advocacy in the entire life of your place of worship: in the services or prayers, in the education programs, in outreach, in faith community gatherings and events, and in its justice work. Also survey the congregational resources that might be available to further meet children's needs; not just financial resources, but in-kind resources and human resources. Make a plan that draws on your congregation's greatest resources to meet children's needs in the congregation and community.

Many faith traditions have publications and other resources that can help you strengthen and extend your work with and for children and justice throughout the life of your place of worship, such as the Union for Reform Judaism's *Lirdof Tzedek: A Guide to Synagogue Social Action*; the Roman Catholic Church's *Catholic Campaign for Children and Families: Parish Resource Manual*; the United Methodist Church's *Putting Children and Their Families First: A Planning Handbook for Congregations; A Church for All God's Children*; and *Safe Haven for Children, Hope for Congregations and Communities* are just a few examples. See the resource section in this manual for more publications that can help your congregation make a holistic plan to strengthen and expand its work with and for children.

Build Relationships with Elected Leaders to Help Them Be Voices for Children's Justice

Help members build relationships with legislators to urge them to protect the needs of children, especially those in greatest need. When key justice concerns arise, gather concerned members to prepare for visits with elected officials. The following pages provide tips for visits with members of Congress. Contact your faith group's Washington or public policy office, if it has one, for information on key concerns and legislative action alerts. The Children's Defense Fund also provides information and alerts at www.childrensdefense.org/action.

Meeting with Your Legislators

Before Your Visit

Begin planning for your visit. Don't worry if you have butterflies in your stomach at the thought of meeting with your legislator for the first time. It would be unusual if you didn't. Know that the best way to communicate with your legislator is to make a personal visit. You probably will enjoy the experience—and the legislator will appreciate the time you spent communicating your views. So take a deep breath and begin planning! First, decide on the issues you want to discuss.

Make an appointment. When making an appointment, explain what issue you would like to discuss. If the legislator is unavailable, the aide who deals with your issue often will be knowledgeable and influential in helping to form the member's views. Don't feel slighted if you end up meeting with the aide. He or she can be very influential and, if your meeting goes well, may also encourage your legislator to meet with you in person the next time.

Do your homework. Study the legislator's voting record on a number of issues, using CDF Action Council's nonpartisan Congressional Scorecard (www.cdfactioncouncil.org) and other sources, so you can comment on something positive, if possible, and know if the particular issue is one on which the legislator tends to agree or disagree with you. If there is a bill that interests you, know its status and whether your legislator has taken a position on it.

Remember the experts! Parents, grandparents, service providers, educators, religious and business leaders, police officers, doctors and nurses, and others who witness children's needs on a daily basis are children's best advocates. They really are the experts when it comes to how bills and policies will affect children, and it's important that policy makers have a wide variety of people to call upon when they have questions about their work's impact on children. Children's advocacy groups often seek out these everyday experts to present the most compelling information during legislative visits. Tell of personal experiences you have had, if possible, to illustrate your point.

Be prepared. Before meeting with the legislator or aide, plan and organize your presentation and practice what you are going to say. If you are going with other people to the meeting, get together beforehand to make sure that you all have the same purpose. Take along helpful information to back up your arguments: newspaper articles about the problems children face, statistics, or a fact sheet. CDF can provide some of the information you need. Call the Religious Action Division at (202) 662-3555 or visit CDF's Web site at www.childrensdefense.org/religiousaction.

During Your Visit

Make your message concise. You may think your meeting is for 30 minutes and then arrive to find the legislator's schedule so tight that you get only five minutes. Know exactly what you want to say and be prepared to say it quickly, if circumstances demand that.

Present solutions. People often feel overwhelmed by problems they consider too massive and diverse for corrective action so don't just talk about the problem. Share one or two concrete ideas for ways to improve the lives of children in your community. Tell your legislator what it will take to ensure that all children get the help they need.

Talk about what works. Using success stories of real children and families who are being helped by Head Start, child care, job training, or health insurance will strengthen your argument and counter claims that all government programs are ineffective.

Search for common ground. Don't be exclusive or judgmental. Keeping in mind the wide range of viewpoints in Congress and in every community and state legislature, frame your messages carefully to include words and themes that will reach new audiences and persuade them to become new allies. Children's advocates care as much as anyone about efficiency, accountability, fiscal responsibility, and personal responsibility. Use themes like these to frame your message.

Be honest. It's fine to say you don't know the answer to a question and to promise to provide information later by phone, fax, or email. This also gives you another opportunity to contact their office.

Following Your Visit

Build a relationship. The better your communication, the more seriously you will be taken, and the more willing the representative and his or her staff will be to rely upon you and your judgments.

Follow up your visit with a letter thanking the legislator for the time spent listening to your concerns. Enclose any documentation you had agreed to provide to bolster your position, and briefly restate your views.

Provide additional information. Send articles, write letters with further information, or offer assistance in thinking through solutions that could work in your community.

Call periodically with updates. It's important to stay in touch, and a good way to do that is to call your legislator's office from time to time with new information.

Invite them to speak. Invite the representative or the staff person who handles children's issues to speak before your congregation or a community group in which you are involved.

Invite them to a site visit. Invite the legislator to visit a successful child-serving program with which you work, such as an after-school program, conflict resolution program, or Head Start class.

Show broad support for your concerns. If your legislator or aide disagrees or is noncommittal, don't threaten or argue after you have made your case, because it is counterproductive. A better strategy is to plan another visit bringing others along to show more community support for your position, to put together a bunch of letters from constituents, or to think of another tactic such as a letter to the editor. Persistence often pays.

Watch how your legislator votes and respond. If the legislator votes with your position on the issue, recognize that vote with a written "thank you." Such recognition may influence his or her next vote on children's issues. It also lets your legislator know that you are watching closely. If the legislator votes against your position, write or call to express your disappointment and urge reconsideration of the issue the next time it comes up for a vote.

Section 12

As you plan your Children's Sabbath, initiate new long-term programs and commitments and reinvigorate existing efforts to help children and families draw on the wealth of resources provided by faith communities and the Children's Defense Fund. The social justice, governmental affairs, or human services divisions of your denomination or faith tradition's national and regional offices can often provide you with resources, advocacy ideas, and policy statements to assist you in your efforts on behalf of children. In addition, your community and state have children's advocacy and social service agencies that can provide useful information and resources.

Resources from the Children's Defense Fund

Be sure to visit CDF's Web site at www.childrensdefense. org for up-to-date information, action alerts, and resources. The Religious Action section of CDF's Web site provides information about the Children's Sabbath, the Samuel DeWitt Proctor Institute for Child Advocacy Ministry, and more.

Sign up for the Children's Defense Fund's e-newsletter (www.childrensdefense.org/newsletter) to receive brief monthly updates on events, resources, and actions, including those of particular interest to faith communities.

All of the following may be ordered by visiting the Web store at www.childrensdefense.org or by calling (865) 457-6466.

Katrina's Children: Still Waiting 2007
In 2006, CDF released *Katrina's Children: A Call to Conscience and Action*, a report highlighting the trauma and heartrending stories of young Katrina evacuees struggling with their devastating losses. As our nation's attention has moved on to the next big story, thousands of Katrina survivors are still scattered across the country or crowded into "temporary" trailers waiting to return home. This second "call to conscience and action" looks at where Katrina's children are now and what still needs to be done to help them get their lives back and address their health and mental health needs, especially as it relates to chronic and acute traumatic stress disorder. Report is available for free by calling (865) 457-6466 or it can be downloaded from www.childrensdefense.org.

In Harm's Way: True Stories of Uninsured Texas Children
Texas has the highest rate of uninsured children in the nation, 20.2 percent, compared to 11.6 percent nationally. In this report from CDF Texas, families lacking health coverage tell their stories, from frustrating to frightening, of the overwhelming obstacles they encountered in trying to get medical care and health insurance for their children. This report is dedicated to Devante Johnson, who went without health coverage for four months while struggling against cancer of the kidneys. He died at the age of 14 in March 2007. The report can be downloaded for free from the CDF Web site at www.childrensdefense.org.

The State of America's Children 2005
This edition of CDF's analysis of the status of children in America puts a special focus on child poverty and the nearly 13 million children who are poor, and includes the latest developments and data related to family income, child welfare, child health and the State Children's Health Insurance Program (SCHIP), early childhood development, education, and juvenile justice. Foreword by Marian Wright Edelman offers both vision and challenge. The 2005 edition can be downloaded for free from www.childrensdefense.org

I Can Make a Difference
Marian Wright Edelman has drawn from a variety of cultures and peoples to compile these timeless stories, poems, quotations, and folktales that speak to all children to let them know they can make a difference in today's world. Illustrated by Barry Moser, the book highlights 12 values children and youth can aspire to achieve. Available in bookstores and through CDF. HarperCollins Publishers, hardcover $19.99

Lanterns: A Memoir of Mentors
Marian Wright Edelman, founder and president of the Children's Defense Fund, shares powerful stories about the mentors in her life from her childhood through the Civil Rights Movement to the founding and building of CDF. She pays tribute to the extraordinary personal mentors who helped light her way: Martin Luther King, Jr., Robert F. Kennedy, Fannie Lou Hamer, William Sloane Coffin, Ella Baker, Mae Bertha Carter, and many others. She brings home the importance of mentoring, caring about, and standing for children every day. 180 pp., 1999. Hardcover $20.00, softcover $14.00

The Measure of Our Success: A Letter to My Children and Yours by Marian Wright Edelman
A touching and moral message from Marian Wright Edelman to her sons—a message both introspective and compelling that all of us can use in our daily struggle to find the right balance. She passes on a family legacy based on service to others and the 25 lessons for life she wants most to impart to her sons. 97 pp., 1992. Hardcover $12.00, softcover $9.00

Guide My Feet: Prayers and Meditations on Loving and Working for Children by Marian Wright Edelman

Marian Wright Edelman offers inspiration, prayers of thanksgiving, pleas for guidance, and pledges of commitment. Beacon Press, 210 pp., 1995. Hardcover $17.95, softcover $10.00

Hold My Hand: Prayers for Building a Movement to Leave No Child Behind by Marian Wright Edelman

An inspiring collection of heartfelt prayers of thanksgiving, prayers of petition, and pledges of commitment that will move and encourage you. Also includes information on CDF's Leave No Child Behind® movement. CDF, 92 pp., 2001. $6.95

"A Prayer for Children" video

This moving poem by Ina Hughs is read by Marian Wright Edelman, along with footage of children, creating an inspirational three-minute video that may be used in worship, educational programs, or to begin or end a meeting. $6.00

Holding Children in Prayer: A Lenten Guide

Each spring renew your spirit and your commitment to children with this Lenten Guide offering daily lessons, reflections, and prayers to encourage and strengthen your commitment to continue serving and advocating for children. CDF, 60 pp., 2005. $2.00

Holding Children in Prayer: An Advent Guide

During the holiday season keep children in your thoughts and prayers with this Advent Guide. Includes Lighting the Advent Candle, Scripture Reading, Reflection, Prayer, and Act in Faith for every day of Advent. CDF, 72 pp., 2001. $2.00

I'm Your Child, God: Prayers for Our Children

by Marian Wright Edelman. Contemporary, multi-cultural prayers for children and teens dealing with the complexities of growing up in today's world, accompanied by stunning illustrations by Caldecott Honor Medal winner Bryan Collier. 2002, 90 pp., $19.99

Faith and Tax Credits Toolkit

A toolkit for the faith community that provides detailed information on the Earned Income and Child Tax Credits and contains tools for reaching out to the faith community. CDF, 4 pp., 2007. Available online at www.childrensdefense.org.

Did Your Members of Congress Protect Children? The 2006 Children's Defense Fund Action Council Nonpartisan Congressional Scorecard

This Scorecard documents how well your state's congressional delegation voted to protect the children in your state and the nation in 2006. Based on crucial votes that affected the lives of millions of children in America, the CDF Action Council names the best and worst Senators and Representatives in protecting children. Download the 2006 edition free at www.childrensdefense.org

Dream Me Home Safely: Writers on Growing Up in America

This book tells the stories of the many ways children make a place for themselves in their families' hearts and in the world. With insight, skill, great humor, and zestful candor, the writers offer a glimpse of their childhood selves. Written by some of America's most outstanding authors (Anna Quindlen, Alice Walker, Joyce Carol Oates, and many others), this compilation highlights the complexities and preciousness of childhood and the importance of family and rituals in the lives of children. Houghton Mifflin, 2003. $13.00

Other Resources

Our Day to End Poverty: 24 Ways You Can Make a Difference by Shannon Daley-Harris and Jeffrey Keenan with Karen Speerstra

Imagine ending poverty at home and around the globe in our own lifetimes. With creativity this book invites us to look at our very ordinary days, from waking up in the morning to going to bed at night, and to begin to think about combating poverty in new, inventive ways. San Francisco: Berrett-Koehler 2007.

Amazing Grace: The Lives of Children and the Conscience of a Nation by Jonathan Kozol

This book draws extensively upon poverty as spoken through the voices of children and their families who live in the South Bronx, the poorest congressional district in the United States. New York: Crown, 1995.

The following are Unitarian Universalist Association resources and/or other resources available through the UUA Bookstore. Phone: 1 (800) 215-9076, email: bookstore@uua.org

Common Fire by Laurent A. Parks Daloz, et al., Beacon, 1997

Landmark study reveals how we became committed to the common good and sustain our commitments in a changing world. Discussion guide available online at http://www.beacon-press.org/client/uu_guides/2005dg.cfm

The Best Things in Life Aren't Things: Celebrating What Matters Most by Joann Davis

Through inspirational essays on family, faith, friends, virtue, service, community, and the beauty of the natural world, the author explores and celebrates the real stuff of life. She reminds us that life is a spiritual exercise that brings fulfillment when we savor the intangibles that are often right in front of us. Beacon, 2003.

How Much Do We Deserve? An Inquiry into Distributive Justice by Richard Gilbert

"It is my intent to bridge the gap between scholars in economic and theological/ethical disciplines and concerned laity and clergy." Draws on Jewish, Christian, Buddhist, humanist, and other traditions to reflect on ethical and economic issues. Can be ordered online at www.uua.org. Skinner House, 2001.

The Prophetic Imperative: Social Gospel in Theory and Practice by Richard Gilbert

Explores the connection between spirituality and social action. Helpfully presented in two parts, "Theoretical Foundations" and "Social Gospel in Practice." Contains vital advice and models to help congregations engage in effective justice work. Can be ordered online at www.uua.org. Skinner House, 2000.

Poems to Live by in Uncertain Times, Joan Murray (ed.)

Sixty poems by an international mix of distinguished poets, including W.H. Auden, Czeslaw Milasz, Bertolt Brecht, Yehuda Amichai, Mary Oliver, Miquel de Unamuno, Gwendolyn Brooks, Billy Collins, Yusef Komunyakaa, and Sharon Olds. In six sections: death and remembrance, fear and suffering, affirmations and rejoicings, warnings and instructions, war and rumors of war, meditations and conversations. Beacon, 2001.

You Can't Be Neutral on a Moving Train: A Personal History of Our Times by Howard Zinn

Acclaimed historian Zinn has both chronicled and participated in some of the most important social movements of our time. His experiences speak to the future as much as to the past, showing in vivid detail how small actions can effect historic change. Beacon, 1995.

The People Speak: American Voices, Some Famous, Some Little Known, Howard Zinn (ed.)

Collected dramatic readings that celebrate the enduring spirit of dissent. Here, in their own words, are Christopher Columbus, an unnamed Lowell mill girl, Frederick Douglas, John Brown, Mark Twain, Malcolm X, a Gulf War resister, a family member of a victim of the September 11 Twin Towers attack, and many others. Includes commentary by Zinn. HarperCollins, 2004.

Bahá'í Resources

The following resources all are available from Bahá'í Distribution Service: 1(800) 999-9019 or http://www.bahaibookstore.com/index.cfm:

* *In Service to the Common Good* by the National Spiritual Assembly of the Bahá'í's of the U.S., 56 pages, 2004.
* *For the Betterment of the World* by the Bahá'í International Community, 32 pages, 2002.
* *Foundations for a Spiritual Education, Research of the Bahá'í Writings*
* *Family Life* and *Bahá'í Education*, compiled by the Research Department of the Universal House of Justice
* *To Be a Mother* and *To Be a Father*, both compiled by Wendi Momen, George Ronald Press
* *When We Grow Up* by Bahiyyih Nakhjavani, George Ronald Press
* *The Brilliant Stars: The Bahá'í Faith and the Education of Children* by H.T.D. Rost, George Ronald Press
* *The Virtues Project Educator's Guide: Simple Ways to Create a Culture of Character*, Jalmar Press
* *Healing Racism: Education's Role*, Editors: Nathan Rutstein, Michael Morgan, Whitcomb Publishing
* *On the Front Lines: Bahá'í Youth in Their Own Words*, Editors: Heather Brandon, Aaron Emmel, George Ronald Press
* *ONE Magazine: Wealth & Poverty, Vol. 2.5*, Editor: The Bahá'ís of Eliot, Maine
* *Youth: Channels for Change: A Compilation of Extracts from the Writings of the Bab, Baha'u'llah, Abdu'l-Baha, Shoghi Effendi and the Universal House of Justice Relating to Youth*

Protestant Resources

Thus Far On the Way: Toward a Theology of Child Advocacy by the Reverend Dr. Eileen W. Lindner

Based on sermons and speeches that Rev. Lindner delivered over more than a decade at CDF's Samuel DeWitt Proctor Institute for Child Advocacy Ministry each July, this superb new book develops a theology of child advocacy, skillfully weaving together theology, church history, biblical exegesis, and more, with Lindner's classic stories and humor that move the reader through laughter and tears to faithful action.

Foreword by Marian Wright Edelman. Louisville: Presbyterian Publishing House, 2006. Available from Presbyterian Distribution Services 1 (800) 524-2612 and amazon.com.

Congregational Health Ministries Resource Packet
An information packet containing resources useful in developing congregational health ministries using the parish nurse, lay counselor, participatory approach and congregations as healing community models. Packet available through the United Methodist Church, www.umc.org. $3.50

Health for All: A Congregational Health Ministries Resource
Manual for congregational use exploring health issues and factors that promote a healthier life for all. Each chapter contains a Bible study, information case study, discussion questions, and suggestions for action. Available through the United Methodist Church, www.umc.org. $6.50

A Church for All God's Children
In 1996 the Council of Bishops called upon The United Methodist Church to reshape its life in response to the crisis among children and the impoverished and in faithfulness to Jesus Christ. Congregations are invited to undertake specific actions to make their churches more responsive to the needs of children and their families in the church and community. This packet contains resources (checklist, guidelines, resource list, and reporting form) for churches that want to participate and to qualify as a "Church for All God's Children." The packet, which was sent to every United Methodist congregation, is available on The United Methodist Web site at www.umc.org/initiative.

Putting Children and Their Families First: A Planning Handbook for Congregations
This book offers strategies for assessing children's needs in the congregation and the community; identifying the strengths and assets of children, families, and communities; and developing a plan for comprehensive ministries. It also provides a biblical framework for ministry and suggestions for implementing new ministries. General Board of Global Ministries, The United Methodist Church, $4.75 plus postage and handling. To order, call 1 (800) 305-9857.

Community with Children and the Poor: A Guide for Congregational Study
This six-session study guide for use by small groups in a congregational setting is based on the United Methodist Bishops' Letter Community with Children and the Poor and was prepared by the Task Force for the Bishops' Initiative on Children and Poverty. Sessions focus on the Bishops' Initiative, Community with the Poor, Economic Globalization, Global Debt, the State of Poor Children in the U.S., and Where Do We Go from Here. Nashville: Cokesbury, 2003. To order, call 1 (800) 672-1789.

The Child-Friendly Church by Boyce Bowdon
One hundred and fifty examples of how churches of various sizes and settings are faithfully ministering to and with children and the impoverished. Models include ways churches attract children and their families, models that help children grow as disciples of Christ, models that enable churches to minister to their communities, and models for ministry to and with the poor. Concludes with consideration of what it takes to make a child-friendly church. Nashville: Abingdon Press, 1999. 142 pages, $10.00

Children's Ministries: Ministries That Help Children Grow in Faith by Mary Alice Gran
A practical resource that helps children's ministries leaders understand elements of that ministry and how it fits within the mission of the congregation and the United Methodist Church. Sections include children in the life of the congregation, ministry in the community and world, and more. Nashville: Cokesbury, 2004. 40 pages, $2.75

Listen to the Children! (35-minute video)
This video takes a look at the lives of children—their needs, fears, and hopes. To create this video, children at four church settings in diverse communities were given video cameras. Hear children's own messages to us through singing, dance, drama, and interviews. The United Methodist Church, $12.50 plus postage and handling. To order, call 1 (800) 305-9857.

The United Methodist Women's Campaign for Children, Phase III
The third phase of this campaign is focused on advocacy in public school education. A brochure and booklet are available from the Service Center, 7820 Reading Road, Cincinnati, Ohio 45222-1800. To order, call (513) 761-2100 or email Scorder@gbgm-umc.org.

United Methodist Women's Division Action Alerts
Updates on legislative issues that address concerns of United Methodist Women including children's issues. Receive by contacting the Women's Division, Office of Public Policy, 100 Maryland Ave., N.E., Suite 530, Washington, DC 20002. For

other information about current campaigns related to children's issues, contact the Women's Division, Office of Community Action, 15th Floor, 475 Riverside Drive, New York, NY 10115.

Seeing Children, Seeing God: A Practical Theology of Children and Poverty by Pamela D. Couture

A holistic theology that incorporates the reality of poverty and the plight of children, this book is a resource for theologians, pastors, and other church leaders. Nashville: Abingdon Press, 144 pp., $15.00

Safe Haven for Children, Hope for Congregations and Communities

From the Evangelical Lutheran Church in America, a folder of tools and information to help Lutheran churches become "Safe Havens" for children in the community. Folder includes an emblem identifying the congregation as a Safe Haven for Children, a reproducible congregational resolution to become a Safe Haven, a certificate, and practical materials spelling out how congregations can be safe havens for children in poverty, needing child care, at risk of abuse, and more. Evangelical Lutheran Church in America. Published by Augsburg Fortress Publishers, 1999, ISBN 6-0001-0865-6. $2.50. To order, call 1 (800) 328-4648.

Our Ministry of Healing: A Study of Health and Health Care Today

This 60-page book is available for download from www.elca.org/dcs/ministryofhealing.html.

Introducing Caring for Health bulletin insert

Bulletin insert offering suggestions for bringing the social statement to life in your congregation. Download from www.elca.org/socialstatements/health/bulletin.

That We May Speak: Our Ministry of Action

A step-by-step guide to help congregations choose an issue and begin a ministry of advocacy. Download from www.elca.org.

Decade of the Child

A brochure, newsletter, and range of other resources are available to help congregations participate in the General Assembly designated "Decade of the Child" and lift up the special gifts and needs of children and youths, birth to 18, within the church, beyond the church, and throughout the world. For more information, call 1 (888) 728-7228 and ask for the Presbyterian Child Advocacy Office or write to: The Decade of the Child, The Child Advocacy Office, Presbyterian Church (U.S.A.), 100 Witherspoon Street, Louisville, KY 40202-1396.

Light a Candle for Children Prayer Vigil Project brochure

This brochure provides information about the Light a Candle for Children project coordinated by the Christian Church (Disciples of Christ) in which congregations are encouraged to pray for children and learn more about children's needs. People in the congregation and/or community are invited to take one of the 40 days to light a candle and spend the day in prayer for children. For information, visit http://www.homeland ministries.org/FamilyandChildren/candle.htm.

Building Assets in Congregations: A Practical Guide for Helping Youth Grow Up Healthy

This guide offers everything you'll need to create a congregation that builds assets—young people's strengths. Perfect for youth workers, clergy, volunteers, and others, this practical book includes: worksheets for assessing and planning your current priorities and programs; strategies and ideas for introducing assets into youth programs; tips for creating intergenerational programs and parent workshops; and ten reproducible bulletin inserts. Search Institute, 1998, 176 pp., #113. $23.95. To order, call 1 (800) 888-7828 or log on to www.search-institute.org.

Jewish Resources

Judaism and Health Care Reform

This packet available from the United Synagogue of Conservative Judaism is intended to help you and your congregation become advocates for just, adequate health care reform. The material includes traditional Jewish sources, a contemporary text for study, suggestions for action, information about health care reform organizations, and additional resources for program planning. Visit www.uscj.org/Social_Action_Resour5405.html.

The Religious Action Center Web site, www.rac.org, has a variety of advocacy resources including information on issue areas including children and poverty, legislative reviews and agendas, and links to write letters to the President and Congress. You can also join RAC's Advocacy Network and sign up to receive emails; RACNews delivers *Chai IMPACT* Action Alerts, the RAC's Weekly Legislative Update, all RAC press statements, program announcements, Web updates, and other timely information to anyone with an email address. "Social Action" is an interactive electronic social justice activists' discussion group, where you can share your successes, learn from others, and discuss pressing issues of the day with other committed social justice activists.

K'hilat Tzedek: Creating a Community of Justice

K'hilat Tzedek is a discussion guide intended to help congregations through a process of reflection to determine where their social action programs fit into the scheme of congregational life, and how they can become models of integrated, justice-seeking congregations. The *K'hilat Tzedek* process will invigorate and deepen your congregation's social justice work.

Speak Truth to Power: A Guide for Congregations Taking Public Policy Positions

A publication to assist congregations in taking public policy positions, created by the Commission on Social Action of Reform Judaism (CSA) and the Ida and Howard Wilkoff Department of Synagogue Management of the Union for Reform Judaism (URJ).

Lirdof Tzedek: A Guide to Synagogue Social Action

Whether you are looking to expand a successful social action program or are working to build one, this guide is an important resource for you and your congregation. *Lirdof Tzedek* provides step-by-step guidelines for all aspects of synagogue social action programming, from establishing the appropriate structures within the congregation to effecting change on the local, regional and national levels.

2004 Get Out the Vote Program Plan and Action Manual

It is not too soon to start planning for Get Out the Vote efforts for the 2008 election. Get Out the Vote 2004 aims to demystify the registration process, to focus communal energy on the privilege and responsibility of voting, and to provide information to plan a successful voter engagement effort in advance of Election Day. While this guide was designed for use by Jewish congregations and communal organizations that wish to conduct their own voter registration drives, we also encourage you to participate in voter registration drives in the general community. The same procedures and materials that are suggested here for use in the Jewish community can be adapted for use in voter registration activities in the broader community.

Catholic Resources

Health Care for All Campaign Brochure.
Introduced at the 2005 Catholic Social Ministry Gathering, it is available for download at www.usccb.org.

Health and Health Care: A Pastoral Letter of the American Catholic Bishops.
This statement issued in 1981 addresses the message of the Gospel and tradition, responsibility for health, formal health apostolate, and public policy. It is available for download at www.usccb.org.

Catholic Campaign for Children and Families: Parish Resource Manual.
This comprehensive resource includes practical planning and support materials, clip art, bulletin quotes, liturgical and preaching guides and models to help parishes integrate a focus on children and families into all aspects of parish life. Includes the Bishops' Statement, "Putting Children and Families First: A Challenge for Our Church, Nation, and World," a resource developed by committees on domestic social policy, international policy, and marriage and family life. A video is also available. Also available in Spanish, $6.95. To order, call the U.S. Conference of Catholic Bishops at 1 (800) 235-8722 and ask for publication number 525-9.

Renewing the Vision: A Framework for Catholic Youth Ministry.
The U.S. Conference of Catholic Bishops addresses the call to personal discipleship, evangelization, and leadership. Offered as a "blueprint" for the continued development of effective ministry with young and older adolescents, this framework is an affirmation of the faith, gifts, energy, and fresh ideas of young people, a Christ-centered vision, and a call to empower young people. Available in English and Spanish, 61 pp., $5.95. To order, call 1 (800) 235-8722.

Organizations

The following key national Catholic social ministry organizations are associated with the USCCB and provide valuable resources to support the Catholic community in its work on poverty and health-related concerns:

Catholic Campaign for Human Development: For information and educational materials on poverty in the United States, go to www.povertyusa.org. For information on the Church's program to support self-help groups in low-income neighborhoods, go to www.usccb.org/cchd.

Catholic Charities USA: For parish social ministry resources, advocacy materials, and information on how the Catholic community serves people in need throughout the United States, go to www.catholiccharitiesusa.org.

Catholic Health Association: For resources and information on Catholic health care and efforts to provide accessible and affordable health care for all, go to www.chausa.org. Its framework for health care reform published in April 2000 is *Continuing the Commitment: A Pathway to Health Care Reform.* In addition, it has an extensive resource catalog of health-related publications and other resources for the Catholic community.

Catholic Relief Services: For advocacy and educational materials on international issues as well as information on the relief and development efforts of the Church in the United States at sites around the world, go to www.catholicrelief.org.

USCCB Department of Social Development and World Peace: For parish resources and educational materials as well as advocacy resources and general information on the U.S. bishops' efforts to address issues of justice and peace, go to www.usccb.org/sdwp.

USCCB Migration and Refugee Services: For parish resources, advocacy materials, and general information on programs of the Church in the United States to support and resettle immigrants and refugees, go to www.usccb.org/mrs.

There are many additional organizations within the Catholic community and beyond that offer programs and resources for understanding and responding to poverty. Throughout the country, there are many *diocesan and parish programs* that offer essential help to poor people who are struggling to live in dignity. In addition, *state Catholic conferences* and *diocesan social ministry* offices work on justice issues and provide helpful information to schools and parishes. Catholics join with many ecumenical, interfaith, and other groups to defend human dignity. For more information, go to www.usccb.org/sdwp.

USCCB Statements on Health Care and Economic Issues
USCCB documents outlining policy criteria on a range of key issues related to health care and poverty include:

- *Health and Health Care*
- *A Framework for Comprehensive Health Care Reform*
- *A Catholic Framework for Economic Life*
- *A Commitment to All Generations: Social Security and the Common Good*
- *A Decade After "Economic Justice for All": Continuing Principles, Changing Context, New Challenges*
- *A Jubilee Call for Debt Forgiveness*
- *Called to Global Solidarity*
- *Economic Justice for All*

- *Food Policy in a Hungry World*
- *Homelessness and Housing: A Human Tragedy, a Moral Challenge*
- *In All Things Charity*
- *Moral Principles and Policy Priorities for Welfare Reform*
- *Putting Children and Families First*
- *Welcome and Justice for Persons with Disabilities*

These documents can be ordered from USCCB Publishing by calling toll-free 1 (800) 235-8722 or obtained by visiting the U.S. bishops' Web site. Also available on the USCCB Web site (www.usccb.org) are recent testimony and action alerts on these and related issues.

Unitarian Universalist Association Curricula

In Our Hands, Grades 4-6: A Peace and Justice Program
by Barry Andrews and Pat Hoertdoerfer, Unitarian Universalist Association, 1990
Explores the concepts of peace and justice. 16 sessions.

*** *The Bully, the Bullied and the Bystander: From Preschool to High School – How Parents and Teachers Can Help Break the Cycle of Violence* by Barbara Colororsa, Quill, 2003
It's a deadly combination: bullies who get what they want, victims who are afraid to tell, bystanders who either watch, participate, or look away, and adults who see these incidents as a normal part of childhood. Parenting educator Colororsa provides the tools to break this cycle of violence.

In Our Hands, Grades 1-3: A Peace and Justice Program
by Samuel Goldenberg, et al., Unitarian Universalist Association, 1989
Explores peace and fairness through active learning. 16 sessions.

Race to Justice: A Racial Justice and Diversity Program for Junior High by Robin F. Gray and José A. Ballester y Marquez, Unitarian Universalist Association, 1995
Program affirms human diversity through role-playing, real-life stories, and games. 15 sessions.

Weaving the Fabric of Diversity by Jacqui James and Judith A. Frediani, Unitarian Universalist Association, 1996
Take stock of the "isms" that may be holding you back from embracing diversity: racism, heterosexism, ableism, classism, and ageism. Eight-session program for adults to learn strategies for increasing diversity in their congregation.

** Resource for teachers and parents

Resources for Children

Black Is Brown Is Tan by Arnold Adolf, Harper Trophy, 2002
The winning portrayal of a loving family—a brown-skinned mother, white-skinned father, two children, and their various relatives—beautifully illustrated with watercolors by Caldecott Medalist Emily McCully. Ages 4-8.

Bucketful of Dreams: Contemporary Parables for All Ages
by Christopher Buice, Skinner House, 1994
A charming cast of characters brings values such as diversity, justice, faith, and empowerment to life in 18 original parables. Playful cartoon illustrations by the author. All ages.

The Kids' Guide to Working Out Conflict: How to Keep Cool, Stay Safe, and Get Along by Naomi Drew, Free Spirit, 2004
Proven, practical ways to avoid conflict and defuse tough situations. Includes tips for how to counter bullying, calm down, reduce stress and tension, let go of anger, and eliminate put-downs and other hurtful language.

What Do You Stand For? A Kid's Guide to Building Character by Barbara A. Lewis, Free Spirit, 1997
Guided exploration of issues of honesty, empathy, integrity, respect, and more. With quotations, activities, problem-solving exercise, true stories, and reproducible handouts. Ages 11 and up.

What If Nobody Forgave? And Other Stories by Colleen M. McDonald (ed.), Skinner House, 2002
"From Buddha to Jesus to the Sufi masters, spiritual teachers have used stories to convey basic messages about truth and right living." This edition contains 11 new stories (19 in all) that echo the seven Unitarian Universalist Principles. Each story is followed by discussion questions, activities, and a reading list. All ages.

Different Just Like Me by Lori Mitchell, Charlesbridge, 1999
While April is waiting for the days to pass before she visits her grandmother, she encounters all sorts of different, interesting people. By the time she returns from her visit, she realizes that people—like the flowers in her grandmother's garden—have different needs and come in many colors, shapes, and sizes. Ages 4-8.

Ten Amazing People and How They Changed the World
by Maura Shaw, Skylight Paths, 2002
Profiles of Black Elk, Dorothy Day, Malcolm X, Mahatma Gandhi, Martin Luther King, Jr., Janusz Korczak, Mother Teresa, Albert Schweitzer, Thich Nhat Hanh, and Desmond Tutu show kids that spiritual people can have an exciting impact on the world around them. Includes a map showing the place of origin for each individual and a timeline. Ages 6-10.

If the World Were a Village by David J. Smith, Kids Can Press, 2003
What if we imagine the whole world as a village of just 100 people? The shrunk-down statistics about everything from religion to language, electricity to water quality, and literacy to money help children gain a better understanding of the world's peoples and their ways of life. Includes two pages of games, activities, and thought-provoking questions to teach "world-mindedness." Ages 7 and up.

Jimenez, Francisco. *The Circuit: Stories from the Life of a Migrant Child*
Bunting, Eve. *Smoky Night*
Bunting, Eve. *The Wall*
Cronin, Doreen. *Click, Clack, Moo (Cows That Type)*
Cuyler, Marge. *That's Good, That's Bad*
Lasley, Kathryn. *She is Wearing a Dead Bird on Her Head*
Howe, James. *The Misfits*
Leonni, Leo. *Swimmy*
Leonni, Leo. *Frederick*
Mochizuki, Ken. *Baseball Saved Us*
Mochizuki, Ken. *Passage to Freedom*
McKissack, Patricia. *Honest-to-Goodness Truth*
Muse, Daphne. *Prejudice – A Story Collection*
Na, An. *A Step from Heaven*
Nye, Naomi. *Sitti's Secrets*
Rembert, Winfred. *Don't Hold Me Back: My Life and Art*
Stieg, William. *The Real Thief*
Seuss, Dr. *Sneetches and Other Stories*
Seuss, Dr. *Horton Hears a Who*
Seuss, Dr. *Lorax*
Seuss, Dr. *Butter Battle Book*

Jeffrey Keenan is strategic initiatives manager, Adobe Systems and actively volunteers in his community.

Shannon Daley-Harris is a freelance writer, editor, and consultant who has worked with the Children's Defense Fund, the Robert Wood Johnson Foundation, and the National Council of Churches.

Karen Speerstra is president of Sophia Serve, a coaching service for writers and publishers.

This book was conceived and developed under the direction of Criterion Ventures, a national firm that incubates and scales social ventures that make for a better world.

Publication date: June 2007
$14.95, paperback original
192 pages, 5 1/2" x 8 1/2"
ISBN 978-1-57675-446-7
(or 1-57675-446-4)
Item #94467-754

New book from Berrett-Koehler Publishers

Shannon Daley-Harris and Jeffrey Keenan
with Karen Speerstra

Our Day to End Poverty
24 Ways You Can Make a Difference

- Offers practical, easy steps anyone can take to help end extreme poverty
- Cleverly organized around the tasks we undertake in a typical day
- Helps you connect your daily experiences to those of people around the world

"As we go about our busy daily lives, Our Day to End Poverty challenges readers to see just how many ways we can find to make a difference. With hundreds of action suggestions, this valuable resource reminds us how small steps can add up to help solve some of the world's most difficult problems."

—Marian Wright Edelman, President, Children's Defense Fund

*O*ur Day to End Poverty invites us to look at the twenty-four hours in our very ordinary days and to begin to think about poverty in new and creative ways. Inspired by the landmark bestseller *50 Simple Things You Can Do to Save the Earth,* this book offers scores of simple actions anyone can take to help eradicate poverty.

Each chapter takes a task we undertake during a typical day and relates it to what we can do to ease the world's suffering. We begin by eating breakfast—so the first chapter focuses on alleviating world hunger. We take the kids to school—what can we do to help make education affordable to all? In the afternoon we check our email—how can we ensure the access to technology that is such an important route out of poverty? The chapters are short and pithy, full of specific facts, resources for learning more, and menus of simple, often fun, and always practical action steps.

Anne Frank wrote, "How wonderful it is that nobody need wait a single moment before starting to improve the world." Let's get started. It is our day to end poverty.

2007 National Observance of Children's Sabbaths®

Evaluation Form

Let us know how you celebrated the Children's Sabbath!

Please detach and return this evaluation form to:

The National Observance of Children's Sabbaths
Children's Defense Fund
25 E Street, NW
Washington, DC 20001

About You and Your Congregation

Name _____

Address _____

City, State, Zip _____

Congregation (if not part of address) and Religious Affiliation _____

Telephone (indicate day or evening) _____   Fax _____

Web site _____   Email _____

Please describe your congregation: its membership (number, racial/ethnic makeup, number of children, and so forth) and location (urban, suburban, rural) _____

Is this the first time your congregation has celebrated a Children's Sabbath?   ❏ Yes   ❏ No

If not, in which years (1992-2005) has your congregation participated? _____

About Your Children's Sabbath

Who took the lead in proposing and planning the Children's Sabbath in your congregation?
(Please describe their role, e.g., senior pastor or rabbi, lay person, committee member, youth group leader)
How many other people helped significantly in the planning?
How did your congregation observe the Children's Sabbath? What activities, services, or events were held, and approximately how many persons participated in each?

_____

_____

Please underline all that apply to your celebration:

1. Focused the worship service, liturgy, or prayer service on children through sermon, prayers, music, or other.
   Was it for a single congregation, ecumenical group (different Christian congregations), or interfaith gathering (Christians, Jews, Muslims, and members of other faith groups)?
2. Involved children and youths more fully in the service.
3. Led educational programs focused on children's concerns for preschool, elementary, middle school, high school, and adult classes.
4. Held special outreach and advocacy activities.

Briefly describe any or all of these events (use additional paper if necessary). Please feel free to enclose any bulletins or other materials from your Children's Sabbath. We would love to see what you did!

_____

_____

What follow-up is planned? That is, how will your congregation incorporate the commitment to children generated by your Children's Sabbath into the ongoing life of your congregation this year? Please be specific.

_____

_____

What support would you like from CDF for your follow-up efforts or your involvement in the Children's Sabbath next year? _____

_____

_____

Did any other congregations in your community hold Children's Sabbaths events? Tell us about them if possible.

_____

_____

About the Children's Sabbaths Manual

Please rate the Children's Sabbaths manual sections.

1. Very useful	2. Somewhat useful	3. Not very useful	4. Didn't use	5. Plan to use at later date

| ____ Section 1 | ____ Section 3 | ____ Section 5 | ____ Section 7 | ____ Section 9 | ____ Section 11 |
| ____ Section 2 | ____ Section 4 | ____ Section 6 | ____ Section 8 | ____ Section 10 | ____ Section 12 |

What resources or changes would you like to see in the Children's Sabbaths manual?

_____

About Spreading the Word

How did you learn about the National Observance of Children's Sabbaths?
1. Denomination/faith group _____
2. Religious organization or community group (specify which) _____
3. CDF (publication, mailing, meeting, Internet Web site, other) _____
4. Media coverage (please specify) _____
5. Other _____

How did you publicize your Children's Sabbath events? (Underline all that apply)
1. Print coverage: (name and date of publication; send clipping if possible)
   Community newspaper
   Denominational newspaper/faith group newspaper
   Congregational newsletter or bulletin
   Other _____
2. Broadcast coverage (name of television/radio station) _____
3. Other _____
4. Did not actively publicize the Children's Sabbath

What individuals do you know or what professional networks are you a part of that might be interested in receiving material about the National Observance of Children's Sabbaths?

_____

Organization	Denomination/Affiliation

Address

City	State	Zip

Telephone	Fax

Web site	Email